Prospering Together:

The Economic Impact of the
Aboriginal Title Settlements in B.C.

Edited by
Roslyn Kunin, Ph.D.

Canadian Cataloguing in Publication Data
Prospering together
Includes bibliographical references
ISBN 0-9682343-0-5
1. Indians of North America–British Columbia–Claims.
2. Indians of North America–British Columbia–Land tenure.
3. Indian title–British Columbia–Economic aspects.
4. Indians of North America–British Columbia–Government
relations. 5. British Columbia–Economic conditions–1945-*.
I. Kunin, Roslyn, 1941-. II. Laurier Institution (Vancouver, B.C.)
E78.B9P76 1998   333.2   C98-910065-0

Production: Peanut Butter Publishing
Plain English Editor: Dianna Bodnar
Copy Editor: Lynne McNeill
Final Editor: Suzanne Bastedo
Text Design: Fiona Raven
Cover Design: Gordon Finlay
Cover Photograph: Ann Chatwin
Cover Art, *Hanookwee*: Art Thompson

First printing January 1998

10 9 8 7 6 5 4 3 2 1

The Laurier Institution

THE LAURIER
INSTITUTION

Suite 608, 1030 West Georgia Street
Vancouver, B.C. Canada V6E 2Y3
Tel: (604) 669-3638
Fax: (604) 669-3626

Printed in Canada

Table of Contents

The analysis and views presented herein are
the responsibility of the authors and do not
necessarily reflect the opinion of the Institution, its Board of Directors or its members.

THE LAURIER
INSTITUTION

The Laurier Institution

The reality of contemporary Canada is a celebration of cultural diversity, a concept which, unfortunately, tends to be surrounded by many myths and misunderstandings. The Laurier Institution was established in 1989 for the express purpose of exploding those myths in order to create a foundation for greater understanding.

The Laurier Institution is a national non-profit organization founded by business and community leaders in Vancouver. In recognizing the importance of cultural diversity to the building of a strong united Canada, they sought to bring about increased tolerance and mutual respect as a basis to social progress.

This institution is non-partisan, has no political or formal business affiliations, and relies entirely on membership fees and donations. Since its inception, it has carried out several major national and provincial research studies. These include an investigation into the effects of immigration on the housing and job markets, an enquiry into the causes of youth gangs, and a project examining the integration of youth into the education system.

In the view of its executive director, Dr. Roslyn Kunin: "The purpose of the Laurier Institution is to encourage informed public discussion. Only by providing people with the facts can we hope to dispel the myths that cloud the issues of a culturally diverse society. There is advantage to assembling the facts to help people make up their own minds on the fundamental political issues of this nation."

As part of its commitment towards achieving a better, more tolerant Canada, the organization convenes monthly breakfast/lunch meetings to provide a platform for cultural and political leaders.

For more information, please contact:
The Laurier Institution
Suite 608, 1030 West Georgia Street
Vancouver, B.C.
Canada   V6E 2Y3
Tel: (604) 669-3638
Fax: (604) 669-3626

Acknowledgements

First, thanks must go to these generous organizations and individuals whose financial support made this project possible.

Organizations

BC Hydro
BC Tel
First Nations Summit
Government of Canada - Ministry of Indian and Northern Affairs
Government of British Columbia - Ministry of Aboriginal Affairs
Vancouver Foundation
Air Canada
Bank of Montreal
Ellis Foster
Gordon Capital
Hong Kong Bank of Canada
Prospero International
Terminal Forest Products
Vancouver Airport Authority
Vancouver Stock Exchange
MK Wong & Associates

Individuals

Maurice & Tama Copithorne
Mr. & Mrs. Fletcher
Mr. Danny Gaw
Mr. & Mrs. McCloy
Mrs. McMaster
Mr. David M. Rosenberg

Second, thanks to the authors, not only for the high quality of their work, but also for their patience and perseverance through the rigorous academic review process to which their original drafts were subjected and through all the details and deadlines entailed in producing this book.

The reviewers are much appreciated for detailed and valuable comments that greatly enhanced the quality of this study. Biographies of both authors and reviewers can be found at the back of the book.

Diana Douglas and Elliott Wolf and their team at Peanut Butter Publishing offered the expertise and the hand-holding necessary to convert the preliminary manuscript to final book form.

The Board of Directors of the Laurier Institution were instrumental not only in initiating this project, but also in providing the momentum to turn it into a reality. Especially to be thanked are the Chairman, Milton Wong, the Vice-Chair, Barbara Brink, and the Secretary and Legal Counsel, Eugene Kwan.

Finally, thanks to Ann Roberts, Executive Assistant at the Laurier, who looked after all the details and kept everything together.

Roslyn Kunin, Ph.D.
Executive Director
Project Director

Foreword

We Canadians see ourselves as fair-minded, tolerant, and sensitive. We pride ourselves on being a mosaic where everyone can retain their uniqueness rather than an American-style melting pot within which all are homogenized. We identify strongly with our much praised social safety net which insures that basic needs are met for all people.

Still, there is one group in Canadian society which has been pressured to "melt" into the larger society and has not benefited proportionately from the national prosperity. That group is the First Nations.

Prospering Together: The Economic Impact of the Aboriginal Title Settlements in B.C. describes the less than glowing history of First Nations in British Columbia — how their rights were limited and their access to land reduced. It then presents the current treaty negotiation process in an accurate and understandable way.

This book deals with tough questions such as: What should settlements cost? How could they be paid for? How will First Nations self-government work and will it fit into Canada's existing legal framework?

The authors do not steer away from difficult issues such as the many differences among First Nations themselves, the need for trained people if First Nations are to be able to benefit from self-government, and possible sources of tension between First Nations and other groups in the community.

One point becomes very clear in this book. There will be significant, but tolerable, costs to negotiating and implementing treaty settlements. However, the costs of not negotiating treaties would be very much higher. In that case, uncertainty would continue to hamper the economic and social development of both First Nations and British Columbia. Our freedom to make choices and solve problems might well be limited by legal precedent as specific issues are brought to the courts for resolution.

The authors of this book are knowledgeable in their fields and have done their homework. They present their ideas clearly and fairly.

I urge everyone concerned about the well-being of First Nations and the well-being of British Columbia to read this book.

Thomas R. Berger, OC, QC

The First Nations treaty process has become a subject of concern, anxiety, and debate all 'round. This book offers an informed, reasoned, balanced background and a factual description of the issues on the table.

I found this book an extremely efficient means of understanding the complexities, urgencies, and necessities of achieving a fair agreement for all the citizens of British Columbia.

Al Thompson
President and Chief Executive Officer,
Air BC

Introduction
and Summary

About 3% of the people in British Columbia belong to a First Nation. But almost 100% are influenced in one way or another by what is and is not happening to First Nations people. This is not only because we are all neighbours in this province, but also because we must share its land and resources. We must live together in a way that will allow all of us to prosper in the future.

This has always been true, but never more so than now. First Nations people, who have always claimed Aboriginal title to their traditional land and resources, now have a more educated and articulate population to express their claims. The Canadian constitution of 1982 and the Canadian courts have recognized and backed these claims. A large part of the general population has also shown some degree of support. We have become more aware of how First Nations people have been treated in the past and of their social and economic conditions now—well below the Canadian average by just about any measure.

The process to settle treaties in British Columbia is bringing these issues to a head. Its purpose is to settle First Nations' claims and to put into place formal agreements between First Nations and the federal and provincial governments, in most cases for the first time.

Many have welcomed the treaty-making process as a way to provide justice to First Nations people, to set up a formal legal framework for business and other activities, and to provide a degree of certainty where none has existed before. Not all are happy about it, however. Fears and concerns have been expressed on all sides.

First Nations people are worried that at the end of the process they may not have enough access to resources to ensure their communities will survive both culturally and economically. Other British

Columbians are afraid that at a time when all resources are scarce, a disproportionate amount of money, attention, and special rights will go to the First Nations, to the disadvantage of the rest of the population.

When people's pocketbooks and livelihoods are likely to be affected, emotions often run high. More extreme views, not always based on fact, seem to be the ones to get media attention, which only worsens the situation.

The purpose of this book is to help improve the treaty-making process itself by helping British Columbians understand both the process and its results. It gives both the negotiating parties and the public a factual description of the issues on the table, some background and history to put those issues into context, and informed opinions of what the outcomes of the treaty process are likely to be.

As is true in any genuine negotiation, the exact outcome cannot be foreseen. Nor do we want to prejudice the result by speculating on it. However, we can set out the issues and scope of the negotiations.

The following chapters do just that. Each has been written by a specialist on the subject.[1] (Biographies of the authors appear at the back of the book.) Most have allowed their work to be edited into plain language, so that it is clear and easy to understand for the general reader, yet is still technically accurate. Each chapter covers a different aspect of the issues around treaty settlement:

- Chapter 1 sets the historical context of the book by describing the relationship between First Nations and European newcomers from the time of contact in British Columbia.
- Chapter 2 examines why settling treaties by negotiation is preferable to doing so through legal action. It outlines the history of the legal struggles to establish and define Aboriginal rights.
- Chapter 3 compares First Nations' concepts of land and resource tenure to those of the larger Canadian society, and explains how these differences affect treaty negotiations.
- Chapter 4 looks at how treaty settlements may affect who can get access to land and resources, who will profit from them, and who will manage them for the common good.
- Chapter 5 considers how settling First Nations' treaties may affect the investment and use of capital in British Columbia.

- Chapter 6 examines the demands that treaty settlements and self-government will place on Aboriginal education, and how this education is likely to affect employability and income levels in First Nations communities.
- Chapter 7 focuses on how transferring control of health care services to First Nations communities will affect both the physical and economic health of Aboriginal people.
- Chapter 8 outlines how self-government may work in practice, and the implications it has for both First Nations and non-aboriginal communities.
- Chapter 9 analyzes how the financial costs of treaty settlements might be borne—a particularly important issue in the current economic environment of government cutbacks.

Chapter 1: Divided Past, Common Future

Ken Coates' title for Chapter 1, "Divided Past, Common Future," both describes the tortuous history of First Nations land claims struggles, and offers the hope that all the peoples of British Columbia are moving toward a more harmonious future.

Coates begins by describing the two great migrations that brought people to the province. The first was the ancient movement of human beings from Asia into the Americas through what is now Alaska, 10,000 or more years ago. These were the ancestors of First Nations people. The second was the flow of Europeans to what they called the "New World," which began around the 15th century.

What followed was a repeated pattern of European "discovery," struggles, and domination, which finally pushed the First Nations to the very edges of mainstream society.

British Columbia followed this basic pattern with a few variations. Until about 100 years ago, First Nations formed the majority of the population in British Columbia. In spite of this, the newly arriving settlers and miners paid little attention to them. Because they feared the First Nations would prevent them from getting access to resources or settling the land, they ignored them, pushed them into specified settlement areas or reserves, and tried to assimilate them into the European cultures. But the First Nations refused to disappear.

Historians generally agree that, of all the early British Columbia leaders, Governor James Douglas treated Aboriginal peoples with the most respect for their rights and needs. But even so, he made treaties with only 14 First Nations groups on Vancouver Island, and dictated their terms himself. In some cases, First Nations people signed a blank piece of paper. Nevertheless, the very act of making treaties recognized that First Nations groups had some autonomy and at least some basic rights.

Douglas' successor, Joseph Trutch, had different views. Rather than allow First Nations their own small but viable share of the economy, Trutch tried to restrict their access to land and other resources. After British Columbia joined Confederation, the provincial government only followed his example.

These actions pushed the First Nations to the economic margins of British Columbian society. Their rights were limited and they were denied basic freedoms like assembly and free expression, and also prohibited from cultural practices such as the potlatch. First Nations children were taken from their families and placed in residential and day schools, to "assimilate" them into the dominant white culture.

Various First Nations leaders tried to fight back in order to express and enforce their traditional rights to land and resources, but with no real success. The Nisga'a, for example, have been actively pursuing their rights for many decades, even travelling to London in 1913 to present their case before British parliament. But the stalemate continued. First Nations sought to exercise their rights, and federal and provincial governments essentially ignored them.

After World War II, broader worldwide changes in social structures meant that church leaders, academics, and others began to support the First Nations' consistent demands for rights and treaties. Strong feelings against racism of any kind and the increasing international emphasis on human rights contributed much to this change of heart. The belief took hold that it was right not to assimilate diverse cultures, but to allow them to continue their own cultural practices. This change has been gradual and is by no means complete. But it enabled First Nations people to get or regain the right to vote, to gather in groups, and to practise their own cultures.

Coates also talks about the legal struggles to establish aboriginal rights to lands and resources (described more fully in Chapter 2). Coates goes on to describe the current treaty-making process involving First Nations and the federal and provincial governments. The fact that these parties have agreed on a process, have begun to put it into practice and are working toward a common goal of reaching mutually acceptable treaties to resolve land claims and other issues is what will take the people of this province, First Nations and non-aboriginal, from a divided past into a common future.

Chapter 2: Why Settle Aboriginal Land Rights?

In Chapter 2, Harry Slade and Paul Pearlman explain why we should negotiate and settle issues of aboriginal title outside of the courts. They do this by clearly reviewing the case law on this complex issue. (For details on all the cases they discuss please refer to the chapter itself.)

The authors begin by discussing the 1993 B.C. Court of Appeal decision that First Nations rights to land and resources still exist, but do not exclude others from having access. The case is now under appeal. Slade and Pearlman then outline the cases and laws that confirm Aboriginal rights are limited to activities that are central to their distinctive culture.

Current Aboriginal rights to land are tied to the rights the First Nations had in the land before the arrival of Europeans. The government cannot now change these rights, though it was able to completely eliminate them in the past through an act of Parliament. The Crown had this right because it held—and still holds—the ultimate title to the land. But even though the Crown ultimately owns the land, that ownership is not outright—it must still acknowledge Aboriginal rights to it. The *Constitution Act, 1982* guarantees these Aboriginal rights, so now even the Crown cannot extinguish them.

Because of their unique origins, Aboriginal rights to land are different from other forms of land title. One of these differences is that they are "inalienable." That is, First Nations cannot transfer their rights to anyone but the Crown.

A First Nation must prove it has Aboriginal rights to a certain territory by showing that its ancestors were members of an organized society, and that they were the only ones to occupy that land at the time of the establishment of British sovereignty or, in some cases, at the time of first contact with Europeans.

Section 35(1) of the Canadian constitution recognizes and confirms Aboriginal rights (which makes Canada unique among other countries). These rights are special; they are given only to Aboriginal people, for the reason that they were the first inhabitants of the country. Therefore, these rights must not only consider the Aboriginal point of view, but also fit within the framework of the common law of Canada. The law has not yet smoothed out the differences between these two perspectives.

The courts have heard a number of cases in which Aboriginal peoples have claimed the Aboriginal right to engage in certain activities such as hunting and fishing. The courts have found that such activities must be integral to the particular First Nations' culture. What form the activities take can change over time, but they must still be rooted in the traditional culture. The courts do not generally consider cultural practices that came about as a result of European influences to be Aboriginal rights.

In general, activities that are the subject of Aboriginal rights and, as such, are protected by common law and now by the Constitution, permit Aboriginal people to sustain themselves by traditional cultural practices. The Crown cannot eliminate these rights. First Nations cannot transfer them to anyone but the Crown. However, the courts have not yet defined all the characteristics of Aboriginal rights. And they are very reluctant to do so. Some courts have recommended negotiation to solve these issues. If negotiation fails, then the parties involved can resort to legal solutions.

The Constitution also implies that the government can no longer extinguish Aboriginal rights even by passing an act of Parliament that clearly and plainly intends to do so. But the Crown can pass laws that limit Aboriginal rights for valid objectives, like preserving resources. To determine whether such laws or objectives were valid, the courts would have to examine the context of current relations between the Crown and First Nations people. The courts have not yet conclusively dealt with defining Aboriginal interests and rights.

What does this mean for third-party interests like resource-based companies and sports fishers? Here, too, the authors suggest that parties use negotiation rather than the legal system to resolve unsettled issues.

Because the Constitution confirms Aboriginal rights and First Nations can only transfer rights to the Crown, the Crown appears to have certain duties, such as consulting with First Nations before taking steps that may interfere with Aboriginal rights.

If negotiations do not take place at all, or do not lead to agreements, then legal action could result in very specific definitions of Aboriginal rights. These could severely limit the areas open to negotiation and therefore also limit opportunities for solutions beneficial to all parties. Negotiated treaties, then, may also serve the important function of more flexibly determining which activities will and won't be permitted. This would bring clarity to the types of economic development that would be possible, reducing long-standing uncertainties. For these reasons, treaty settlements are in the interests of all British Columbians, First Nations or not.

And the interests of all must be taken into account as the federal Crown negotiates settlements. The province has an obvious interest and role in treaty making, if only because the land rights it can grant can affect Aboriginal rights. The guiding principles of a democratic society also dictate that the Crown must both consider the interests of all segments of society in treaty negotiation, and clearly demonstrate that treaty settlement is in the public interest.

Slade and Pearlman conclude by describing two extreme positions. The first is that no one but Aboriginal peoples can use the province's land and resources and that Aboriginal peoples are required to obey only First Nations' laws. The second is that the government can act as it pleases because First Nations no longer have any special rights. Neither of these can prevail, for the simple reason that the other side would never accept them.

But somewhere between these extremes is an acceptable negotiated settlement that takes into account such realities as resource constraints. Since the negotiation process will involve reallocating resources, disputes will inevitably occur. Such specific issues can be settled in the courts without limiting negotiations in other areas.

The First Nations' goals are to gain self-government and access to the land and resources within their traditional territories. Both federal and provincial governments aim to create certainty through resolution and to clearly define what exactly Aboriginal self-government and rights to land and resources will mean. Both are within reach.

Chapter 3: Land and Resource Tenure

Chapter 3 compares First Nations' concepts of land and resource tenure to those of the larger Canadian society, and explains how differences between the two affect treaty negotiations.

Greg Poelzer notes both that First Nations' ideas about political community, government, and land ownership are linked closely together, and that they are very different from those of the larger Canadian society. How to reconcile these differences is a major task of negotiating treaty settlements. The work gets more complex when we recognize that because the First Nations themselves are so diverse, each First Nation may need different forms of land tenure and self-government.

Poelzer also points out that treaty settlements will create an additional level of government in Canada. This could be a scary thought for Canadians. Many already feel overgoverned by the federal and provincial governments. (Municipal and local governments are not independent, but are under the authority of the provinces.) However, these fears may be unjustified. As many other chapters also point out, First Nations governments, though independent, will cover areas not too different from those of existing municipal and local governments. Their ability to be independent will also be reconciled with existing provincial and federal laws.

Any political community can exist, make, and carry out decisions with or without governments. Governments provide stability and authority, but principles of kinship and consensus can also be used to make collective decisions.

Like political decision-making, territoriality (how communities use and control land and resources for political ends) is part of any organized community. However, it doesn't have to be based on ownership. For example, communities can also use land as a means of political control through a system of rights to exclude others, and rights to use of the land or its resources. These rights can be permanent or temporary (see Chapter 2).

Because they were traditionally people who lived with boundaries that were often only roughly defined, First Nations ideas of territoriality are largely based on more general non-ownership rights. However, leadership styles varied considerably among the groups, from the more common egalitarian style found in many Interior First Nations, to the much more hierarchical style of West Coast groups.

But large as the differences are among First Nations, there is a much wider gap between First Nations as a whole and the larger Canadian society. In our European-based society, decision-making is formal, structured, and impersonal. Territoriality is precise and fixed, with clearly defined borders. Governments keep authoritative order throughout the very specific territory.

However, there is one link between the more defined modern Canadian social structure and less-specific First Nations structures. Our Canadian federalism is based on reconciling federal and provincial governments, each of which has its own level of autonomy.

Poelzer is optimistic that a political solution that allows First Nations and non-aboriginal communities to peacefully co-exist within the terms of the Canadian federation is possible and likely. Treaties with individual First Nations groups will vary. Principles of full ownership need not apply to all territories. Rights to use and profit from land and resources may be more appropriate in some cases, leading to unique partnerships with the provincial government.

Poelzer concludes by reminding us that Canada is already a collection of political communities with some quite distinct cultures. If we apply what we have learned in building this country so far, along with some goodwill, we can also accommodate First Nations communities within this country.

Chapter 4: How Settlements Will Affect Access to Natural Resources

In Chapter 4, Paul Mitchell-Banks looks at who will control and profit from resources in a post-treaty world. He also considers who will have the responsibility and authority to protect the environment, allocate scarce resources, and ensure that those profiting from renewable resources indeed renew them. Finally, he examines how First Nations government relates to resources and resource management.

The Sechelt Self-Government Agreement and the Nisga'a Agreement-in-Principle stand as examples and precedents of how some of these issues may be resolved. Mitchell-Banks, however, is careful to point out that the Nisga'a settlement is unique. The Nisga'a First Nations live in an area of B.C. that has few non-aboriginal residents. Their traditional lands are large and continuous.

Settling the interests of non-aboriginal residents, and dealing with scattered traditional lands and overlapping claims by different First Nations groups will make other treaties more complex to resolve. Many more people have proprietary ownership of lands in other areas. These and other lands with other legal rights already attached are not on the negotiating table.

Mitchell-Banks begins by looking at subsurface resources, which include minerals and other materials. With respect to Nisga'a traditional lands, the Nisga'a own these resources and will be able to trade the related rights. The exception is uranium, which the government will still control for health, safety, and defense reasons. However, on all lands held in "fee simple" (proprietary ownership), the provincial Crown will own the mineral rights, as it does on other fee-simple lands in the province.

To manage claim staking and resource development on their traditional lands, the Nisga'a could set up structures parallel to those of the Province. The provincial government could even collect the royalties on behalf of the Nisga'a. This system would avoid the cost of unnecessary duplication. It also would provide guidance on management to the Nisga'a and other First Nations peoples who do not yet have the expertise to take full control of developing and managing these resources. Joint ventures, partnerships, and the use of accounting and management firms are other possible ways for First Nations to benefit from their mineral resources in the short term.

The Nisga'a Agreement-in-Principle is much more specific on how forest resources will be transferred. They will gain full control of these gradually over a period of years, with the annual allowable cut to be negotiated. The Nisga'a cannot build primary timber-processing facilities for several years, to minimize disruption to exiting operations. They have also agreed not to sell raw logs, even though other proprietary owners can generally sell such logs, and selling them in this state is a quick way to generate funds. Finally, the Nisga'a can set environmental and conservation standards, but they must meet or exceed existing government standards. This condition applies generally and is not restricted to forest resources.

Future treaties will likely follow the broad principles of the Nisga'a Agreement-in-Principle, as they apply to forestry, though they may be complicated by higher levels of pre-existing rights to forest resources. As in mining, First Nations' ability to effectively use their forest resources will be limited in the short run by the lack of trained First Nations personnel. At present in B.C., there are only four Aboriginal Registered Professional Foresters. Mitchell-Banks does note, however, that partnerships and joint ventures between Aboriginal groups and forestry companies have been successful in many locations, and that such partnerships could well become more common in British Columbia.

Because the Nisga'a's territory is such a large continuous area, the Agreement specifies that the Nisga'a government will allow the public reasonable public access to it. Of course, the condition is that people must not destroy or damage any resources on the land. Such rights of public access do not exist on other freehold land in the province, where owners can exclude "trespassers." In fact, where the First Nations territories are likely to consist of several smaller parcels of land, future treaties may not adopt this principle.

Rights to maintain and use roads through both Nisga'a and Sechelt territories are set out in an arrangement that will avoid confrontations between Aboriginal and non-aboriginal users. Since the use of road-blocks has been one way for some First Nations groups to raise awareness about issues of concern to them, road access is a crucial and controversial issue.

As anyone who has been following the media knows, use and conservation of fish stocks is also complicated and controversial. For the Nisga'a, the complications are reduced because their territory is so isolated. Their agreement gives them a percentage of the commercial salmon fishing catch, which they can sell, as well as rights to fish for other species for sustenance. It also sets up a joint committee of federal, provincial, and Nisga'a governments to decide how to manage the fish stocks.

Fishing resources will not be as easy to settle in other treaties. Some among First Nations groups have conflicting claims for fishing resources due to conflicts among those who share a waterway.

As with fish other than salmon, the Nisga'a will be able to harvest other wildlife for their own use or to trade among First Nations people. Here, too, a joint committee of First Nations and other government representatives appears to be the best way to deal with overall management and environmental issues. Other treaties have followed this precedent, which will most likely continue to be the model for future settlements. It preserves traditional hunting rights, and makes use of both traditional First Nations knowledge and more quantitative government data.

Like self-government in general, First Nations' management of resources will be initially challenging because of the limited number of trained, experienced, and qualified First Nations people. They will have to rely on outside assistance as Aboriginal people get trained, and as First Nations communities develop capable governments that can operate according to Aboriginal cultural principles, yet conform with Canadian and British Columbian legal frameworks. Only then will First Nations be able to fully manage resources and self-government to the benefit of all involved.

Chapter 5: Investment and Capital Productivity

In Chapter 5, Steven Globerman considers how settling First Nations treaties could affect the investment and use of capital in British Columbia. It focuses mainly on the possible consequences to financial investment, but also pays attention to the effects treaty settlements may have on economic factors like the availability of technical expertise, a skilled labour force, and modern transportation facilities. Both will be an important influence on how much real income or spending power British Columbians will have in the future.

First, Globerman assumes that investment will create a net benefit; that is, that any related costs such as pollution or government subsidy won't outweigh the gains from the project. Then he looks at which factors encourage investors and which influence the level of their investment.

Risk and uncertainty always reduce investment. Many expect treaty settlements will reduce the uncertainty about how resources on Crown lands can be used, and thus increase investment. However, some argue that changes in systems of land tenure and ownership will create uncertainties of their own.

But risk and uncertainty are not the only relevant factors. Operating costs and financing costs also influence investors' decisions. An investment becomes more attractive if the expected revenues increase and costs decrease. Overall costs depend upon the price of the resources, material, and energy used, and how efficiently they are used. Factors that generally influence operating costs are the availability and quality of resources, government policies, and competition. Increasing the availability or quality of resources (including skills of workers) lowers costs. So does access to information and financing. Taxes, government regulations, and environmental requirements increase costs.

The same factors that influence cost also determine how productive the capital is. Government regulations tend to reduce productivity. Competition, on the other hand, tends to increase it by encouraging producers to use the most economical assets in the best ways, including new technologies. Uncertainty about property rights tends to reduce productivity by making investors reluctant to invest as much capital as necessary to achieve the best results.

How does all of this tie into treaty settlements?

Arguments have been put forward on both sides about how treaty settlements will affect environmental and business regulations. Some have suggested that First Nations will have a "preservationist bias" and a tighter regulatory system, which would limit investment. Others feel that under self-government, First Nations will create regulations that will encourage industrial and commercial development. There may be few changes at all. The 1996 Agreement-in-Principle with the Nisga'a Nation specifies that environmental standards have to meet or exceed those specified in existing legislation.

Treaty settlements will also affect the finances of the B.C. government. The money for the treaty settlements will have to come from increased taxes or reduced government services. This could reduce the overall level of investment in the province.

Based on the research of Nobel Laureate Robert Coase, Globerman offers an interesting theory on the impact of transferring land and other assets to First Nations. He believes that if the costs of making the transfer are low, it will have no impact, either positive or negative, on resource use.

Globerman carries this idea forward to say that any changes to environmental regulations or elsewhere after settlements are made would likely have little impact on investment. Studies of international business show that other factors are far more influential in investment decisions. The mining industry is one of the most concerned about such regulations, and even they pay far more attention to factors like the availability of low-cost ore.

One change that is fairly certain is the redistribution of income. Transferring assets to First Nations will also transfer the income from those assets to First Nations people. If these First Nations people pay a lower rate of income tax on these assets than the previous owners, government revenues will drop. This could be offset if First Nations found a way to earn a higher rate of return on the resources, or if income to First Nations increases to the point where the taxes they owe are equal to those paid by the previous owners.

Transferring assets and responsibilities will also bring other changes. As previously mentioned, how productive the invested capital is depends on other complementary assets, especially managerial and technical expertise and skilled labour. Globerman recognizes that at present, First Nations people have less education, training, and skills than other Canadians (see Chapter 6). If treaty settlements require the use of lower-skilled First Nations workers, this will reduce investment and productivity. Of course, skilled workers can be brought in to work on projects in the short term, while First Nations take steps to educate their people to assume full management. In fact, there are advantages to using First Nations workers on local projects, especially in more remote areas. They are familiar with the area and its residents, and so are more likely to remain settled there. And investors may save on the high transportation and settlement costs of bringing a workforce to a new site.

Globerman agrees with earlier studies that found the uncertainties of treaty settlements have dampened investors' willingness to invest in provincial resource-based activities, particularly in the mining industry. When the question of who has long-term ownership of assets has no clear answer, investors have trouble getting financing. Overall, the uncertainty of whether and how treaties will be settled is discouraging some investment in B.C., though how much is difficult to say.

To get a clearer picture of what may happen, it is useful to look at past experiences in British Columbia and elsewhere. The review of each case study shows how different each set of circumstances is. However, some tentative conclusions are possible. Because each different region will have different types and numbers of resources, First Nations groups should have the flexibility to choose the economic development strategies they prefer. The administrative structures governing any new political questions should also be easy to understand and efficient.

In the end, Globerman concludes that we must acknowledge that First Nations treaty issues are not the only factors influencing investment in B.C. We must also take into account uncertainty about future government policies on the environment and economic development, and on bitter conflicts between environmental groups and resource companies. We must also carefully weigh the social costs of developing natural resources. Globerman suggests that what we need is a careful study of how existing public policies may discourage investment after treaties are settled, and direct attention to the broader issue of how British Columbia will be able to compete for scarce investment capital in the future.

Chapter 6: The Impact of Aboriginal Title Settlements on Education and Human Capital

We have noted more than once that the First Nations will need a well-trained population in order to benefit from treaty settlements and the opportunities resulting from them. Unfortunately, they have not yet developed such a pool of skilled people. Stephen McBride and Patrick Smith begin Chapter 6 by painting a familiar and grim statistical picture of the economic and social conditions that are responsible. These include unemployment rates three times higher than those for other Canadians and much lower levels of income. In 1991, about one-quarter of First Nations people in B.C. had annual incomes below $2,000. An additional one-third had annual incomes between $2,000 and $10,000.

The authors point out that while education is no doubt necessary to improve these economic and social conditions, it is by no means enough. However, education is still a significant tool to help overcome income disparities and other problems like unemployment, alcohol abuse, and violence.

The differences in the amount of formal education Aboriginal peoples have obtained compared to other Canadians are large. A far higher proportion of First Nations people have lower literacy levels, while comparatively few have any post-secondary education or university degrees.

Organizations like the Canadian Labour Force Development Board, and the International Labour Office point out that the world of work has become more difficult, more competitive, and more demanding. Better jobs and higher incomes largely depend on having higher education. In general, we have far more unskilled workers than we need and far fewer specialized workers. And government programs to deal with these imbalances are being cut back.

To develop a strategy for educating First Nations people in a post-treaty world, McBride and Smith say we must address two major issues. First, if First Nations people are to obtain their fair share of opportunities in the increasingly demanding labour market, their general levels of education must be brought up to the Canadian average. Second, any educational system for First Nations people must incorporate the languages and cultures specific to those peoples. To do this, First Nations must play a greater role in running their own educational systems.

Smith and McBride go on to describe various federal strategies for helping First Nations to do this, and analyze how successful they have been. They also carefully examine the Agreement-in-Principle between the federal government and the Mi'kmaq Nation in Nova Scotia, which was the first to give a First Nations group control over the education of their children. This agreement is expected to lead to a final settlement that will form part of an overall self-government package.

McBride and Smith also give some attention to another agreement often mentioned in these chapters—the February 1996 Agreement-in-Principle with the Nisga'a in British Columbia. This Agreement concentrates most heavily on land and resource issues (see Chapters 2 and 4), but it does give the Nation legal authority over education and other areas related to training, especially those concerning language and culture.

The clear trend in both these Agreements-in-Principle and in the other developments McBride and Smith discuss is that Aboriginal people must be involved in developing and implementing any program for their improvement, whether in their own separate educational institutions or in conjunction with others. Developing and financing these activities will require co-operation between First Nations and all levels of government. And all must be based on the principles of recognition, respect, and responsibility.

As with so many other fields discussed in this book, there will be no one "right" or "best" way to create and deliver educational services. Each First Nations group will have to develop the systems that will best meet their own needs. After so many decades of control by outsiders, it is time to determine what goals First Nations want their educational systems to achieve, as well as how they want to get there.

Chapter 7: Unlocking the Medicine Chest

Health is a central issue in treaty settlements both in terms of the people who will live under them and of the new economic and social structures they will create. Lee Morrison and David Fish begin by looking at the health and well-being of First Nations people compared to other Canadians and British Columbians. They then consider how treaty settlements may affect this health status. Finally, they examine strategies that would allow the First Nations to take over the management and delivery of their own health care services. Such strategies will have to be negotiated along with land claims and self-government.

The health status of First Nations people in British Columbia can only be described as desperate, regardless of which measures we examine. Life expectancy is about ten years shorter for men and six years shorter for women than it is for other men and women in the general B.C. population. The gaps are even wider if we look at the number of years that people live free of major disabilities.

First Nations birth rates are twice those for other British Columbians or Canadians, but teenage birth rates are four times higher, leading to more stillbirths and premature babies. The survival rates for First Nations newborns equals that of the general population, likely the result of good medical care available at the time of birth. However, older babies have a much higher than average risk of early death.

Further up the age scale, death rates for First Nations people are twice those of the rest of the B.C. population, with rates for traffic accidents and alcohol-related deaths five or more times higher. Both environmental and social factors contribute to these higher death rates. In addition to high mortality rates, more frequent occurrences of disabilities and chronic diseases steal many productive years from First Nations communities and diminish the quality of life for First Nations people.

What lies behind such sobering statistics? Morrison and Fish maintain that the government policies limiting First Nations' access to economic resources and their limited participation in the mainstream society contributed to their dismal health picture. They feel that with the settlement of land claims, First Nations will be able to control the path of their own economic development by blending traditional cultural values with those of the larger Canadian society. How well they will be able to do so depends on how viable and complete the self-government process is, and whether they have access to adequate natural resources and capital.

Results will take time, maybe more than one generation. But there are already communities that have taken the first steps to educate young and old; to improve diets and nutrition; to deal with alcohol, drugs, and violence; and to provide better housing, safe water, and all the other factors that lead to healthier, happier, and more prosperous communities.

How is the transfer to occur? Morrison and Fish assume that federal and provincial governments will continue to provide resources for First Nations up to at least current levels. They do note, however, the limitations on funding implied by the federal government's "envelope" system of capping the amount of funds available for any specific use. Morrison and Fish also expect that health services not currently provided by governments to the general population (non-insured health benefits and services such as prescription drugs and dental care) would continue to be funded by the government for First Nations people. These and other health services would be administered by First Nations communities under self-government arrangements.

The actual transfer of management to individual First Nation communities will be a complex and difficult process. One problem would be that First Nations people may lose the portability of benefits now available to First Nations across Canada.

Another problem is expense. But Morrison and Fish point to several ways to save costs as First Nations begin to deliver their own health services, such as setting up local pharmacies. Strategies like this will create local employment and economic development and save on hefty transportation costs. This "new money" may well remain within the First Nations economy; however, the government or tax payers that originally provided these resources may not see any of the savings.

Transferring control of health care resources will no doubt be one of the more challenging components in the whole complex treaty negotiation process. But there is no doubt that it is essential to improve the health and well-being of First Nations people to at least the Canadian or British Columbian average. Greater access to resources, more education, and greater autonomy all work together as steps to better health and the advancement of First Nations communities.

Chapter 8: Degrees of Separation

As we noted in Chapter 1, First Nations never gave up on their quest for self-government. However, it has only been within the last 30 years that governments and non-aboriginal communities have begun to recognize First Nations' rights. Even with such recognition, there are still many crucial questions yet to be answered about how Aboriginal self-government will actually work.

Will First Nations pay taxes? Will they be financially accountable? How will they relate to other levels of government? In Chapter 8, Ken Coates tries to answer these and other questions.

He begins by answering the most basic question: Can Aboriginal people govern themselves? His answer is a firm yes. First Nations communities in B.C. governed themselves effectively for thousands of years before the Europeans arrived. After that, paternalistic systems such as the *Indian Act* and the residential school system ruled First Nations. First Nations chafed under these systems, but objected to a proposal in 1969 that would have ended the *Indian Act* and removed all special recognition of First Nations people. Instead, the First Nations continued to seek cultural and economic independence through land claims settlements and self-government.

Eventually, Aboriginal rights were guaranteed by the 1982 constitution (see Chapter 2). But the defeats of both the Meech Lake and Charlottetown accords meant that First Nations would need to use less dramatic means to pursue these rights.

One approach that the federal government has put forward has been community self-government. Many Aboriginal peoples feel that this limited amount of independence does not go far enough in recognizing First Nations' autonomy. However, it has been applied with some success in the Sechelt area (see Chapter 4).

There are also limitations in the federal government's current approach to First Nations self-government, which Coates spells out in detail. These include leaving international issues and broad national areas, such as defense, in the hands of the Canadian government. But they also ensure that the *Canadian Charter of Rights and Freedoms* will continue to apply in Aboriginal communities.

Some First Nations have objected to some of these conditions and to the lack of First Nations input into the process. Nevertheless, the federal government is making headway in trying to settle both self-government and land claim issues. In British Columbia, these both come under the umbrella of treaty negotiations.

Many First Nations communities have not been waiting for all the complexities of political, legal, and treaty issues to be ironed out in order to get on with self-government. They have been taking small but determined steps forward to exercise their autonomy in specific areas like education. Only some of these attempts have been successful so far, but First Nations are learning what does and does not work and are making progress nevertheless.

Although First Nations have long maintained (and non-aboriginal groups are now coming around to agree) that self-government is both necessary and desirable, there is no obvious or easy way to get there. Coates lists 11 of the many challenges to be faced:

- The first challenge is recognizing that self-government is not a cure-all. It will not solve all past, present, and future problems, and it will be more difficult, time-consuming, and costly to achieve than many want to admit. We must remember that the perfect is the enemy of the good, and not turn our backs on the whole process because it does not meet unrealistic expectations.
- The second challenge will be to reduce the weight of all the various government bureaucracies that First Nations now have to deal with. They will have to develop efficient and effective structures of their own.
- Self-government will both symbolically and practically remove the heavy hand of paternalism from First Nations people. Allowing Aboriginal communities to design their own approaches to government, and accepting the results of that process will require patience and open-mindedness.
- Combining the systems and beliefs of the larger Canadian society with First Nations' methods of operations will be the next challenge. Many Canadians take for granted established civil services, public tendering of contracts, and detailed procedures for government accountability. Some First Nations have not used these systems, but integrate cultural practices such as prayers and ceremonies in the process of government.
- The "politics of smallness" can produce some big problems that some people mistakenly think to be unique to First Nations. In small communities, all government decisions, especially budgetary ones, affect individual citizens directly and obviously. Keeping personal relationships at arm's length from government activities becomes close to impossible. Privacy is a very rare commodity. These factors make governing a small community very different from regulating larger, more impersonal societies where govern-

ments seem far away and it is possible for decision-makers to be anonymous.

- Coates' next challenge is one that comes up over and over again in connection with resource development. Do First Nations communities have the trained people to actually implement self-government? In the short run, the answer appears to be no. However, no one seems to be willing to even ask this question, let alone try to answer it. This is a shame, since over time and with some planning, First Nations can develop the needed expertise in their people.

- Geography is yet another challenge for First Nations governments. Many communities are small and widely dispersed in remote areas, with limited access to roads or other means of communication. Large numbers of community members have moved from these communities to cities. For smaller bands, having more than half the members living away from their home communities is not unusual.

- Money always presents challenges. The answer to the question of who pays the unavoidable costs of self-government will have to be worked out among the federal government, the provincial government, and each First Nation. Once the money has been allocated, those who provide the funds, including taxpayers, will want to see some financial accountability. But because First Nations governments may not have the same financial principles and systems that most Canadians are used to, this in itself could be a challenge. Issues will also arise when First Nations leaders start taxing their own people. The feelings will be very different from when all Aboriginal peoples could stand together seeking funds from higher levels of government. Yet another challenge will be to make sure that any new government system will be financially stable over the long term.

- The concerns that non-aboriginal municipal, local, and regional governments have about First Nations self-government are many and serious, but have not yet received enough attention. Yet, as Coates points out, these local governments will likely feel the effects of changes brought by treaties and long after federal and provincial officials have left the negotiating table and gone home. Their worries are about levels of taxation, access to services, and other issues about "level playing fields" for all. If negotiators do not deal with these concerns up front in a way that is fair to both sides, it could poison relationships between First Nations people and their non-aboriginal neighbours throughout the province.

- First Nations people in British Columbia are looking at developing governments at a time when the trend is to move toward deregulation. In the larger Canadian society, governments are reducing spending, funding, and the services they provide. First Nations do want to see the higher-level governments become less involved with local Aboriginal issues to make room for more autonomous forms of Aboriginal government. However, they will have to deal with the possibility of reductions in the levels of program support and funding provided. (Chapter 7, on the implications of transferring health care services, touches on this challenge.)

- Another major shift in Canadian society is the movement away from collective rights toward more individual rights. As they protested in 1969, First Nations groups have rightly feared that treating all people as individuals, and only as individuals, could result in the disappearance of Aboriginal cultures and the end of their existence as separate peoples. It may be harder for First Nations to express these concerns to a larger society where individualism is becoming more highly prized.

We can see that many of the questions about self-government still remain unanswered. But even considering that much is still unknown, Coates does foresee that the number and strength of independent Aboriginal communities in British Columbia will grow. He also sees the development of more equal relationships between First Nations and other British Columbians. However, movements in this direction may well face criticism by those in the media and in private circles who are opposed to its progress.

Self-government is not an end in itself, but a means to larger ends, such as preserving First Nations culture and autonomy, and establishing healthy communities. It is not a magic solution to all problems. But if expectations are realistic, it can help First Nations people take control over their lives.

Chapter 9: Financing First Nations Treaty Settlements

In Chapter 9, Brian Scarfe turns to the question that has many fearful Canadians clutching their pocketbooks: How are Aboriginal title settlements to be paid for? He admits that his answer to this daunting question is more general than specific. Like the authors of preceding chapters, he refers to the Nisga'a Agreement-in-Principle, but does not see it being used as a model.

Scarfe's purpose in this chapter is to set up a financial framework that will allow Aboriginal claims to be settled in a way that is politically workable and broadly acceptable to both First Nations and other Canadians. As in other chapters, he addresses the issues primarily from a British Columbia perspective.

Recently, the government of the Province of British Columbia has moved away from its long-held position that the federal government was the only governing body with any financial obligations to First Nations people. It has now joined with the federal government and First Nations groups in a process aimed to resolve treaty issues. The cash costs will be paid primarily by the federal government. The provincial government will make its major contribution in the form of Crown lands. Crown lands could be transferred to First Nations groups in the form of proprietary fee-simple ownerships. But Scarfe feels that transferring various rights to use much of the lands would be both more consistent with First Nations' traditional methods of land use, and more acceptable to other Canadians.

It goes without saying that the costs of treaty settlements will ultimately be carried by taxpayers. However, third parties, including those now using and profiting from Crown land resources, will also pay part of the cost of treaty settlements. Their access to the resources will be limited or the cost of such access will increase. Therefore, they should have input into any negotiation process.

Finally, First Nations themselves will bear part of the cost of treaty settlements. Government services now provided to them will be reduced, and their tax obligations will increase.

Scarfe next describes in some detail the issues of land use and resource tenure that come up when the user does not hold the land as a proprietary owner. He feels that such tenure (rather than freehold of the land) should apply to much of the Crown land that would be transferred to Aboriginal people's use.

The transfer of rights to use resources from the provincial Crown to First Nations might actually have little effect on current resource users. Instead of paying the provincial government for access to the resources, they would simply pay similar fees to First Nations groups. In this case, the cost would be carried by British Columbia taxpayers, who would face higher tax rates or lower services as a result of the decline in provincial tax.

Taxpayers will also have to provide funds for governments to finance cash transfers to First Nations communities. Scarfe's financial framework (shown in chart form) shows that this flow would be at least partly offset by a reduction in government services to First Nations, and by any increased taxes they paid.

As previously mentioned, the Province will transfer property rights to First Nations. Any resulting loss in provincial revenue will again have to be paid for by taxpayers, who would also have to pay the cost of any settlements to previous resource users whose rights have been limited.

Scarfe's chart describes the patterns of the treaty settlements, but does not try to measure the amount of funds involved. To do so would be beyond the scope of this book, and practically impossible until the terms of several actual treaty settlements have been finalized.

Scarfe recommends that the federal government should shift its provision of services to First Nations people to Aboriginal governments as they are set up. First Nations governments should have at least the powers of municipalities, including the right of taxation, to generate the funds to support them. But Scarfe does not recommend that First Nations people pay full taxes to the provincial and federal governments, at least in the short term. The money they save could then be used to establish local government and services.

Finally, like Mitchell-Banks, Scarfe cautions against using the Nisga'a Agreement-in-Principle as a model for future settlements.

Differences in geography and sizes of First Nations are among the factors that need to be taken into account.

We must accept some responsibility. Scarfe concludes: "Given the unfortunate history of discrimination against First Nations peoples in B.C., most non-aboriginal people understand that redistributing resources is only just, and essential to redressing past wrongs." Such justice will be expensive. But if we are to build both trust and opportunities for development, the costs must not go beyond what society can bear.

Conclusion: What Can We Expect from Treaty Settlements?

It seems that we have provided far more questions than answers on treaty settlement. Nevertheless, certain themes recur through the chapters of this book that allow us to build at least a skeleton of principles upon which treaty settlements will be built.

First, treaty settlements will not be quickly and easily reached in a way that completely satisfies the parties. The road will be long and hard, and the results less than perfect. However, they will still be an improvement over the present uncertainties.

Second, the path of negotiation, difficult though it is, is preferable to allowing the courts to make very specific judgments that could limit future options. Having said that, treaties must be set within the framework of existing Canadian law and systems of government.

First Nations people will also have to obtain enough skilled and experienced people if they are to get the most benefits from self-government and increased access to resources. They can acquire these resources by training their own people or by hiring help from outside their communities.

Finally, according to the authors of this book, transferring resources to the control of the First Nations will not cause major disruption to the larger society. There will certainly be changes to incomes, tax bases, and so on. However, the consensus is that for settlements to work, they must be politically acceptable. The public must see them as fair.

One measure of fairness would be to ensure that First Nations people have a level of self-government that allows them to maintain their culture and enjoy economic prosperity similar to other Canadians. The evidence in this book shows that the treaty settlement process can help us reach this goal, so we can all prosper together.

Notes

1. Each chapter has been reviewed by another researcher in the field. Nevertheless, each author is ultimately responsible for the accuracy of their research and for the validity of their analysis and conclusions.

1

Divided Past, Common Future:

The History of the Land Rights Struggle in British Columbia

By Ken Coates

The conflict over the rights of aboriginal peoples in British Columbia is not solely a product of our time. The dispute has its genesis in the early years of European settlement. It is a conflict that speaks to the difficulties in reconciling fundamentally different philosophical and cultural systems. Historically, the conflict has focused on rights to land, sea, and resources. However, the ultimate solution lies in a much wider political and legal reconciliation between aboriginal and non-aboriginal societies. Addressing the problem will require an appreciation of the historical relationship between aboriginal and non-aboriginal people, and an understanding of how this history has shaped the political and legal reality of today. (*The Report of the British Columbia Claims Task Force,* June 1991).[1]

British Columbia's ongoing and heated debate over the land rights and political status of the First Nations now focuses on close to 70 separate negotiations across the province. Historic tensions between First Nations peoples anxious to retain control of traditional territories and non-aboriginal peoples and governments equally determined to limit First Nations' rights to their historic lands are as high as ever. Even now, as federal and provincial governments support the negotiations process, opponents continue to try to convince government officials to back away from their repeated public commitment to resolve the land rights issue "once and for all."[2]

This chapter sets the context for those to follow by examining the history of the relationship between Aboriginal and non-aboriginal peoples, from the time First Nations originally encountered Europeans. As the British Columbia Claims Task Force pointed out, understanding how history has shaped current political and legal situations is the first step to resolving conflicts over rights to the province's land and resources. The sections that follow examine

- relations between Aboriginal peoples and newcomers in world history
- patterns of encounter in B.C.
- approaches colonial governments have used to deal with First Nations in the past, including attempts to socialize them into European culture
- how Canadian governments pushed First Nations to the margins of the country's life from 1871 to World War II
- Aboriginal land rights campaigns after World War II and the emergence of the modern treaty process
- why understanding past history is important to understanding land claims issues today.

Relations between Aboriginal Peoples and Newcomers in World History

British Columbians are proud of their province's uniqueness, invoking it as something of a mantra. From its confrontational, combative political culture to its image as the land of hot tubs and cappuccino bars, British Columbia stands apart from the rest of Canada. So does the province's history. It is bound up in the conflicts of the Pacific, shaped as profoundly by influences from the north and south as those from the east and west, heavily influenced by both fear of Asia and Asian immigration. It is also a "have" province in a country of increasingly poor cousins. Historians and novelists have played on this theme, highlighting British Columbia's differences and documenting the repeated rivalries that have resulted in the national image of the province as "Lotus Land." So it is not surprising that the history of relations between

Aboriginal peoples and newcomers has typically been presented in a similar way, strongly emphasizing B.C.'s deviations from national norms. This has, in turn, fueled British Columbians' perceptions of the land claims process. It is strikingly different in scale and intensity than in the rest of the country.

Historians studying relations between Aboriginals and newcomers have typically presented their findings by nation and by region. The lives of First Nations people in California were shaped by different processes, events, and personalities than those of First Nations people in central Canada. Similarly, Canadian government policy on Aboriginal peoples is sharply different from policies in Russia or Nicaragua. Historians' emphasis on local developments thus is considerably justified. It is, however, only part of the story. The expansion of Europe onto Aboriginal lands is also a global story, connected by ideas, images, and assumptions about Aboriginal peoples. The history of encounters between First Nations and newcomers in B.C. is unique, and reflects the particular cultures, circumstances, and systems of the people in the region. But it also has important connections to events in other parts of the world.

We can hardly explain the complexities of the contact between Aboriginal peoples and newcomers on a world scale in a few short paragraphs. However, a few generalizations will help set the stage for the situation in B.C. We begin with the two greatest migrations in world history. The first was the original settling of North America. First Nations' accounts of how human beings arrived on "Turtle Island" emphasize spiritual and mythical experiences that led individual cultures to their place on the land. For the more scientifically minded, evidence points to a grand migration of people from Eastern Siberia at least 10,000 years ago and possibly earlier.[3] Most historians generally accept that Aboriginal peoples reached what is now called Alaska and moved to the south, then east, and then north, discovering vast new lands and resources. The process took thousands of years as, pushed on by the same combination of local shortages and a desire to explore that has long motivated humankind, First Peoples continued the shift across the continent. Regional cultures emerged as the settlers adapted to local resources and opportunities, and rubbed against neighbouring peoples (through conflict, trade, intermarriage, and diplomacy).

The second great wave of expansion began in the 14th and 15th centuries, when Europeans began to push beyond the frontiers of their knowledge and understanding. This was a complex and contentious process. Driven by a desire to spread the gospel, to increase the power of king and country, and to locate the now proven treasures of the New Worlds, European explorers fanned out across the globe. In some places, they discovered opportunities for settlement, in others for trade. In still others, they found only lands that seemed ill-suited for European habitation.

Through various means, from armed conquest to peaceful integration (more the former than the latter), European societies sought to develop the commercial potential of the new lands and to bring the wonders of their own civilization to the original inhabitants. They created images and stereotypes of the First Peoples that were sometimes positive, but more often harsh and unflattering, to justify occupying their territories and dispossessing them. In some areas, the local residents fought back, only to be devastated by European weapons or diseases. From time to time, as in New Zealand, the newcomers discovered a formidable foe and decided that a formal treaty was preferable to conflict (although in New Zealand they ended up with both).[4]

The extension of Europe overseas resulted in the widespread dislocation of Aboriginal peoples, particularly in those zones best suited for agricultural settlement. On vast sweeps of land in North America, Australia, South America, and Africa, colonizers moved in, occupying Aboriginal territories and forcing the established residents to become outsiders. In slightly less attractive areas (including much of Canada until the last half of the 19th century), Aboriginal peoples remained on the land. If goods like furs and fish were available, they traded with the newcomers. The diseases that were also exchanged, especially the spread of "virgin soil epidemics" to Aboriginal lands, devastated local populations, making the newcomers' expansion easier.

Colonial governments played a major role in European occupation of Aboriginal territories. They provided military power, legal justification (if needed), and local governments to control and restrain any protests. Methods varied from fighting wars of conquest, supporting the campaigns of Christian missionaries, negotiating treaties with larger Aboriginal groups, creating and regulating reserves or reservations, and trying to assimilate First Peoples through education, to making laws and restricting traditional cultural practices. Governments were often heavy-handed, but some colonial administrators discovered that they could handle Aboriginal peoples with less harsh measures.

For many decades, historians presented Aboriginal peoples as passive victims in this process (if they discussed the topic at all). They misread the situation. First Peoples proved to adapt remarkably well to the changes brought by European expansion. Some events, like destructive diseases and military conquest, were difficult to resist, although there were many armed struggles around the world. More often, Aboriginal peoples either avoided the encroaching settlement and retreated to remote regions, or accepted some level of integration with the newcomers.

First Nations in Canada participated actively and creatively in the fur trade. The Maori joined South Seas whaling ships and worked in the gold fields. The Inuit likewise joined whalers in the Arctic and, when that trade declined, traded in silver fox. Far from helpless in the face of European invasion, First Nations responded creatively to the opportunities and challenges presented.

Historians have also proposed the "fatal impact" theory from time to time, suggesting that the arrival of Europeans was the beginning of the end for an isolated, backward people. They were far too pessimistic. Aboriginal people showed considerable resiliency in dealing with the changes brought by newcomers. Disease was indeed a killer, and wars caused great disruption.[5] But most First Nations societies overcame vigorous attempts to assimilate them, and even survived losing much of their traditional lands.

In Canada, First Nations groups responded by becoming active in the fur trade and post-fur trade economies, relocating to accommodate agricultural settlement, negotiating treaties with the federal government, and initially accepting Christian education. Newcomers did little to help them. In fact, they encouraged First Nations to remain segregated from the dominant society, which widened the gap between the peoples. But the First Nations persisted in their struggle to survive as distinct cultures.

Relations between Aboriginal peoples and newcomers is a vast drama, often a tragedy, played out across the continents and around the globe. What occurred in British Columbia differed from other situations, but it followed a broad global pattern: first occupation by Aboriginal peoples, European "discovery," conflict and accommodation, eventual domination by outsiders, and then the forcing of First Peoples to the margins of society, economics, and politics. As with European stereotyping of Aboriginal cultures, these global experiences and attitudes coloured the newcomers' understandings of regional societies. Because they expected to find "barbarians," "savages," and "heathen," that's just what the newcomers found. Methods used by government to handle Aboriginal peoples in B.C. are also similar to world patterns, though B.C. relied much more heavily on models from the British Empire than those of other imperial powers. The uniqueness of British Columbia is in the details of each interaction. Otherwise, it fits well with the global pattern of discovery, conquest, incorporation, and marginalization.[6]

Patterns of Encounter in British Columbia

Experiences resulting from first contact have played a major role in shaping regional relationships between Aboriginal peoples and newcomers. Until the last part of the 19th century, First Nations people made up the majority of B.C.'s population. In the early years after first contact, newcomers worried about their potential power and slowly moved to establish footholds in the land. When the fur-trade era ended, newcomers began to settle and develop the frontier during the gold rush of the 1850s and 1860s. Incoming populations quickly overwhelmed the First Nations, pushing them to the margins of economic and social life. First Nations struggled to hold onto their traditional lands and participate in the economy of the rapidly changing environment, but found that governments paid little attention to their needs and goals.

From the beginning of contact to World War II, European settlers paid very little attention to the First Nations, except to consider them as a direct opportunity or a serious threat. Racism spurred provincial and federal governments to push Aboriginal peoples into becoming irrelevant. The First Nations responded in more flexible and innovative ways than many newcomers expected. However, newcomers' increasing populations and their political and military edge ultimately worked against the First Nations. In this way, patterns of encounter and government intervention in B.C. were similar to those in other parts of the colonial world.

Government Approaches to Dealing with Aboriginal Peoples

Global comparisons of colonial government

The expansion of Europe overseas brought sweeping changes to Aboriginal peoples, particularly those in accessible, temperate zones. (Peoples in more remote arctic, desert, and mountain regions generally did not feel the full weight of newcomer encroachment until the 20th century.) When European countries established colonial footholds in the New World, they discovered that occupying territories and subjugating Aboriginal peoples would be much more difficult than they expected. (The speed of the Spanish through Mexico and the wealth they discovered there had raised their hopes.)

Treaties of friendship or co-existence, or at least practical understandings based on shared economic benefits, allowed the colonists and Aboriginal peoples to occupy the same or adjoining territories. Colonial administrations also often made formal diplomatic relationships and military alliances with Aboriginal leaders to get support against other nations. Such strategic treaties were an integral part of European expansion.

The growth of European migrations in the 19th century increased pressure on colonial governments to ensure that land was available for incoming populations to use safely and easily. This meant either forcing Aboriginal residents to move, or, as in New Zealand, negotiating a formal treaty with Aboriginal leaders. A battery of government officials were assigned to manage Aboriginal affairs. One of their top priorities was to ensure that First Nations peoples did not interfere with newcomers' uses of land and resources. Most often, they restricted First Peoples to small allotments of land, and gave them opportunities to assimilate into European culture, usually by making alliances with church organizations.

If few settlers wished to occupy an area, Aboriginal peoples could resume some of their activities, which typically had some connection with the new commercial economy. However, when large numbers of newcomers arrived to capitalize on the availability of land, colonial administrators redoubled their efforts to keep Aboriginal peoples "in their place," and if possible, to encourage them to assimilate into the colonial mainstream.

This was an era of European paternalism, powered by strong Christian convictions and an unchallenged belief in the superiority of European social, political, and economic culture. The idea that colonial administrations ran the affairs of their people like a father runs the lives of his children took various forms. On some occasions, it appeared as the harsh hand of the disciplinarian, and at others it was the more gentle touch of the kindly parent. Behind the government stood a population of settlers who feared Aboriginal uprisings, or who simply had hostile and discriminatory attitudes towards the peoples whose lands they now occupied. Given these undercurrents and tensions, colonial administrators saw themselves as buffers between "childlike" Aboriginals and avaricious and potentially disruptive settlers.

Uncomfortable with situations that could make them unpopular in both camps, government officials opted for policies that separated the two groups. They created reserves or reservations, controlled the movements of Aboriginal peoples, restricted key cultural practices, and forbade Aboriginal peoples from consuming alcohol. Where possible, they promoted intermarriage and integration, hoping and believing that time would solve the Aboriginal "problem."

The First Peoples proved to be surprisingly hard to manage. Resentments developed as Aboriginal communities lost land and access to resources. In some areas, particularly where government controls and influence were weak, violence often erupted between Aboriginal people and settlers, eventually damaging the less powerful First Nations. Paternalism proved very strong, however. Colonial governments did not soon give up the idea that they knew what was best for the small, vulnerable Aboriginal populations. The pattern of domination established in the early decades of contact was reinforced by educational, economic, and administrative policies. Non-aboriginal settlers wanted the assurance that their use and occupation of First Nations lands would not be interrupted.

Each colonial administration had a wide selection of examples for how to deal with aboriginal peoples. Experiences ranged from the American frontier's legacy of military combat, to New Zealand's treaty negotiations, Australia's informal methods of dispossession, and the tightly run colonial administrations found on many Pacific Islands. All assumed that European control (with a few exceptions, as in Fiji) was both desirable and inevitable, and readily dismissed local inhabitants' land rights. Their priorities were to settle the land, develop the economy, and keep the peace among races—by force, if necessary.

The British colonial government and First Nations in the Pacific Northwest

British colonial administration came to British Columbia relatively late in the day. After an initial period of rivalry among Spain, Britain, and the United States over control of the Northwest, the colonial powers fell back into accepted territories.[7] This changed with the Oregon Treaty of 1846, which divided British holdings in the area, and passed the only lands where significant numbers of Europeans had settled into American hands. Britain and its commercial handmaiden, the Hudson's Bay Company, retreated to the north and re-established a corporate and colonial foothold at Fort Victoria, on Vancouver Island. The governor of Vancouver Island (1846) and British Columbia (established in 1858) was James Douglas, a forward-looking, experienced man who symbolized the union of government and business in the Northwest.[8]

Under Douglas, and drawing on the experience of the New Zealand Company, the government took careful steps towards removing Aboriginal claims to land and resources. Douglas had long experience in the fur trade, a commercial enterprise that was based on European familiarity with Aboriginal cultures. His background and his sympathy for First Nations people determined how he approached treaties.

By signing a series of small, local agreements with First Nations groups, Douglas tried to eliminate aboriginal claims to the land, and to make sure that European settlers had full rights of access. He drew very heavily on the New Zealand Company example—British Columbia treaties were almost identical to New Zealand documents. As with the Treaty of Waitangi, early B.C. treaties clearly did not intend to allow the First Nations to keep any strong, lasting land rights. This choice to minimize powers appears even more deliberate when we consider that Douglas did not draw on treaty examples from closer to home. The Robinson treaties, signed in southern Ontario in 1850, set the precedent of annuities and reserves, yet Douglas did not use this model.[9]

The Douglas treaties made from 1850 to 1854 were on a small scale, involving only 14 First Nations groups on Vancouver Island.[10] Governor Douglas had little money to spend, and settlers made few demands for land beyond the immediate areas of Fort Victoria and Nanaimo. As a result, he did not continue the treaty process around the rest of Vancouver Island or onto the mainland. The treaties were not the result of negotiations. In the most flagrant instance, Douglas had the First Nations sign a blank piece of paper, then added the text later. The central elements of each were the same:

> The condition of our understanding of this sale is this, that our village sites and enclosed fields are to be kept for our own use, for the use of our children, and for those who may follow after us; and the land shall be properly surveyed hereafter. It is understood, however, that the land with these small exceptions, becomes the entire property of the white people for ever; it is also understood that we are at liberty to hunt over the unoccupied lands, and to carry on our fisheries as formerly. We have received in payment [amounts varied depending upon the size of the reserve].[11]

After the B.C. gold rush began, tens of thousands of miners and settlers flooded the region, which sparked a series of violent confrontations between the newcomers and the First Nations. Douglas was no longer able to continue the treaty process.[12]

Except for Treaty 8, signed in 1898 and covering a large portion of the northeast corner of the province, the Douglas treaties were the only efforts to formally restrict First Nations land before the Nisga'a Agreement-in-Principle in 1996. But Douglas did not restrict his activities to formal treaties. He also moved quickly to establish small residential reserves for First Nations people, particularly those dislocated by the arrival of newcomers. Anxious to carve out a niche for First Nations people, and seriously concerned about the potential spread of violence northward from Oregon and Washington, Douglas encouraged First Nations groups to identify lands that they wished to set aside for their use. He also allowed individuals to claim land as freehold, as could any incoming settler. As long as Douglas remained in office, which he did until 1864, he could capitalize on the trust he had developed with First Nations people and the authority he possessed as governor to protect Aboriginal land rights in a limited way.

James Douglas was not a benign paternalist, but rather a practical man who worried about the future role of First Nations in British Columbia. He was replaced by Joseph Trutch, Chief Commissioner of Lands and Works. After B.C. joined Confederation in 1871, Trutch became lieutenant-governor of the province.

In Trutch's mind, First Nations people were an impediment to progress, and their control of key pieces of land throughout the province a serious economic disadvantage. He believed that the Douglas treaties were not a foundation to build on, but simply promises of friendship. Trutch felt about B.C. the way Australian settlers felt about Australia: it was land without an owner. He had none of Douglas' compassion, nor even the gentle paternalism shown at that time by governments in other parts of the country.

Trutch felt that First Nations' claims to the land could and should be dispensed with quickly. He didn't worry about whether the people displaced sank economically or socially. Like many others of his day and background, Trutch believed that the First Nations had few long-term prospects in a province that was as rich in resources and developing as quickly as British Columbia. He also believed that First Nations people were not using the land as intensively as it should be used. His idea, common at the time, was that any land that was not physically occupied and was not "developed" should be open to all comers. This idea of "permanent" occupation and development was alien to a people who mostly resided in small, seasonal camps.

With his hands on the government controls, Trutch began to reduce and eliminate reserves, and to cut back on Aboriginal rights to own land. He reduced the land allocation per person for new reserves from 160 acres per family to a miserly ten acres per family. Step by step, Trutch moved to constrain and push aside the First Nations people of British Columbia.

If Joseph Trutch has become the symbol of government policy and British Columbian attitudes in this period, it is with good reason. As Robin Fisher has argued:

> Trutch's actions, moreover, involved a break with the usual British policy. In her haphazard way, Britain seems to have developed a policy whereby, if territory was occupied in a regular way, aboriginal possession was recognized, and therefore had to be

extinguished before settlement could proceed. There was some kind of threshold over which Britain would recognize native rights to the land. The land ownership concepts of the Australian aborigines, for example, were not sufficiently clear for Britain to recognize, whereas those of the New Zealand Maori were. Given this threshold, then, were the concepts of territory and ownership of British Columbia's Indian sufficiently precise to be recognizable? It seems clear that they were. There were variations in different parts of the colony, but the Indians had precise concepts of territorial boundaries or ownership of specific areas. Douglas knew the Indians well enough to be aware of this aspect of their society and he tried to recognize it in his policy. When it was financially possible he compensated the Indians for giving up their rights to the territory. His attitude was sustained by the imperial government and he was clearly in accord with British policy throughout the rest of North America. Trutch, on the other hand, was not the least interested in Indian social usages. He denied that they had any rights to the land at all.[13]

The effects of the shift from Douglas to Trutch were not immediately evident, and would not be so for many years, except to the First Nations peoples displaced by government action. Nevertheless, this period marked a vital transition in government policy. Douglas tried to use the offices of government to buffer the First Nations from the trauma of the collapse of the fur trade and the rapid expansion of the settlement and mining frontier. His measures, though largely ineffective, attempted to carve out a small niche for First Nations people within the evolving colony. Trutch shared no such views, and moved very quickly after assuming office to promote a very different idea of how the province's lands and resources should be used. And it was Trutch's perspective that B.C. carried into Confederation.

Pushed to the Margins: Government Dealings with First Nations in B.C. from 1871 to World War II

The story of how British Columbia was courted by the newly founded nation of Canada has been told well and often. When B.C. finally surrendered to Canada's generosity, it had collected a fine set of endowments that both caused resentment in the rest of the country and bred an attitude of grievance and expectation within B.C.—hence its reputation as the "spoilt child of Confederation." Because the First Nations were very prominent in B.C. at the time of the negotiations, representing over half the population, the federal government opened up the touchy matter of responsibility to Aboriginal peoples. British Columbia agreed to very limited obligations. In the agreement for Confederation, a simple but potent phrase stated that the Canadian government was expected to adopt a policy toward the First Nations that was "as liberal as that hitherto pursued by the British Columbia Government."[14] The wording created nothing but mischief.[15]

Under Trutch, British Columbian policy was anything but "liberal." In accepting responsibility to administer First Nations' affairs in the province, the federal government was actually not accepting much of a duty. Trutch ensured that the federal government did not make any effort to extend the policy on the prairies, where the first of the numbered treaties were being signed in the 1870s, west of the mountains. He said to John A. Macdonald:

> The Canadian treaty system as I understand it will hardly work here—we have never bought out any Indian claims to the lands nor do they expect we should—but we reserve for their aid and benefit from time to time tracts of sufficient extent to fulfill all their reasonable requirements for cultivation or grazing. If you now commence to buy out Indian title to the lands of British Columbia—you would go back on all that has been done here for 30 years past and would be equitably bound to compensate the tribes who inhabited the district now settled and farmed by white people equally with those in the more remote and uncultivated portions. Our Indians are sufficiently satisfied and had better be left alone as far as a new system towards them is concerned.[16]

After Trutch's initial efforts, First Nations people had little land remaining. As new reserves were created in northern and remote regions, the government followed the pattern of offering them only small bits of real estate. In addition, what lands were granted were restricted by concerns for the needs of newer settlers. The federal government took few steps to protect existing First Nations reserves, and carved off portions that were not being used "productively," that were required for other purposes, or that they decided to be more than the First Nations group really needed. Canada was in the middle of a growth spurt, planning dozens of railway projects, new town sites, and countless development projects. First Nations people and their landholdings were seen as an obstacle to progress. And with both governments involved in the process of restricting Aboriginal land rights, the First Nations had few ears for their complaints.

However, the federal government in particular did not opt entirely out of the lives of First Nations people. In fact, at the same time it reduced Aboriginal landholdings, the government began an extensive series of programs in other areas. British Columbia had been roughly divided into areas of religious authority based largely on the right of first arrival. Working with the Christian churches, the federal government set up a small network of residential and day schools, designed to uplift First Nations children from the "depravity" of their surroundings and culture, and to give them the skills necessary to survive in the new economy and society.[17] Agencies were opened across the province to provide some measure of government influence over First Nations' affairs (although, particularly in the North, the areas involved were so large that practical control was very difficult).

The government also began a campaign to eliminate certain "undesirable" cultural activities. The potlatch, the core of the economic and social system of Northwest Coast First Nations, was banned in 1884. Many First Nations found ways to sidestep the regulation, demonstrating a continued pattern of resistance that had long been their response to settlement and government. But this legislative attack on the centrepiece of coastal culture was a bitter cut. When the government used its authority to close down potlatches and to imprison First Nations people for practising their traditions, as they did in the 1920s, it was a forceful demonstration of the power the state could wield over its people.[18]

By the 1920s, First Nations had been pushed out of most main sectors of the B.C. economy and had a much reduced role in its mainstream society. The fur trade remained active, but only in the Far North. Many Aboriginal groups worked in coastal fisheries, but were gradually losing out to Japanese and Chinese labour. Government regulations further eroded the ability of First Nations fishers to profit from the fishing industry.[19] Many First Nations people had long moved up and down the coast, from the Alaska Panhandle to Puget Sound, to search for trade and job opportunities. Many from the Georgia Strait area played an active role in the Washington State hop industry. But these opportunities declined as the non-aboriginal population increased. First Nations workers were displaced by those more acceptable to employers.

Hemmed in on small, largely residential reserves, lacking secure access to land or resources, increasingly displaced from the workplace, and kept to the margins of society by deeply entrenched racial biases, the First Nations of British Columbia found themselves pushed into irrelevance in their own homeland. Christian missionaries and school teachers continued their systematic assault on the First Nations' languages, culture, and spiritual beliefs, cutting younger people off from the lifestyles and values of their elders.[20]

Within 50 years of Confederation, First Nations had been forced out of the main life of the province.[21] Few pleaded their cause to government or the general public; few even gave much thought to the decline in Aboriginal culture. Governments took a leading role in placing First Nations people on the margins—the province by its unbending commitment to limited land rights, and the federal government by its extensive program of assimilation and "civilization." Voices were raised in protest, largely Aboriginal, but few listened. There was no James Douglas in a position of authority in the first half of the 20th century to support them, and no indication that government policy or public attitudes would soon change.[22]

However, in the northwest corner of B.C., First Nations' protests about losing their land rights were not ignored.[23] In the late 1890s, after gold was discovered in the Klondike River valley of the Yukon District, miners began to pour through northern routes to the far northwest. Several of these passages passed through the region north and west of Edmonton. First Nations people around the post at Fort St. John protested the invasions. At one point, they gathered some 500 people to prevent the North West Mounted Police and a group of miners from crossing their territory. As they had done previously when First Nations land rights and claims clashed with development priorities, the federal government moved quickly to start a treaty process. David Laird, Lieutenant-Governor of the Northwest Territories, was assigned late in 1898 to head the treaty expedition.

The task of getting signatures on Treaty 8 started in the Northwest Territories in 1899, but did not extend to northern British Columbia until the following year. Efforts in B.C. did not go well. As one government official wryly noted, "a great many of them [First Nations peoples] have a great antipathy to treaty."[24] Other groups, especially those in the northern reaches of the treaty region, withheld their consent for another ten years. Efforts to include groups missed in earlier visits and those initially reluctant to sign continued through to 1914.

The treaty itself was a limited document that was based on the assumption that the First Nations would continue their harvesting lifestyle and that there was little need, as in the south, to shift them onto residential reserves. The terms of the agreement offered blocks of land (one square mile for a family of five), annual grants, farming supplies, and education in return for the First Nations' surrender of their right to traditional territories.[25]

British Columbia was not directly involved in the transfer of land. In 1907, the province had given the federal government 3.5 million acres in return for federal assistance in building railways in the south. Agricultural settlement began in 1912. In 1914, the federal government started setting aside reserve lands in the southern portions of the Treaty 8 region in British Columbia. Other First Nations groups—Fort Nelson, Laird River, McLeod Lake, Ingenika (then called Fort Grahame and including Fort Ware), and Findlay River—lived outside the Peace River block, and therefore could not receive land directly from the federal government. The issue went to the McKenna-McBride Royal Commission, which had been established to examine the Indian land questions in British Columbia. For the bands in isolated areas, the Commission put off the matter until they had more information on band sizes and patterns of residence. In fact, bands in the Fort Nelson district did not receive land allotments until the early 1960s. The Commission granted others a series of small reserves.

The Treaty 8 experience was not repeated across the rest of the province. The unique combination of the rush to the Klondike, the need to settle land rights in the area northwest of Edmonton (only part of which lay in British Columbia), and the availability of the Peace River block convinced the federal government to act. The province participated little in the process, but did agree with the recommendations of the McKenna-McBride Royal Commission on granting small reserves to a few bands. B.C.'s pattern of moving reluctantly on such matters continued after World War II. Creating reserves for the Fort Nelson band was delayed by a long discussion over mineral rights to oil and gas reserves in the area.

By the end of the 19th century, the promising legacy of James Douglas had been swept aside, replaced by the more restricted agenda of Joseph Trutch. The construction of railways, expansion of agriculture, development of mining deposits, and the expansion of towns and cities took precedence over First Nations' land needs. First Nations were seen primarily as an impediment to the province's proper development. The federal government resisted interfering with provincial affairs, doing so only in the northwest, where circumstances made action both desirable and possible. First Nations were for the most part on their own in demanding attention to their land claims and rights, and found few allies in their efforts to secure control of traditional territories.

In other parts of the country and in other parts of the British Empire, settlers sought to take over the lands of Aboriginal peoples as cheaply and efficiently as possible. In most places, governments stepped in and imposed some form of treaty or settlement process. British Columbians (like Australians) established early on their opposition to wide recognition of First Nations' rights. The fact that local politicians and administrators were able to proceed with such a concerted anti–First Nations land policy was a sign of the low priority this issue had in London and Ottawa. Perhaps the issue was even more practical. On the Canadian plains and in New Zealand, governments faced the possibility of armed uprisings. Only rarely was that an issue in B.C. Whatever the explanation, at the end of the 19th century British Columbia had a well-established policy of pushing First Nations' demands for land and resources into the background, no doubt in the hope and expectation that they would remain there.

Aboriginal Land Rights Campaigns in the 20th Century

Aboriginal land rights now have a prominent place on the international and domestic political agenda. But 100 years ago, the issue attracted virtually no political attention. It was sustained only by the firm belief among the First Nations that they still had a spiritual and cultural claim to the lands and resources that had supported their people for generations. The shift from one extreme to the other was far from logical or consistent. It depended on continuing pressure from Aboriginal people, occasionally interrupted by government orders and interference. And government indifference was really overcome only in the last 25 years. The difficulty and length of the process is a testament to the importance of this issue to the First Nations people, and of government reluctance to accept their concerns as legitimate.

The First Nations' struggle for land rights in B.C.

The fact that federal and provincial governments did not recognize Aboriginal land claims did not make First Nations' rights any less real to the people themselves. Even before outsiders (mainly missionaries and lawyers) alerted them to the possibilities of appeal through legal and parliamentary channels, First Nations across British Columbia had a strong conviction that the land and resources still belonged to them. Responses varied across the province in the years after Confederation. First Nations in isolated areas and away from population centres had less direct interference in their lives and with their land than those near towns and cities. Land rights were less of a concern where the people remained on the land and had little competition for resources. Typically, when land and resources were in demand for railways, mines, forestry, or commercial fishing, the commercial frontier arrived quickly and with little regard for First Nations' occupation and use of traditional territories.

First Nations people protested, of course, and routinely demanded both more land and more attention from both governments. The federal government was sympathetic, but felt its hands were tied by provincial stubbornness. In 1887, First Nations leaders from the North Coast presented their case to Premier Smithe. He dismissed their entreaties with a phrase that would echo in the observations of Chief Justice A. McEachern 100 years later: "When the whites first came among you, you were little better than the wild beasts of the field."[26] The governments agreed to investigate Aboriginal demands, but later rejected them as being the complaints of a few unpatriotic leaders. The First Nations did not back down. Led by several members able to function effectively in the newcomers' world, they continued to press their case. In 1906, the Salish sent three chiefs to London to argue their case, and the next year the Nisga'a formed a special committee to address the land question. In 1909, two Aboriginal organizations were formed: the Interior Tribes of British Columbia and the Indian Rights Association (for Coastal groups).

The major government action on land rights in the early 20th century was the establishment of the McKenna-McBride Royal Commission in 1912. The Commission was to examine the reserve allocations across the province, supposedly to standardize the allotments and to make sure that the First Nations had the land that they needed. Despite First Nations' protests, the government made no effort to broaden its mandate to consider the broader question of treaty rights in British Columbia. The Commission took its work seriously. Some reserves were increased in size; many others were cut back. This was particularly the case near towns and cities, where the Commissioners found that valuable land was not being actively used. They did not ask or get permission from the affected First Nations, violating the terms of the *Indian Act* and the principles of natural justice.

First Nations groups had been active in pressing their case. A group of Interior chiefs, meeting at Kamloops in 1910, petitioned the federal government for greater compassion in handling land rights:

> What we know and are concerned with is the fact that the British Columbia Government has already taken part of our lands without treaty with us, or payment of any compensation, and has disposed of them to settlers and others. The remaining lands of the country, the Government have claim to as their property, and ignores our title. Out of our lands they reserved small pieces here and there, called Indian Reserves, and allowed us the occupancy of them. These even they claim as their property, and threaten in some places to taken away from us, although we have been in continuous occupancy and possession. . . . We never asked for part of our country to be parceled out in pieces and reserved for us. It was entirely a Government scheme originating with them.[27]

The Nisga'a in particular continually pushed the federal government for action. When that failed, they launched an appeal to the British government in 1913. It had no immediate effect, but did signal to both levels of government that the First Nations were far from ignorant about conditions elsewhere in the country, and had not abandoned their claims to traditional lands.

The formation of Aboriginal organizations—which was difficult in itself due to historical differences between Interior and Coastal bands, language and cultural barriers, and various conflicts between First Nations leaders—increased the pressure, especially on the federal government. The Allied Tribes of British Columbia, the first province-wide organization, was formed in 1916. It brought forward specific proposals to recognize Aboriginal land rights and to negotiate treaties with the First Nations. Under the leadership of Peter Kelly and Andrew Paull, it began to be prominent in federal-provincial political relations. Federal authorities established a joint committee of the Senate and House of Commons to hear the proposals. The First Nations made the first of many difficult journeys to Ottawa, but found the audience far from receptive. The committee rejected First Nations' demands as being unreasonable. To make matters worse, the government changed the *Indian Act* to make it illegal for First Nations to meet, raise money, and hire lawyers to challenge federal authority on land and traditional rights. It was a shocking setback from what many believed was a promising process. Instead of securing recognition of their rights to the land, First Nations found themselves legally prohibited from so much as discussing the matter.

Government regulations had little effect in stopping the potlatch and other cultural activities, and could not easily prevent Aboriginal people from pursuing their land claims. The law, however, blocked public action and ensured that the federal and provincial governments would pay little attention to protests from First Nations. Federal restrictions on First Nations cultural and political activities were lifted in 1951, following yet another set of hearings by a joint committee of the House and Senate. Nevertheless, the government still did not abandon its determination to assimilate Aboriginal peoples or to listen to demands for treaty negotiations. Freed from *Indian Act* prohibitions on meetings, First Nations organized more publicly and expanded their networks (which ironically were reinforced through contacts made in Native residential schools) to try to develop province-wide support for their claims. Internal difficulties persisted. Conflicts in culture, language, and personality often interfered with developing a coherent provincial First Nations position on land claims and rights. But over time, the political skills and following of First Nations organizations grew.

During the first half of the 20th century, the two basic elements in the history of First Nations land rights continued. Aboriginal peoples were committed to resolving their claims, and provincial and federal governments paid no attention to their demands. At no time did the First Nations surrender their claims or abandon the cause, even though the federal government prevented them from organizing to pursue their goals. First Nations' belief that their cause was legitimate proved to be immovable. But so did the position of the two governments.

There was virtually no electoral constituency for First Nations rights. Status Indians did not have the right to vote, and the number of Aboriginals who had surrendered their status or had it taken from them was very small. There was little political incentive to act. In fact, there was widespread support for segregating and assimilating the First Nations, and for limiting their land rights to the small residential allotments set aside for their use. The two unbending commitments—one sustained by the majority of the population and the authority of the federal and provincial governments, the second by the determination and cultural beliefs of the First Nations—seemed to be at a permanent impasse. Governments expected that over time, if their methods of assimilation worked, First Nations' interest in traditional activities and collective rights would fade. And once they had been fully integrated, or disappeared entirely as a viable culture, the land rights issue would disappear entirely. There were few forces for change in British Columbia and only slightly more across the rest of Canada.

The emergence of the modern treaty process after World War II

Native demands to resolve land rights and claims never stopped in British Columbia, even with concerted government efforts to muzzle First Nations leaders.[28] Government tactics, however, changed over time. By the 1960s, they could count on much more support from within non-aboriginal communities, particularly from the churches and academia.[29] The commitment of First Nations to get a just settlement to their land claims never wavered. The fundamental transformation was much broader, in worldwide changes in attitude to human rights and Aboriginal cultures. We can't trace the shift in support to a single event, personality, or process. It was tied to a complex web of political and social changes.

The experiences of World War II, particularly the intense racial hatreds bred by the Pacific War and mass horror at the discovery of the Jewish Holocaust in Europe, knocked the foundations from systemic racism. Though it now seems unlikely, public declarations of racist attitudes were an integral part of western democratic cultures through the 1930s and 1940s. When the larger population realized the extremes to which racism could be taken, they were ready to find new approaches to cultural relations.

At the same time, the United Nations was created in 1945, and governments began to commit to international conventions on human rights, to decolonization, and to accepting cultural differences. These developments transformed public and political ideas of what behaviour toward minorities was and was not acceptable. Additional motivations to change came from the liberal democracies' growing commitment to the "welfare state," and to raising the standard of living of the nations' poorest people. Changes in attitude ranged from taking a greater interest in traditional crafts to worrying about how economic development projects were encroaching on Aboriginal lands and peoples. Slowly, changed perceptions moved into the global consciousness. Churches that had once been a driving force behind assimilation shifted to defending Aboriginal peoples' right to self-government. Governments that had long ignored First Nations' demands for action began paying more attention to them, even if their old paternalistic streak was still strong. First Nations peoples became more politically active and more public, and even began to establish the beginnings of an international network.

The first major attempt to recognize and respond to Aboriginal concerns was Convention 107 (1957) of the International Labor Organization. Even though the document was assimilationist in tone and few people signed it, it showed that the unique circumstances of Aboriginal peoples were being recognized internationally. With the international spotlight clearly on Aboriginal issues, national governments of all political stripes found it more and more difficult to ignore the needs of their First Peoples.

Canada responded to international concerns by revising the *Indian Act,* granting the vote to First Nations people (and also to Chinese- and Japanese-Canadians), and offering a broad range of economic and social programs through the Department of Indian Affairs. The public also came to a greater appreciation of Aboriginal cultures, though it did so slowly. Some non-aboriginal peoples clung to the belief that First Nations cultures were doomed to disappear and their people should be absorbed into the Canadian mainstream. Old attitudes died hard. As late as 1969, in the White Paper on Indian Affairs, the federal government considered eliminating "Indian status" in Canada, and drafted a plan to integrate the First Nations more fully into the dominant society. At the same time, however, the government was expanding its social, economic, and cultural programs for First Nations. It began a long program of improving housing on reserves, expanding local school options, and otherwise trying to provide better conditions for Aboriginal peoples.

Made bold by international action, and in particular by the radicalism of the American Indian movement, First Nations in Canada became increasingly active and outspoken in their demands for change. Chances for major changes, however, ran up against the Prime Minister's opposition. As Pierre Trudeau argued in 1969, "It is inconceivable I think that in a given society, one section of the society have a treaty with the other section of the society. We must all be equal under the laws. . . . We cannot recognize aboriginal rights because no society can be built on historical 'might-have-beens.'"[30]

On the global scene, the 1970s and 1980s saw continued pressure on international organizations and national governments to listen to Aboriginal demands for action. In 1983, the creation of the United Nations Work Group on Indigenous Peoples (set up by the Sub-Commission on Prevention of Discrimination and Protection of Minorities) was a major step forward in recognizing the special needs and concerns of Aboriginal peoples. The International Labor Organization updated its statement on Aboriginal rights in 1991, but again the document attracted few signatures. A battery of global organizations, like the International Work Group for Indigenous Affairs, Survival International, and Cultural Survival made a special effort to keep Aboriginal affairs on the public agenda.

One landmark event was the 1993 release of the Draft Declaration on the Rights of Indigenous Peoples. The United Nations Work Group on Indigenous Peoples had consulted with Aboriginal groups from around the world in preparation, the radicalism of Aboriginal peoples in the liberal democracies offsetting the more pragmatic approaches of groups in the developing world. The Draft Declaration played a major role in centralizing the Aboriginal rights movement, primarily by bringing representatives together in a major, highly public global forum.[31]

Between the 1950s and the 1980s, the Aboriginal rights movement was transformed from a limited and domestic concern that got little attention even in national politics, to a highly publicized international issue. Some evidence shows that global interest in Aboriginal rights may have hit a plateau at this point. However, the efforts of the past 30 years helped make it impossible or at least unwise for governments to shove First Nations' demands into the background. Arguments that could readily be ignored before World War II now carried the growing weight of national and international opinion. In this atmosphere, First Nations organizations began to chip away at the resolve of the provincial and federal governments, finding cracks in the wall of resistance to First Nations' concerns.

First Nations land claims in British Columbia after World War II

The land is our culture and it is our only future. Before the coming of the Europeans, we lived as one with the land and waters. We have our own systems of government, our own way of managing the land and its resources for the benefit of all. In short we had sovereignty over our own lives and means to live. These are our aboriginal rights. (Grand Chief George Manuel, Shuswap Nation)[32]

Showing the resiliency that had pulled them through years of neglect and oppression at the hands of the federal government, First Nations leaders in British Columbia continued their efforts to get the government to listen to their claims. At postwar hearings of the Special Joint Committee of the Senate and House of Commons, B.C. First Nations made strong presentations about why the government had to acknowledge Aboriginal rights and title. Their appeals were ignored. First Nations did get the right to vote (provincially in 1951 and federally after 1960). But more ambitious plans to address Aboriginal concerns remained in the distant future. First Nations organizations re-emerged (particularly under the guidance of George Manuel) to make repeated but unsuccessful attempts to get government support for their demands.

Faced with federal and provincial governments that refused to consider matters of Aboriginal rights and land title, First Nations turned to the courts more and more. At the most basic level, Aboriginal leaders felt that the Royal Proclamation of 1763 guaranteed Aboriginal title to treaty negotiations. On Vancouver Island, the less dramatic commitments of the Douglas treaties seemed to offer some minor protection for First Nations' rights. A major turning point came with *Regina v. White and Bob,* a case about First Nations hunting rights on Vancouver Island. The defendants argued that the Douglas treaties protected their harvesting privileges, which the courts upheld, right to the Supreme Court of Canada. *White and Bob* (December 15, 1964) marked a turning point for First Nations people in British Columbia, for it confirmed that their arguments about Aboriginal rights and the supremacy of the Douglas treaties were legitimate.

The Nisga'a of northwestern B.C. pressed the matter further, challenging federal and provincial claims that Aboriginal title had expired. They demanded recognition of their existing rights to the land and resources. As with *White and Bob,* the Nisga'a case, *Calder v. British Columbia (Attorney General),* worked its way slowly through the court system, reaching the Supreme Court in 1973. The result solved little. The seven justices split 3/3/1 on the case, with the seventh judge ruling on a technical basis. The fact that three of the Supreme Court judges had accepted the Nisga'a position meant nothing legally. The case had been lost. However, Prime Minister Trudeau, who did not personally accept the notion of Aboriginal land title, was strongly affected by the fact that three Supreme Court justices had taken a contrary opinion.

Legal judgments are not the final word. The pressure of the Nisga'a challenge raised the possibility that a future "all or nothing" court decision could lead to a major reversal for the government. Moreover, public sentiment was shifting decisively toward the First Nations' side. The federal government responded by establishing an Office of Native Claims in 1974. This organization was responsible for negotiating comprehensive land claims submitted by First Nations across the country. The first claim, from the Yukon Native Brotherhood (later the

Council for Yukon Indians), had been accepted by the federal government the previous year.

Ironically, the shift in public opinion only added to the frustrations of First Nations in B.C. Although the federal government opted for modern treaty negotiations, it could only do so for those areas where it had control of land and resources. As a result, First Nations from the Yukon and Northwest Territories found themselves involved in long and costly discussions with federal negotiators. But the national government lacked the authority to negotiate over land and resources within B.C., and the provincial government showed few signs of backing down from its long-standing opposition to such measures. So, while the Nisga'a case greatly advanced the cause of Aboriginal land rights across the nation, it had no immediate impact on British Columbia, except to highlight the continued stubbornness of the provincial government.

The provincial position remained firm and simple. As historian Robin Fisher described the situation a few years ago:

> The provincial government of British Columbia remains quite obdurate. It continues to argue that aboriginal title never existed; or, if it did, it was extinguished before confederation; or, if it was not dealt with before 1871, it is now Ottawa's problem. As well as rejecting the broad issue of title, the province has often blocked the settlement of particular land claims by virtue of its control over Crown lands.[33]

As Ottawa moved toward the First Nations' position, B.C. remained firm. Even major land claims agreements in the North, First Nations protests, and a national decision to entrench "existing aboriginal and treaty rights" in the Canadian constitution in 1982 did not move it. (British Columbia argued that the constitutional change actually reinforced its position on Aboriginal title. The spirit of Joseph Trutch lived on.)

Over time, however, the B.C. government found itself in a vice. It was squeezed by Ottawa, the First Nations, and a growing group of non-aboriginal supporters. A series of court decisions seemed to be tipping the law in the First Nations' favour. Several court judgments in the 1980s and 1990s confirmed what First Nations had been arguing for years—that the federal government had ignored its legal obligations and had not managed Aboriginal affairs with appropriate sensitivity and understanding. Each of the main cases involved either sizable financial compensation for First Nations groups (*Guerin v. The Queen* over the use of Aboriginal land and resources) or reinstating important Aboriginal rights (*R. v. Sparrow* and fishing rights). This only increased the public outcry and the pressure on governments to deal with outstanding aboriginal claims.

The battle lines were firmly drawn in *Delgamuukw v. The Queen*, in which the Gitksan-Wet'suwet'en launched a major challenge to the provincial government's position on land rights. The case lasted longer than any other in Canadian history, and cost the Gitksan-Wet'suwet'en millions of dollars in court and other charges. Never had an Aboriginal group in Canada invested as much in a single court case, culturally as well as financially. Elders presented important cultural information to the courts, their evidence backed up by academics and legal advisors. And then they lost—spectacularly. The final judgment by Chief Justice Allan McEachern, presented to unbelieving audiences in Vancouver and Smithers on March 8, 1991, could not have been more harsh and dismissive. While the decision was tightly argued on matters of law (the bulk of his findings of fact withstood the first appeal), McEachern's final comments included a blatant indictment of Aboriginal culture and completely dismissed most of the social and political information presented by Gitksan-Wet'suwet'en elders. The Gitksan-Wet'suwet'en launched an appeal, but got little encouragement from the British Columbia Court of Appeal.

For opponents of First Nations land claims, the McEachern judgment was convincing evidence that the governments of British Columbia and Canada had no legal obligation to proceed with negotiations. The judgment, combined with other court rulings, did compel governments to consult with First Nations groups on traditional land and resource use before proceeding with development projects. The Gitksan-Wet'suwet'en pursued their appeal. In 1993, the B.C. Court of Appeal supported many of Chief Justice McEachern's findings of fact, but held that the First Nations had "unextinguished non-exclusive aboriginal rights, other than a right of ownership" to some of their lands. The Court also recommended that negotiated settlements were preferable to continued court trials. The Gitksan-Wet'suwet'en launched a further appeal to the Supreme Court of Canada.

The Gitksan-Wet'suwet'en appearance at the Supreme Court was put on hold in 1993 as a result of several major changes in policy at the provincial level that had begun a few years earlier. Because there was growing support across the province for First Nations land claims, and a provincial election was coming up, the provincial government suddenly changed its approach. The Supreme Court of Canada's decision in the *Sparrow* case seemed to undercut the government's argument that Aboriginal rights had been "frozen" in the past. And in the summer of 1990, sparked by the stand-off at Oka, First Nations' political tensions heated up across the country. In the fall of 1990, just before the provincial election, the Social Credit administration of Bill Vander Zalm announced that the provincial government would enter into negotiations with the Nisga'a and would also begin the process of negotiating with other First Nations. The province set up the Ministry of Aboriginal Affairs, under Minister Jack Weisgerber, to handle this work on the government's behalf. The federal and provincial governments, together with the First Nations, established the British Columbia Claims Task Force to advise the government on the treaty negotiation process. The following year, the Task Force's recommendations were accepted. The new treaty process had emerged, founded on the New Democratic Party government's acceptance of Aboriginal rights and the right to self-government.

British Columbia's modern treaty process was drawn directly from the recommendations of the B.C. Claims Task Force, which ended its report with this observation:

> The task force believes that the process of negotiation to establish a new relationship will be positive for the First Nations and for the citizens of British Columbia and Canada. The status quo has been costly. Energies and resources have been spent in legal battles and other strategies. It is time to put these resources and energies into the negotiation of a constructive relationship.[34]

All parties had accepted each of the Task Force's 19 recommendations. One of the key items was the creation of the British Columbia Treaty Commission to oversee the land claims process. This process had six stages for resolving claims:

- statements of intent sent from First Nations to the B.C. Treaty Commission

- preparations for negotiations and preliminary meetings
- negotiation of framework agreements, which list the items for negotiation and the schedule for discussions
- signing of an Agreement-in-Principle by all three parties
- public discussion, legislative debate, and consultations with the First Nations beneficiaries
- implementation of the treaty, as negotiated.

This process began late in 1993. First Nations groups rushed quickly to file statements of intent and to begin negotiations. At the same time, the federal and provincial governments, together with the B.C. Treaty Commission and the First Nations Summit, began a program of public education and consultation to respond to general concerns about the process. In addition, governments accepted the need to negotiate "interim measures" agreements to make sure that areas under negotiation would be affected as little as possible by delays in discussions. For example, one interim measure was to ensure that lands due to be claimed by a First Nation as part of its settlement would not be logged or mined before a treaty could be signed.

Of course, First Nations always have the option to return to the courts. With the *Delgamuukw* appeal not yet concluded, and with other court challenges on hold, B.C. First Nations have the threat of the "all or nothing" legal decision to back their demands. If political will to continue negotiations falters, and the land claims process stalls, First Nations could abandon the negotiations and turn their attention back to the courts. This is the main reason why provincial and federal governments are participating in land claims negotiations. They want to avoid the uncertainty of legal challenges. It is difficult to imagine the land claims negotiations proceeding smoothly if the First Nations did not have at least this potential legal recourse. As has become increasingly common in the province and across the country, when they lack such a legal hold, First Nations peoples have resorted to civil disobedience and the threat of violence, which is hardly a solid foundation for lasting relationships.

British Columbia is now deeply involved in a land claims process that seeks to resolve outstanding First Nations claims to land and resources. At present, the process has strong public support among people who truly wish to give Aboriginal peoples back their power, and who simply want this contentious and controversial matter solved. But there is also considerable public opposition, mostly from the Interior and the North. Many people there feel that the negotiations could well result in significant economic losses for non-aboriginal peoples. The signing of an Agreement-in-Principle with the Nisga'a in February 1996, which took place outside the B.C. Treaty Commission process, has both answered the critics who said agreements were not possible and inflamed those who felt that the governments were overly generous in the settlement.

The negotiation process, now begun in earnest, has assumed a life and authority of its own, and is quickly settling into a firm spot in the political culture of British Columbia. The change from six years ago, when the provincial government would not sit at the negotiating table, or from 25 years ago, when neither level of government recognized that Aboriginal land claims were legitimate, is dramatic. First Nations take a different view and are less impressed. To them, negotiations are only another stage in a long and difficult history of trying to reach a lasting, mutually respectful agreement with the governments of Canada and British Columbia. They are to be forgiven for withholding their enthusiasm until concrete results appear.

The people of British Columbia remain divided over the question of First Nations' land rights and the treaty process. Support for negotiations appears to be strongest in urban areas, where the impact of treaty settlements is likely to be slight. It is weakest in the Interior, Northern, and Coastal areas, where the terms and conditions of the final agreements will likely have an immediate effect on non-aboriginal peoples. The response of the fishing industry to the Nisga'a Agreement-in-Principle is a good illustration of this division; non-aboriginal fishers fear that the treaty will result in severe economic losses. Some still have the lingering suspicion that First Nations will either squander the economic benefits they get from the land claims process, or will become too wealthy from the settlements. These issues, and many others, will continue to influence the process.

Why We Must Understand Past History in order to Understand Modern Land Claims Issues

The attempt to resolve First Nations land claims is really a contest over the past. The issue is whether the injustices and actions of the past should lie under the gravestones of time, or whether society has an obligation to acknowledge past experiences and use them to determine modern policy. Land claims are also practical "tests" of the past. Major court cases and negotiated decisions can often turn on detailed points of historical analysis. Can a First Nations community document its past and demonstrate its use of land and resources? Do the historical records show that politicians knew that they were ignoring their legal obligations when they arranged to remove specific pieces of land from Aboriginal control?

History resonates throughout the land claims debate, providing justification and support for all positions, clearly showing that the past is not a set of "facts," but contested territory. As the debate continues over the resolution of First Nations land rights, British Columbians will hear more and more passionate interpretations of their province's history, offered as justification, counterpoint, or motivation for certain stands on the land claims issues. Examining how each of the parties sees history will help us to unravel the complex conflicts involved.

The First Nations' position: History is a legacy of loss

For First Nations people, the past is a simple, tragic story of loss— lands and resources, freedom and control, and of cultural centres. To be sure, they recognize the importance of certain legal agreements (like the Douglas treaties) and a vast array of government decisions and judgments made over the years. But to most First Nations people, the history of British Columbia is the history of the occupation and seizing of Aboriginal lands by and for non-aboriginal people.

For First Nations peoples, history is also a driving force. The victims of the past live longer and more passionately with their history than those who have benefited from the developments over time. First Nations people think back to experiences of dishonesty, misunderstanding, and painful cultural loss. The passionate positions often taken by

First Nations negotiators come from this legacy of frustration and anger. They have been taught not to trust governments by the sad and sorry lessons of the past 150 years.

The position of supporters: History is motivation and justification

After being long locked away in the memories and oral traditions of the First Nations, the history of Aboriginal dispossession is now more widely known. Writers like Robin Fisher, Paul Tennant, High Brody, and Thomas Berger, joined now by Aboriginal writers like Harry Robinson, have both highlighted the vitality of Aboriginal cultures and drawn attention to the treatment of First Nations in the past. In the process, they have given many non-aboriginal British Columbians a reason to support the Aboriginal cause. Knowing the circumstances of how Aboriginal peoples lost their lands and their access to traditional resources makes it much easier to support claims for land settlements and self-government. Combined with a sense of collective guilt, history sustains non-aboriginal support for First Nations' claims. It is a strong motivation for British Columbians to urge the government to address unresolved land rights questions.

The opponents' point of view: History is irrelevant

Not all British Columbians feel this way, of course. There is a very strong current of opinion in the province that argues that the past is past, and modern generations are not obliged to set right the errors or judgments of their ancestors. Some argue the details of history, as in Mel Smith's impassioned case that governments are proceeding where they have no historical or legal obligation to do so.[35] Most simply do not accept that there is a connection between the realities of the past and the grievances of the present. The argument that history is irrelevant, and that dwelling on decisions made 100 years ago simply prevents Aboriginal peoples from addressing the serious problems that they face in the present, remains deeply entrenched in British Columbia. One fairly common view is that Aboriginal peoples want to gain control of the land so that they can retreat into the past, even though such a belief flies in the face of the evidence that First Nations people adapt well to changing economic, social, and political circumstances.

In the past, people simply did not know about history. Their igno-
rance helped explain their lack of sympathy. Now that the historical
record is much clearer, and the actions of governments in restricting
First Nations access to land more sharply evident, the argument that the
past is irrelevant is more difficult to sustain.

The government position: History limits government responsibility

Governments have listened to the First Nations people, historians,
and lawyers, and have concluded that land claims must be settled. The
fact that it took so long to come to this decision is in itself evidence of
how deep administrative resistance was to First Nations land rights.
Now, having chosen to resolve First Nations claims through negotiations, the federal and provincial governments find themselves wedged
between passionately different interpretations of British Columbia's
past.

In seeking the middle ground (the most stable foundation for policy
in Canada), governments have tried to compromise. They acknowledge
historic injustices and the need to meet legal obligations to sign treaties, while at the same time recognizing the need to settle claims within
tight financial, geographic, and administrative boundaries. In other
words, the government has accepted the judgment of history, but has
decided that the judgment is a duty to honour only its strict legal obligations. Governments are reluctant but committed participants in the
process. They don't oppose First Nations claims, but neither are they
apologetic supporters of Aboriginal concerns.[36]

In the main, governments have chosen a narrow and legalistic interpretation of their obligations. In coming to the negotiating table, they
have accepted the need to respond to Aboriginal demands, but not necessarily for the legal and moral reasons put forward by First Nations.
They answer opponents who are trying to block negotiations by arguing that they are simply trying to secure certainty, so that the economic
development of the province can proceed. By accepting the need to
right past wrongs while limiting their obligations to those legally necessary, both governments are very much sitting on the fence between
conflicting views of history.[37]

Conclusion

The land claims process in British Columbia is both historic and historical. The beginning of negotiations and the potential for settlements could usher in a new era in the province's history. That new era could be one of cooperation and greater mutual understanding, but as the patterns of the past suggest, it could also be one of conflict, frustration, and false optimism. At its core, the land claims debate is a struggle over which interpretation of history will govern the general understanding of the province's past, and whether the current generation is responsible for setting right past injustices. As the negotiations unfold, expect a flurry of historical arguments, disputes, and reworkings of the past. Also expect that these retellings of provincial history will be filled with passion.

The connection between the past and the present also reinforces the sense that the modern land claims process is unique in British Columbia. But the historical reality is that both the occupation of Aboriginal lands and the attempts to constrain, define, and ultimately resolve First Nations land claims fall within broader global patterns. The land claims issue is on the provincial and national agenda at this time only partly because of the determined efforts of the First Nations. They have always demanded attention to their land rights. Its roots really lie in a series of global changes—in attitudes about Aboriginal peoples, in the belief in protecting human rights generally, and in the idea that Aboriginal peoples have specific rights. Canada was brought to the negotiating table as much by changing international attitudes as by reassessing history and the moral imperatives of Aboriginal land claims.

The ultimate message is quite simple. British Columbia is not alone in this process. It is riding a tide of opinion, government policy, and legal decisions that have had a profound effect on the fate of Aboriginal land claims. Like all tides, this one ebbs and flows. Governments edge toward a resolution, only to be pulled back by the shifting waters of public opinion. It is important that British Columbians recognize in the modern land claims process the interplay between the global and the provincial. Broad social and intellectual movements forced non-aboriginal peoples to listen more closely and with greater compassion to the words of the First Peoples and the tangled webs of provincial and federal policy that have defined First Nations land rights in British

Columbia. There is hope, too, in the ability of countries as diverse as Denmark, New Zealand, Australia, and Norway to address and respond to Aboriginal concerns. B.C. stands at a crucial point, one laden with historical meaning. It will either represent a sharp new direction for the province and the First Nations or simply another chapter in a century-long struggle over the right of Aboriginal peoples to a portion of their ancestral lands.

Notes

1. British Columbia Claims Task Force, pp. 1–4.

2. The key texts on the history of land rights and relations between Aboriginals and newcomers in British Columbia are

- Robin Fisher, *Contact and Conflict: Indian-European Relations in British Columbia, 1774–1890*
- Wilson Duff, *The Indian History of British Columbia, Vol. 1: The Impact of the White Man*
- Jean Barman, *The West Beyond the West: A History of British Columbia*
- D. Raunet, *Without Surrender, Without Consent: A History of the Nishga Land Claims*
- F. LaVillette, *The Struggle for Survival*
- H.R. Hawthorne et al., *The Indians of British Columbia*
- Robert Cail, *Land, Man and the Law: The Disposal of Crown Lands in British Columbia, 1871–1913*.

The most important study on the political and legal aspects of land rights is Paul Tennant's *Aboriginal Peoples and Politics: The Indian Land Question in British Columbia, 1849–1989*.

3. Several archeologists have argued that earlier migrations, likely by sea, occurred during the last ice age, when ocean levels were significantly lower. This would mean that habitation sites from that era would now be under many feet of water and would be extremely difficult to locate or investigate.

4. See James Belich, *The New Zealand Wars and the Victorian Interpretation of Racial Conflict*.

5. On the issue of disease as it relates to the early history of British Columbia, see Cole Harris, "Voices of Disaster: Smallpox Around the Strait of Georgia in 1782," and James Gibson, "Smallpox on the Northwest Coast, 1835–1838."

6. There are many studies of Aboriginal peoples in world history. As a starting point, the following books are helpful:

- Julian Burger, *Report from the Frontier: The State of the World's Indigenous People*

- John Bodley, *Victims of Progress*
- Ken Coates and John Taylor, eds, *Indigenous Peoples in Remote Regions*.

7. The best account of the history of relations between governments and the First Nations, and one of the most important books on British Columbia, is Tennant's *Aboriginal People and Politics*. The survey that follows relies heavily on Tennant's descriptions. For a contrary view that is not grounded in a detailed understanding of the historical record, but that does represent a fairly common viewpoint in B.C., see Melvin Smith, *Our Home or Native Land? What Governments' Aboriginal Policy is Doing to Canada*.

8. The major work on this subject is the second edition of Fisher's *Contact and Conflict: Indian-European Relations in British Columbia, 1774–1890*. For a different view of the early period of contact, see Barry Gough's *Gunboat Frontier: British Maritime Authority and Northwest Coast Indians, 1846–90*.

9. I thank Dr. A.J. Ray, from the University of British Columbia, for bringing this point to my attention.

10. Duff, "The Fort Victoria Treaties."

11. The texts of the Douglas treaties are widely available. See Government of B.C., *Briefing Material for Treaty Commissioners, Douglas Treaties, 1850–1854*.

12. Although the treaties were narrow in scope, First Nations people have used them to protect traditional rights (See *R. v. White and Bob*, 1964 and *Claxton v. Saanichton Marina Ltd.*, 1989). One major example is the 1987 injunction secured by the Tswaout Band to prevent construction of a marina in Saanichton Bay. They successfully argued that the construction project would interfere with their traditional right to fish, as guaranteed in the treaty.

13. Fisher, "Joseph Trutch and Indian Land Policy," p. 266.

14. Quoted in Fisher's "With or Without Treaty: Indian Land Claims in Western Canada," p. 56.

15. Barman summarizes the development of relations between First Nations peoples and the steadily increasing non-aboriginal population in *The West Beyond the West: A History of British Columbia*.

16. Trutch to John A. Macdonald, 14 October 1872, as quoted in Dennis Madill, *British Columbia Treaties in Historical Perspective*, p. 37.

17. The residential schools have left a bitter legacy in British Columbia. On this issue, see the very important study by J.R. Miller, *Shingwauk's Vision: A History of Indian Residential Schools in Canada*. On British Columbia, see Celia Haig-Brown's *Resistance and Renewal: Surviving the Indian Residential School*.

18. Historians have engaged in a lengthy debate about the significance of the potlatch laws. Some use them to document the nature and extent of First Nations government. Others claim that they demonstrate the greater power of the colonial system. It does seem clear that most First Nations knew the laws against potlatches were not very significant and applied rarely, and paid relatively little attention to them. The reader can follow this debate in the works below:

- Douglas Cole and Ira Chaikin, *An Iron Hand Upon the People: The Law Against the Potlatch on the Northwest Coast*
- J. R. Miller, "Owen Glendower, Hotspur, and Canadian Indian Policy"
- Tina Loo, "Dan Cramer's Potlatch: Law as Coercion, Symbol, and Rhetoric in British Columbia, 1884–1951."

19. See Dianne Newell, *Tangled Webs of History: Indians and the Law in Canada's Pacific Coast Fisheries*.

20. The major British Columbia studies of missionary activity are David Mulhall's *Will to Power: The Missionary Career of Father Morice* and Clarence Bolt's *Thomas Crosby and the Tsimshian: Small Shoes for Feet Too Large*.

21. One of the few published studies of the evolution of First Nations society in the 20th century (although it unfortunately is not based on documentary sources) is Peter Carstens' *The Queen's People: A Study of Hegemony, Coercion, and Accommodation among the Okanagan of Canada*.

22. For a strongly worded analysis of this process, see Rolf Knight, *Indians at Work: An Informal History of Native Indian Labour in British Columbia, 1858–1930*.

23. For an interesting and provocative study of First Nations in the region, see Hugh Brody, *Maps and Dreams: Indians and the British Columbia Frontier.*

24. Madill, p. 47. See also Rene Fumoleau, *As Long As This Land Shall Last: A History of Treaty 8 and Treaty 11, 1870–1939.*

25. See Richard Daniel, "The Spirit and Terms of Treaty Eight."

26. Government of B.C., *The Indian Law Questions B.C.: A Chronology*, p. 2.

27. Memorial to Sir Wilfrid Laurier from the Chiefs of the Shuswap, Okanagan, and Couteau Tribes, 25 August 1910, as quoted in Mandall and Pinder, pp. 59–60.

28. For the ideas in this section, I am greatly indebted to discussions that have stretched back over ten years now with Al Grove, then a History Masters student at the University of Victoria. I have developed them further in *The Internationalization of Indigenous Rights and the Impact on Maori Claims in New Zealand.*

29. Although a small number of Canadian scholars were interested in Aboriginal issues, they only rarely became politically active on their behalf. This is in sharp contrast to Australia, where an active and earnest group of academics lead the campaign for aboriginal rights.

30. Quoted in Fisher's "With or Without Treaty: Indian Land Claims in Western Canada," p. 64.

31. It is very difficult to imagine the Draft Declaration on Indigenous Rights passing in its current form. The United Nations is generally much weakened, so bringing forward a controversial document would be politically unsound. In addition, the draft would impose conditions that many countries, Canada included, would find unacceptable. Open-ended commitments such as self-determination and return of Aboriginal lands would impose expectations on government that Canadian authorities (who, more than most countries, take commitments made to the United Nations quite seriously) would not be in a position to implement.

32. Union of British Columbia Indian Chiefs, *Aboriginal Rights Position Paper*, p. 15.

33. Fisher, "With or Without Treaty," p. 64.

34. British Columbia Claims Task Force, p. 19.

35. Smith, *Our Home or Native Land?*

36. Opponents of the land claims settlement would certainly disagree with this point. They generally see both the federal and provincial governments as apologists for the land claims process. On the other hand, First Nations feel that government officials are not sympathetic to their cause. If the old saying that governing fairly means that everyone is equally upset at what is being done, then the federal and provincial governments are doing their jobs well.

37. For a study of how history relates to the legal process, see Fisher, "Judging History: Reflections on the Reasons for Judgement in *Delgamuukw v. the Queen.*"

References

Barman, Jean. *The West Beyond the West: A History of British Columbia*. Toronto: University of Toronto Press, 1991.

Belich, James. *The New Zealand Wars and the Victorian Interpretation of Racial Conflict*. Auckland: Penguin, 1988.

Bodley, John. *Victims of Progress*. Mountain View, California: Mayfield, 1990.

Bolt, Clarence. *Thomas Crosby and the Tsimshian: Small Shoes for Feet Too Large*. Vancouver: UBC Press, 1992.

British Columbia Claims Task Force. *The Report of the British Columbia Claims Task Force*. Vancouver: British Columbia Claims Task Force, 1991.

Brody, Hugh. *Maps and Dreams: Indians and the British Columbia Frontier*. Vancouver: Douglas and McIntyre, 1981.

Burger, Julian. *Report from the Frontier: The State of the World's Indigenous People*. London: Zed, 1987.

Cail, Robert. *Land, Man and the Law: The Disposal of Crown Lands in British Columbia, 1871–1913*. Vancouver: UBC Press, 1974.

Carstens, Peter. *The Queen's People: A Study of Hegemony, Coercion, and Accommodation among the Okanagan of Canada*. Toronto: University of Toronto Press, 1991.

Coates, Ken. *The Internationalization of Indigenous Rights and the Impact on Maori Claims in New Zealand*. Wellington: Public Law Office, 1997.

Coates, Ken, and John Taylor, eds. *Indigenous Peoples in Remote Regions*. Thunder Bay, Ont.: Centre for Northern Studies, 1996.

Cole, Douglas, and Ira Chaikin. *An Iron Hand Upon the People: The Law Against the Potlatch on the Northwest Coast*. Vancouver: Douglas and McIntyre, 1990.

Daniel, Richard. "The Spirit and Terms of Treaty Eight." In *The Spirit of the Alberta Indian Treaties,* ed. Richard Price. Edmonton: Pica Pica Press, 1987.

Duff, Wilson. "The Fort Victoria Treaties." *BC Studies* 3 (Fall 1969).

———. *The Indian History of British Columbia, Vol. 1: The Impact of the White Man*. Victoria: Provincial Museum of B.C., 1964.

Fisher, Robin. *Contact and Conflict: Indian-European Relations in British Columbia, 1774–1890*. Vancouver: UBC Press, 1992.

———. "Joseph Trutch and Indian Land Policy." In *Historical Essays on British Columbia,* eds. J. Friesen and H.K. Ralston. Toronto: McClelland and Stewart, 1976.

———. "Judging History: Reflections on the Reasons for Judgement in *Delgamuukw v. the Queen*." *BC Studies* 95 (Autumn 1992).

———. "With or Without Treaty: Indian Land Claims in Western Canada." In *Sovereignty and Indigenous Rights,* ed. W. Renwick. Wellington: Victoria University Press, 1991.

Fumoleau, Rene. *As Long As This Land Shall Last: A History of Treaty 8 and Treaty 11, 1870–1939*. Toronto: McClelland and Stewart, 1975.

Gibson, James. "Smallpox on the Northwest Coast, 1835–1838." *BC Studies* 56 (Winter 1982–83).

Gough, Barry. *Gunboat Frontier: British Maritime Authority and Northwest Coast Indians, 1846–90*. Vancouver: UBC Press, 1984.

Government of B.C. *Briefing Material for Treaty Commissioners, Douglas Treaties, 1850–1854*. Unpublished, n.d.

———. *The Indian Law Questions B.C.: A Chronology*. Unpublished, n.d.

Haig-Brown, Celia. *Resistance and Renewal: Surviving the Indian Residential School*. Vancouver: Tillicum Library, 1988.

Harris, Cole. "Voices of Disaster: Smallpox Around the Strait of Georgia in 1782." *Ethnohistory* 41, 4 (Fall 1994).

Hawthorne, H.R., et al. *The Indians of British Columbia*. Toronto: University of Toronto Press, 1960.

Knight, Rolf. *Indians at Work: An Informal History of Native Indian Labour in British Columbia, 1858–1930*. Vancouver: New Star Books, 1978.

LaVillette, F. *The Struggle for Survival*. Toronto: University of Toronto Press, 1961.

Loo, Tina. "Dan Cramer's Potlatch: Law as Coercion, Symbol, and Rhetoric in British Columbia, 1884–1951." *Canadian Historical Review* 73, 2 (June 1992).

Madill, Dennis. *British Columbia Treaties in Historical Perspective*. Ottawa: Indian and Northern Affairs, 1981.

Mandall and Pinder (Law Firm). *Aboriginal Royal Commission: B.C. Issues*. Unpublished, 1993.

Miller, J.R. "Owen Glendower, Hotspur, and Canadian Indian Policy." In *Sweet Promises: A Reader on Indian-White Relations in Canada*. Toronto: University of Toronto Press, 1991.

———. *Shingwauk's Vision: A History of Indian Residential Schools in Canada*. Toronto: University of Toronto Press, 1995.

Mulhall, David. *Will to Power: The Missionary Career of Father Morice*. Vancouver: UBC Press, 1986.

Newell, Dianne. *Tangled Webs of History: Indians and the Law in Canada's Pacific Coast Fisheries*. Toronto: University of Toronto Press, 1993.

Raunet, D. *Without Surrender, Without Consent: A History of the Nishga Land Claims*. Vancouver: Douglas & McIntyre, 1984.

R. v. White and Bob (1964), 50 D.L.R. (2nd) 613.

Saanichton Marina Ltd. v. Claxton (1989), 36 B.C.L.R. (2nd) 79 (B.C.C.A.).

Smith, Melvin. *Our Home or Native Land? What Governments' Aboriginal Policy is Doing to Canada*. Victoria: Crown Western, 1995.

Tennant, Paul. *Aboriginal Peoples and Politics: The Indian Land Question in British Columbia, 1849–1989*. Vancouver: UBC Press, 1990.

Union of British Columbia Indian Chiefs. *Aboriginal Rights Position Paper*. Vancouver: Union of British Columbia Indian Chiefs, 1979.

2

Why Settle Aboriginal Land Rights?

Exploring the Legal Issues of Litigation and Negotiation

By Harry Slade and Paul Pearlman

To understand why British Columbia should settle the claims of its First Nations, we must first understand what the claims are, and what basis they have in law. This chapter is a very brief overview of Aboriginal rights, including land rights, in B.C. It explains what these rights mean, where they come from, who holds them, and how they are proven in court. The chapter also explains the rights of First Nations and the obligations of the Crown that arise as a result of those rights. In addition, it looks briefly at how these rights might affect other British Columbians. Our intention is to make clear why First Nations' rights are significant, and why it is important to recognize these rights through the current treaty process.

A review of the case law on the subject shows us the nature and focus of the legal issues to date. In 1993, the British Columbia Court of Appeal decided the much publicized case *Delgamuukw v. British Columbia* (1993),[1] the Gitksan's and Wet'suwet'en's land claims case. In that decision, the Court found that the Gitksan and Wet'suwet'en have "unextinguished non-exclusive aboriginal rights" in the territory they claim. However, the Court left the nature, scope, and extent of these rights largely undefined. The result is that, while we know that

British Columbia First Nations hold certain rights in the land and resources of the province, we do not know the extent of these rights or exactly how they will affect other British Columbians. The Supreme Court of Canada will address at least some of these issues concerning the Gitksan and Wet'suwet'en when it hears the *Delgamuukw* appeal in June 1997.

In *Van der Peet v. The Queen* (1996),[2] the Supreme Court of Canada considered the purpose of Aboriginal rights, recognized and affirmed by section 35(1) of the *Constitution Act, 1982*. The Court said that Aboriginal rights are the way the Constitution recognizes the fact that before Europeans arrived in North America, distinctive Aboriginal societies already occupied the land. Recognizing Aboriginal rights was the way the Constitution reconciled that prior occupation with the concept of Crown sovereignty over Canadian territory. The Supreme Court of Canada adopted the following test to identify what constitutes an Aboriginal right protected by section 35(1):

> [I]n order to be an aboriginal right, an activity must be an element of a practice, custom or tradition integral to the distinctive culture of the aboriginal group claiming the right.[3]

Van der Peet and the two other cases decided by the Supreme Court at the same time, *Gladstone v. The Queen* (1996)[4] and *N.T.C. Smokehouse v. The Queen* (1996),[5] all deal with Aboriginal fishing rights. These cases take a comparatively narrow and highly fact-specific approach to the definition of Aboriginal rights. In *Van der Peet,* the Supreme Court describes Aboriginal title as a right. Aboriginal *title* involves a claim to *land* or *territory,* while a *right,* as defined in the fishing-rights cases, refers to an *activity.* It remains to be seen whether the Supreme Court will also apply a narrow approach to the issue of Aboriginal title.

This narrow, fact-specific approach may conflict with the interests of the treaty-making process now in place in B.C., which seeks to resolve the uncertainties over the relationship between the rights and interest of both First Nations and other British Columbians. The goal of the treaty process is to settle the valid claims of First Nations through negotiations that will arrive at a fair resolution for everyone involved. The British Columbia Treaty Commission is the neutral body overseeing the process that is agreed upon by Canada, British Columbia, and First Nations.

An Overview of Aboriginal Rights and Title

The history of Aboriginal rights in Canada

Understanding what Aboriginal rights are begins by knowing what their history is and how they came to be recognized by Canadian common law. The concept of Aboriginal rights is a basic principle of Canadian common law. It began as far back as the 17th and 18th centuries in Britain's imperial policy, and defines the constitutional relationship between First Nations peoples and the Crown. The doctrine governed how the new colonies would apply the common law to First Nations. It set rules about the status of First Nations people living under the Crown.[6] As section 35(1) of the *Constitution Act, 1982* confirms, Aboriginal rights today exist to reconcile the fact that distinct societies of Aboriginal peoples first occupied Canada with the legal principle that the Crown is sovereign over Canadian territory.

The purpose of Aboriginal rights was to ensure that the practices, customs, traditions, and communal rules distinctive to each First Nation were preserved as European nations began settling North America. They guaranteed that these local customs, practices, traditions, and communal rules could continue as long as they were compatible with the Crown's sovereignty. This principle of continuity was affirmed in the early 1800s in a series of United States Supreme Court decisions, which Canadian courts have followed.

As a result of the doctrine of Aboriginal rights, the communal rules and customs of First Nations became enforceable rights recognized by the common law. As such, they survived the introduction of English common law in the North American colonies. However, they were not absolute rights. An Aboriginal right could be extinguished or changed by a valid act of Parliament that showed a "clear and plain" intention to extinguish or change it. As we shall see later on, this all changed in 1982.

First Nations land rights: "Aboriginal title"

Where did Aboriginal title originate?

First Nations land rights, often called "Aboriginal title," are an important aspect of Aboriginal rights. The common law in the United States and Canada has recognized that First Nations have an interest in land that, unlike land held by non-natives in North America and Britain, comes not from a Crown grant, but from the First Nations' own possession and occupation of the land before the arrival of Europeans. Though the Crown could at one time extinguish Aboriginal land title through acts of Parliament (like other Aboriginal rights), the existence of Aboriginal title does not depend on the will of the Crown. Aboriginal title exists because First Nations historically used and occupied the land, and claimed it as their right.

In *Van der Peet*, the Supreme Court of Canada described Aboriginal title as "the aspect of aboriginal rights related specifically to aboriginal claims to land; it is the way in which the common law recognizes aboriginal land rights."[7] The Chief Justice of the Court, quoting from *Calder v. British Columbia (Attorney General)* (1973), went on to note that both Aboriginal title and Aboriginal rights arise from the existence of distinctive Aboriginal communities occupying "the land as their forefathers had done for centuries."[8]

While Aboriginal title to the lands that First Nations used and occupied exists, the Crown continues to hold the underlying title to the land (often called the "root" or "radical" title). The Crown acquired this title by asserting sovereignty over its North American colonies. In spite of this, Aboriginal title continued to exist, and in fact became a burden on the Crown's newly acquired title. Chief Justice Marshall of the United States Supreme Court explained this principle in *Johnson v. M'Intosh* (1823):

> This principle was that discovery gave title to the government by whose subjects, or by whose authority, it was made, against all other European governments, which title might be consummated by possession.

> The exclusion of all other Europeans, necessarily gave to the nation making the discovery the sole right of acquiring the soil from the natives, and establishing settlements upon it.

In the establishment of these relations, the rights of the original inhabitants were, in no instance, entirely disregarded; but were necessarily, to a considerable extent, impaired. They were admitted to be the rightful occupants of the soil, with a legal as well as just claim to retain possession of it, and to use it according to their own discretion; but their rights to complete sovereignty, as independent nations, were necessarily diminished, and their power to dispose of the soil at their own will, to whomsoever they pleased, was denied by the original fundamental principle that discovery gave exclusive title to those who made it.[9]

Chief Justice Marshall again discussed the "principle of discovery" in *Worcester v. Georgia* (1832):

The principle . . . gave to the nation making the discovery, as its inevitable consequence, the sole right of acquiring the soil, and of making settlements on it. It was an exclusive principle, which shut out the right of competition among those who had agreed to it; not one which could annul the previous right of those who had not agreed to it. It regulated the right given by discovery among the European discoverers, but could not affect the rights of those already in possession, either as aboriginal occupants or as occupants by virtue of a discovery made before the memory of man. It gave the exclusive right to purchase, but did not found that right on a denial of the right of the possessor to sell.[10]

The Supreme Court of Canada endorsed these principles in *Guerin v. The Queen* (1984):

The principle of discovery which justified these claims [to sovereignty by various European nations] gave the ultimate title in the land in a particular area to the nation which had discovered and claimed it. In that respect at least the Indians' rights in the land were obviously diminished; but their rights of occupancy and possession remained unaffected. [The Court then quoted the above passages from the *Johnson* and *Worcester* cases.][11]

Thus, while the Crown acquired the root title to the land in Canada, Aboriginal title remained a burden on the Crown's title until the First Nations surrendered their title to the Crown, or the Crown clearly and plainly extinguished it.

What does Aboriginal title mean legally?

What is the burden that Aboriginal land title places on the Crown's title? Defining the nature and extent of Aboriginal title is difficult, since neither the B.C. courts nor the Supreme Court of Canada has yet given any clear definition of Aboriginal title. However, through cases such as *Delgamuukw,* the Australian High Court's decision in *Mabo v. Queensland* (1992),[12] and the Supreme Court of Canada's recent definition of Aboriginal rights in *Van der Peet,* we can at least identify some characteristics of Aboriginal title.

It is now well established in Canadian law that Aboriginal title is an interest in land. As an interest in land, it has the same legal protection as the common law gives to more conventional property interests.

However, Canadian law has not determined the relationship and priorities between Aboriginal title and other interests in land based on Crown grants. So while we know that Canadian law defines Aboriginal title as an interest in land, it has not yet defined its precise legal nature, or its consequences for other interests in the land. Interestingly, in *Mabo,* the Court found that, unless Aboriginal title has been extinguished by a valid legal act, it continues to be a right held by the Aboriginal occupants that they may exercise not only against the Crown but also against the whole world.

Aboriginal title is unlike any traditional common-law property interests that we are familiar with. Courts often refer to Aboriginal title as a *sui generis* interest; that is, an interest of its own kind. Indeed, in his majority judgment in *Delgamuukw,* Mr. Justice Macfarlane acknowledged that the unique nature of Aboriginal rights "has made them difficult, if not impossible to describe in traditional property law terminology."[13] Later in the judgment, he said:

> To stretch and strain property law concepts in an attempt to find a place for these unusual concepts which have arisen in a special context is, in my opinion, an unproductive task.[14]

In that case, based on the evidence at trial, the Court rejected the claim that the First Nation had an interest that amounted to "ownership" of the land. Having rejected the claim of ownership, the Court did not have to define the nature and scope of the First Nation's interest in land, or the consequences of the continued existence of that interest for others.

In *R. v. Sparrow* (1990), the Supreme Court of Canada also cautioned against the use of common-law property concepts to define Aboriginal title:

> Courts must be careful . . . to avoid the application of traditional common law concepts of property as they develop their understanding of . . . the *sui generis* nature of aboriginal rights.[15]

In spite of this lack of a clear definition of Aboriginal title, we can at least identify some characteristics of it. Aboriginal title is a right to land which, according to *Mabo,* can be claimed against the whole world. Furthermore, it is more like a proprietary interest than a personal interest.[16] This is significant. One cannot lose a proprietary interest as easily through lack of use as one can a right of possession.

However, because Aboriginal title is a *sui generis* interest in land, it has certain restrictions on it that other common-law interests in land do not have. The most significant of these restrictions is that the First Nations possessor cannot transfer Aboriginal title to anybody except the Crown. This is because the Crown holds the root title to the land. As we will see later, this "inalienability" of Aboriginal title gives certain obligations to the Crown.

How does a First Nation prove Aboriginal title?

The next questions to be addressed are who holds Aboriginal title, and how do they prove it? Like other property-law interests in land, Aboriginal title to a specific area of land comes from the historical exclusive use and occupation of that land. This principle is reflected in a test that the Federal Court established in *Hamlet of Baker Lake et al. v. Minister of Indian Affairs and Northern Development et al.* (1980) to prove the existence of Aboriginal title.[17] An Aboriginal group must show four elements to prove title. These are that

- the Aboriginal group and their ancestors were members of an organized society
- the organized society occupied the specific territory over which they claim the Aboriginal title
- they occupied the territory to the exclusion of any other organized society
- the occupation was an established fact when England declared sovereignty.

In *Van der Peet,* the Supreme Court of Canada held that courts must use the "time of contact," rather than the time when the British declared sovereignty, to determine Aboriginal rights. However, in Aboriginal *title* cases, when a particular First Nation is claiming the right to occupy and use a particular tract of land as a burden on the Crown's title, the situation may be different. The fact that a particular Aboriginal group occupied the land not only before European contact, but also when the British declared Crown sovereignty, may still be a relevant consideration.

The relationship between Aboriginal title and other Aboriginal rights

Aboriginal title is part of a larger group or "bundle" of Aboriginal rights that includes many other rights, such as the right to fish and hunt. Aboriginal rights, as distinguished from title, protect *activities* that are an "integral part" of an Aboriginal society. The precise bundle of rights held by a First Nation varies from nation to nation.

Defining Aboriginal rights set out in the Constitution

Aboriginal rights in section 35(1)

Canada is unique in that the *Constitution Act, 1982* specifically recognizes and affirms Aboriginal rights:

The existing aboriginal and treaty rights of the aboriginal peoples of Canada are hereby recognized and affirmed (s. 35(1)).

This fact is very important in any analysis of the relationship between Aboriginal rights, the powers of the Crown, and the interests of other parties.

In *Van der Peet,* Chief Justice Lamer began his analysis of Aboriginal rights by stating the purposes of the unique constitutional status that Aboriginal peoples in Canada have. He noted that Aboriginal rights are different from rights under the *Canadian Charter of Rights and Freedoms* because they are rights held only by Aboriginal members of Canadian society. They come from the fact that Aboriginal people are original peoples. The Chief Justice observed:

The task of this Court is to define aboriginal rights in a manner which recognizes that aboriginal rights are *rights* but which does so without losing sight of the fact that they are rights held by aboriginal people because they are *aboriginal.*[18]

He then explained:

More specifically, what s. 35(1) does is to provide the constitutional framework through which the fact that aboriginals lived on the land in distinctive societies, with their own practices, traditions and cultures, is acknowledged and reconciled with the sovereignty of the Crown. The substantive rights which fall within the provision must be defined in light of this purpose; the aboriginal rights recognized and affirmed by s. 35(1) must be directed toward the reconciliation of the pre-existence of aboriginal societies with the sovereignty of the Crown.[19]

After reviewing Commonwealth and United States case law and legal sources, the Chief Justice concluded that the aboriginal rights recognized and affirmed by section 35(1) could best be described as:

1. the means by which the Constitution recognizes the fact that, before the arrival of the Europeans in North America, the land was already occupied by distinctive aboriginal societies; and
2. the means by which the prior occupation is reconciled with the assertion of Crown sovereignty over Canadian territory.[20]

The test to identify Aboriginal rights

For the Court in *Van der Peet,* logic followed that any test to identify the Aboriginal rights recognized and affirmed by section 35 had to focus on identifying the practices, traditions, and customs central to the Aboriginal societies that existed in North America before European contact. Chief Justice Lamer stated the test:

In order to be an aboriginal right, *an activity must be an element of a practice, custom or tradition integral to the distinctive culture of the aboriginal group claiming the right.*[21] [emphasis added]

While he emphasized that courts hearing Aboriginal rights claims must be sensitive to the Aboriginal perspective, the Chief Justice also observed that these rights exist within the general legal system of

Canada, and that to reconcile First Nations' occupation of Canadian territory with Crown sovereignty, courts must weigh the Aboriginal perspective equally with the perspective of the common law. What the practical results of this will be is unknown.

The court's duty to precisely identify the claim

The Court in *Van der Peet* also stated that, to determine whether a First Nations claimant has demonstrated the existence of an Aboriginal right, courts must identify *precisely* what the nature of the claim is. They said that "the nature of an applicant's claim must be delineated in terms of the particular practice, tradition or custom under which it is claimed."[22] In his dissenting judgment, Justice Lambert found that the scope of the Aboriginal right could be determined by an inquiry into the level of exercise of the right that would assure to the Aboriginal claimant a moderate livelihood from utilization of the resource. This was characterized as the "social test." However, the majority of the Court, in *Van der Peet,* rejected the "social test" as too broad. The majority found that the principal focus required an examination of the particular traditions, customs, or practices of the First Nation Aboriginal community in question. In a key passage, the majority said:

> To characterize an applicant's claim correctly, a court should consider such factors as the nature of the action which the applicant is claiming was done pursuant to an aboriginal right, the nature of the governmental regulation, statute or action being impugned, and the tradition, custom or practice being relied upon to establish the right. In this case, therefore, the Court will consider the actions which led to the appellant's being charged, the fishery regulation under which she was charged and the customs, practices and traditions she invokes in support of her claim.[23]

To determine the precise nature of an applicant's claim, a court must examine the nature of the action claimed to be done as an Aboriginal right, and the particular tradition, custom, or practice claimed to create the Aboriginal right.

In *Sparrow,* the Supreme Court of Canada had previously held that government regulations cannot determine the content and scope of an existing Aboriginal right. What the Court may now be saying in *Van der Peet* is that, because one must precisely identify the right claimed, one should carefully consider how the government regulation or statute impacts the activity claimed, and be careful not to define the right any more broadly than is necessary. Thus, for example, the Court concluded in *Van der Peet* that the most accurate definition of the applicant's claim was that she was claiming the Aboriginal right to exchange fish for money or other goods, rather than a right to engage in the commercial sale of salmon.

Determining whether the activity is integral to the distinctive culture

After defining precisely what Aboriginal right is being claimed, the court must then determine whether the activity is part of a practice, custom, or tradition integral to the distinctive culture; that is, it must be a central and significant part of the Aboriginal society's distinctive culture. The Chief Justice in *Van der Peet* stated that a practical way of determining whether a practice, tradition, or custom meets the "integral to the distinctive culture" test is to ask "whether or not a practice, tradition or custom is a defining feature of the culture in question."[24] The same test applies to claims of Aboriginal rights of self-government as shown in *Pamajewon and Jones v. Her Majesty the Queen* (1996).[25]

In *Pamajewon,* where the applicants claimed an Aboriginal right to conduct high-stakes gambling on two Indian reserves in Ontario, the Court assumed that section 35(1) included self-government claims. After referring to the test in *Van der Peet,* Chief Justice Lamer said:

> In so far as they can be made under s. 35(1), claims to self-government are no different from other claims to the enjoyment of Aboriginal rights and must, as such, be measured against the same standard.[26]

Once again, the Supreme Court of Canada had rejected making any broad statement that the Aboriginal right claimed was a general Aboriginal right to manage and use reserve lands. The Chief Justice emphasized that the courts must look at any claim of Aboriginal rights, including any claims to self-government, in light of the specific circumstances of each case, and, in particular, in light of the specific history and culture of the Aboriginal group claiming the right.

The Court then examined the evidence at trial to determine whether participating in and regulating gambling on reserve lands was an integral part of the Shawanaga or Eagle Lake First Nations cultures. Because they had no evidence to show that gambling was of central significance to the Ojibwa people, or had ever been the subject of Aboriginal regulation, the applicants' claims failed. *Pamajewon,* like the British Columbia fishing appeals, emphasizes how much the presence or absence of convincing anthropological and historical evidence will shape not only the trial judge's findings, but also how such cases will ultimately be determined on appeal. Unless the judge made a "palpable and overriding error" in assessing the evidence, an appeal court will not make new determinations of the facts of the case.[27] In future cases, in addition to evidence from First Nations witnesses about their oral histories and traditions, we can expect to see batteries of anthropologists debating whether a particular custom, practice, or tradition was a central or defining feature of the distinctive Aboriginal culture in question.

The requirement of continuity

In the Aboriginal fishing appeals, the Supreme Court of Canada found that the practices, customs, and traditions recognized as aboriginal rights are those that continue the traditions, customs, and practices that existed in the particular First Nations society before European contact.[28] Thus, the focus of inquiry is no longer whether a practice, custom, or tradition was integral to the society at the time of British sovereignty. Chief Justice Lamer summarized his conclusions on this point as follows:

> Where an aboriginal community can demonstrate that a particular practice, custom or tradition is integral to its distinctive culture today, and that this practice, custom or tradition has continuity with the practices, customs and traditions of pre-contact times, that community will have demonstrated that the practice, custom or tradition is an aboriginal right for the purposes of s. 35(1).[29]

A claimant does not need to demonstrate an unbroken chain of continuity between the pre-contact society and the current practice of the activity. The Court must just be satisfied that the particular practice, custom, or tradition "can be rooted in the pre-contact societies of the aboriginal community in question."[30]

In *Gladstone,* the applicants were able to meet this requirement by providing evidence that, before contact with Europeans, trading in herring spawn on kelp was a significant aspect of their society, and that they had traded in this way to an extent that could be described as commercial. Expert testimony in the form of the diary of Alexander McKenzie, who gave a first-hand description of the Heiltsuk trade in herring spawn on kelp in 1793, and the diaries of an early 19th-century fur trader all suggested a trade of herring spawn on kelp in "tons." They provided the evidence that the applicants had a "commercial" trade in herring spawn on kelp that was an integral part of their distinctive culture both before and after contact.

The Court also stated that its flexible approach to the concept of continuity avoids taking the "frozen rights" approach to defining Aboriginal rights. In other words, practices, customs, and traditions may evolve into modern forms, as long as the applicants can show such modern forms are rooted in the pre-contact Aboriginal society.[31]

Proving claims without written records

The Court in *Van der Peet* recognized the difficulties in proving claims that have their origins in pre-contact times, and for which there were no written records. Chief Justice Lamer stated:

> The courts must not undervalue the evidence presented by aboriginal claimants simply because that evidence does not conform precisely with the evidentiary standards that would be applied in, for example, a private law torts case.[32]

This passage shows the courts are willing to accept evidence of oral history and tradition, when this evidence meets the tests of reliability and necessity.

First Nations Rights and Title in B.C.: The Decision in Delgamuukw

The right claimed in *Van der Peet* had to do with fishing rights, not Aboriginal title. It remains to be seen whether the principals stated by the Supreme Court in *Van der Peet* concerning Aboriginal rights will be applied to issues over the nature and proof of Aboriginal title. The Supreme Court heard the appeal in *Delgamuukw,* which raises the question of Aboriginal title, in June 1977. The Court's decision has not been released as of the date of this paper.

The decision

Delgamuukw appealed the trial decision that

- the Gitksan and Wet'suwet'en (the applicants) did not prove their claim of ownership of and jurisdiction over the claimed territory
- the applicants had proven only their Aboriginal rights for "non-exclusive sustenance purposes" (rights to engage in certain activities to earn a living) in a portion of the territory, and not their Aboriginal title (an Aboriginal interest in their traditional territory)
- all the applicants' Aboriginal rights were eliminated by the time that British Columbia joined the Canadian federation in 1871.

The Court of Appeal dismissed the Gitksan and Wet'suwet'en's claim to ownership by a majority decision. The applicants did not prove "ownership" on the terms set out in the Statement of Claim. However, the Court changed the trial judge's final order. It ruled that the Gitksan and Wet'suwet'en had established non-exclusive Aboriginal sustenance rights within part of the territory over which they claimed ownership and jurisdiction, and that these rights had not been eliminated before 1871.

Two Justices of the Court wrote dissenting decisions that would have allowed the appeal, but not on the basis that the Gitksan and Wet'suwet'en had established an exclusive right of ownership and jurisdiction over the territory. They found that the Gitksan and Wet'suwet'en had established Aboriginal title and rights of self-government over some of the territory.

Four out of five of the Court Justices wrote reasons for decision. (Justice Taggart agreed with Justice Macfarlane's reasons for judgment.) The other Justices who wrote reasons were Justices Wallace, Lambert, and Hutcheon. These Justices differed on

- what the legal issues were
- what decision they made on those legal issues they agreed on.

We will see that the fact that the majority of the Justices took a different view on what the issues were from the two who wrote minority decisions is important in understanding the final decision.

The issues and findings

The Justices in the majority (Macfarlane, Taggart, and Wallace) differed from the minority (Justices Lambert and Hutcheon) in determining which were the issues they had to decide. This occurred in two significant areas:

- "ownership," or aboriginal title
- "jurisdiction," or Aboriginal self-government.

The Gitksan and Wet'suwet'en had stated their claim as "ownership" and "jurisdiction." None of the Justices accepted their definition of Aboriginal rights as ownership or jurisdiction. The majority dismissed the claim to ownership and jurisdiction on the basis that they felt the evidence did not support the claim of ownership. They also stated that the common law does not protect Aboriginal rights of jurisdiction, as the applicants claimed.

The majority found that the applicants' claim at trial was for ownership and jurisdiction, and for Aboriginal sustenance *rights*. Their view was that the applicants had not put forward a claim to Aboriginal *title,* but a claim of complete "ownership" in the full legal sense of that term. Similarly, the majority treated the claim to jurisdiction as a claim to rights or government that would extend to regulating the rights of all people within the claimed territory.

Justice Lambert's minority decision, on the other hand, treated the claim of "ownership" as a claim to Aboriginal title. His judgment also dealt with Aboriginal rights. In addition, both Justices Lambert and Hutcheon treated the claim to "jurisdiction" as a claim to rights of self-government or self-regulation. Justice Hutcheon did not expressly state the claim to "ownership" was a claim to Aboriginal title, but concluded that the Gitksan and Wet'suwet'en had established "aboriginal rights to land."

The differences of opinion between the majority and minority on the issues are important. The majority did not believe the Gitksan and Wet'suwet'en case involved a claim of Aboriginal title, as an interest distinct from "ownership." The same appeared to be the case with the claim for jurisdiction. The majority rejected the claim to "jurisdiction," but did not deal with the issue of a more limited form of aboriginal self-government or self-regulation. Only the decisions of the minority Justices dealt directly with proof of Aboriginal title and the existence of powers of self-regulation. They also addressed the issue of how Aboriginal title and government fell short of full ownership and plenary jurisdiction. As a result, the case did little to clarify the issues around the existence, nature, and scope of Aboriginal rights to land.

After disposing of the Gitksan and Wet'suwet'en claims to ownership and jurisdiction, the majority of the Court discussed whether the applicants had proof of, and legal protection for, Aboriginal rights. Because they dealt with sustenance rights rather than title or land rights, the two majority judgments (Justices Macfarlane and Wallace) focus on Aboriginal practices and activities. This contrasts somewhat with Justice Lambert's approach. In dissent, he spoke about an interest in land that reaches beyond the right to take part in specific practices or habits, though he also discussed rights to engage in specific practices such as hunting and fishing.

This does not mean that the majority and dissenting opinions failed to address the same issues altogether. All dealt with the issues listed below.

Did the Royal Proclamation apply to B.C.?

Four of the five Justices found that the *Royal Proclamation of 1763* did not apply in British Columbia. One Justice expressed no opinion on the matter.

The Justices found that the Proclamation reflected British colonial policy, but was not relevant to the determination of the First Nations' Aboriginal rights.

Were the rights claimed proprietary or personal?

Three members of the Court found it was not appropriate to define the First Nations' interest as being proprietary or personal. They decided it is an interest *sui generis* (on its own), and that it was best to determine the nature and scope of Aboriginal rights on the specific facts, based on the evidence at trial. A fourth Justice agreed with this view.

How did the applicants have to prove Aboriginal rights and title?

The common thread through the reasons for decision was that Aboriginal interests should be determined by asking what elements members of the organized society regarded as integral parts of their distinctive culture. The majority excluded any practices that became common as a result of European influences.

To prove an existing Aboriginal right, the majority decided the applicants must give evidence that a practice

- is integral to the distinctive culture of an Aboriginal society of which some of the applicants' ancestors were members
- existed as an Aboriginal right when the British declared sovereignty, and it had not been extinguished before 1982.

Justice Macfarlane stated that to determine what specific territory First Nations used or occupied, they must prove that their ancestors used and occupied the area enough to support the belief that the area was their traditional homeland.

Were the Aboriginal rights extinguished before 1871?

The Court unanimously rejected the notion that the Gitksan and Wet'suwet'en's Aboriginal rights and title were extinguished before 1871. It found that the Province of British Columbia did not have the power to extinguish Aboriginal interests after 1871, except in cases where the federal government had clearly and plainly given the Province the power to extinguish them.

The Court also stated that section 88 of the *Indian Act,* which extends provincial laws of general application to Indians, does not clearly and plainly authorize the province to extinguish Aboriginal rights and title. However, Justice Macfarlane left open the questions of whether valid provincial grants might infringe upon Aboriginal rights, and, if so, whether the First Nations group or person affected would have any recourse. Aboriginal rights and title could not be extinguished after 1982, except by the consent of the First Nations groups affected.

What was the nature of the rights held?

The majority of the Justices in *Delgamuukw* found that the Gitksan and Wet'suwet'en had unextinguished, non-exclusive, Aboriginal sustenance rights. These rights were protected by the common law, and as Aboriginal rights under section 35(1) of the *Constitution Act, 1982*. The Court did not define the rights specifically, but left definition to negotiation. If the parties did not reach agreement, definition would have to come through further legal proceedings. The Court urged the parties to negotiate a resolution of the outstanding issues.

The dissenting Justices also discussed the characteristics of Aboriginal title in a general way. Justice Lambert quoted from the decision of the Australian High Court in *Mabo,* which found that an exclusive Aboriginal title gives its holder the rights to own, occupy, use, and enjoy their lands "as against the whole world."[33] Justice Hutcheon found that Aboriginal rights to land "were of such a nature as to compete on an equal footing with proprietary interest."[34]

The Court left it to further court proceedings to determine whether there had been any legal interference with specific Aboriginal interests. It also left open the question of how to resolve any conflicts between existing Aboriginal interests and the rights of those holding interests in land under provincial grants.

"Frozen" vs. evolving rights. The majority found that Aboriginal rights must reflect Aboriginal practices at the time of British sovereignty. For the purposes of this case, this was 1846. The Court concluded that such traditional rights could be exercised by using modern methods.

In dissent, Justice Lambert defined rights as "evolving," because using them now might involve adapting the right to fit modern times. For example, say that at the time of sovereignty, a First Nation had the right to kill all the deer they wished, for whatever purpose they wished. The modern form of that right would still be to kill all the deer the First

Nation wished, for whatever modern purpose they wished, as long as they met modern-day conservation requirements.

Justice Lambert also found that if an Aboriginal right was defined as the exclusive right to occupy, own, use, and enjoy land, the modern form of the right would include modern uses, even if that particular use did not exist at the time of sovereignty. This is contrary to the Supreme Court's approach in *Van der Peet*. There the majority found that for a practice, custom, or tradition to be recognized and protected as an Aboriginal right, it must have been rooted in the practices of the Aboriginal community before European contact.

Exclusive vs. shared rights. The Court in *Delgamuukw* found that Aboriginal rights—for example, the sustenance rights of hunting and gathering—could be held by more than one Aboriginal society. To obtain rights to occupy specific lands, however, a community would need proof that they had exclusive possession, not only in pre-contact times, but perhaps also at the date of sovereignty.

Justice Lambert suggested the possibility of shared exclusive Aboriginal title. This would enable more than one Aboriginal society to share rights to occupy land and to exclude all others.

The significance of the decision

Clearly, *Delgamuukw* did not establish a defined set of enforceable Aboriginal rights for the applicants. As mentioned, the Court left it to the parties to negotiate their specific rights, and, if necessary, to return to the courts to seek a definition.

Nevertheless, the decision is conclusive in the finding that the First Nations did not have the form of ownership and jurisdiction that they claimed in their pleadings, and sought to prove at trial. Despite this result, First Nations can still pursue claims of Aboriginal rights, title, and self-regulation. As the Supreme Court's recent decisions in *Van der Peet, Gladstone,* and *N.T.C. Smokehouse* illustrate, each First Nation must prove that the customs, practices, and traditions that it claims as Aboriginal rights were integral to its distinctive culture before European contact. The specific bundle of Aboriginal rights or title held by one First Nation may be quite different from the rights held by others.

It is, of course, possible that the Supreme Court could change any of the B.C. findings on appeal. It may also consider whether to deal with the questions about Aboriginal title and self-government that the two dissenting Justices in *Delgamuukw* addressed.

At this point, however, the most important ruling in *Delgamuukw* is the Court's conclusion that Aboriginal interests were not generally extinguished before 1871.

The Government's Power and Duties Concerning Aboriginal Rights

The fiduciary duty of the Crown

Earlier (under "First Nations Land Rights"), we saw that, because the Crown assumed "radical title" to North America, First Nations cannot transfer their title in the land to anybody except the Crown. Because this "inalienability" limits the powers of First Nations to deal with their land, the Crown owes a "fiduciary duty" to the First Nations to protect their interests. The Supreme Court of Canada confirmed this duty in *Guerin:*

> The nature of Indian title and the framework of the statutory scheme established for disposing of Indian land places upon the Crown an equitable obligation, enforceable by the courts, to deal with the land for the benefit of the Indians. This obligation does not amount to a trust in the private law sense. It is rather a fiduciary duty. If, however, the Crown breaches this fiduciary duty it will be liable to the Indians in the same way and to the same extent as if such a trust were in effect.

> The fiduciary relationship between the Crown and the Indians has its roots in the concept of aboriginal, native or Indian title. The fact that Indian bands have a certain interest in lands does not, however, in itself give rise to a fiduciary relationship between the Indians and the Crown. The conclusion that the Crown is a fiduciary depends upon the further proposition that the Indian interest in land is inalienable except upon surrender to the Crown. . . .

The surrender requirement, and the responsibility it entails, are the source of a distinct fiduciary obligation owed by the Crown to the Indians.[35]

In *Sparrow,* the Supreme Court found that this fiduciary duty to protect First Nations' interests applies not only to dealings in land, but to the entire relationship between the Crown and First Nations. Speaking for the Court, Chief Justice Dickson and Justice La Forest said:

> The *sui generis* nature of Indian title, and the historic powers and responsibility assumed by the Crown constituted the source of such a fiduciary obligation. In our opinion, *Guerin,* together with *R. v. Taylor and Williams* (1981), 62 C.C.C. (2d) 227, 34 O.R. (2d) 360 (C.A.), ground a general guiding principle for s. 35(1). That is, the government has the responsibility to act in a fiduciary capacity with respect to aboriginal peoples. The relationship between the government and aboriginal is trust-like, rather than adversarial, and contemporary recognition and affirmation of aboriginal rights must be defined in light of this historic relationship.[36]

The fiduciary duty places significant obligations on the Crown in its dealings with First Nations, specifically on how the federal government uses its powers under section 91(24) of the *Constitution Act, 1867*. It gives the federal government the authority to deal with "Indians and lands reserved for Indians." As we will see in the next section, the duty to protect First Nations interests plays an important role in reconciling federal powers and Aboriginal rights.

The Crown's power to affect Aboriginal rights

As we stated earlier, Aboriginal rights are not absolute. Before section 35(1) of the *Constitution Act, 1982,* which recognized and affirmed existing Aboriginal and treaty rights, Aboriginal rights could be extinguished or altered through valid acts of Parliament, as long as the legislation shows a *clear and plain intention* to extinguish the right. This need to show a clear and plain intention was specified by Justice Hall in 1973, writing for half of a split Court in the Supreme Court's landmark decision in *Calder*. The Supreme Court later affirmed the decision in *Sparrow:*

But Hall J. in that case stated that the "onus of proving that the Sovereign intended to extinguish the Indian title lies on the respondent and that intention must be clear and plain." The test of extinguishment to be adopted, in our opinion, is that the Sovereign's intention must be clear and plain if it is to extinguish an aboriginal right.[37]

Sparrow found that federal government fishing regulations that had the *effect* of repealing the Aboriginal right to fish for food, social, and ceremonial purposes did not eliminate the right, because acts of Parliament that are merely not consistent with Aboriginal rights do not show a clear and plain intention to extinguish them. Remember that in *Delgamuukw,* the B.C. Court of Appeal also found that Aboriginal rights had not been extinguished before B.C. entered into Confederation. After Confederation, the province did not have the authority to extinguish them. Only the federal government can do so, under section 91(24) of the *Constitution Act, 1867.*

In 1982, Canada's constitution was amended to include section 35. It significantly limits the powers of the Crown to interfere with Aboriginal rights. It also likely removes the power of the Crown to unilaterally extinguish Aboriginal rights. Yet, because of the federal government's powers under the *Constitution Act, 1867,* the Crown still has the ability to enact legislation concerning First Nations peoples. This power enables the Crown to make laws that might limit or infringe upon an Aboriginal right.

Parliament's powers to affect Aboriginal rights are limited. Any action must comply with the conditions of section 35 and the fiduciary duty of protection that the Crown owes to First Nations. The Crown must justify any government regulation that limits Aboriginal rights. The Supreme Court set out the test for justification in *Sparrow*. It includes the following conditions:

- The legislation must have a valid objective. The preservation of a resource to which Aboriginal people have access as a matter of right would be a valid objective. The preferential allocation of the resource to people who do not have a constitutionally protected right would not.
- "The way in which a legislative objective is to be attained must uphold the honour of the Crown and must be in keeping with the

unique contemporary relationship, grounded in history and policy, between the Crown and Canada's Aboriginal peoples."[38]

- Because Aboriginal history, society, and rights are complex, any test must consider the particular circumstances of the case at hand.[39]

How much the specific facts in a case will shape the test for justification is illustrated by the Supreme Court's recent decision in *Gladstone*. The applicants had established an Aboriginal right to harvest and sell herring spawn on kelp commercially. The Aboriginal fishing right was therefore not limited, as was the Aboriginal right in *Sparrow* to fish only for food, social, and ceremonial purposes. In *Gladstone,* the Court suggested that to justify placing limits on technically unlimited Aboriginal commercial fishing rights, the Crown could do so (after first considering conservation principles) if the limits were to achieve valid objectives like economic and regional fairness, and the recognition that other people also relied on and participated in fishing. It observed that *"in the right circumstances,* such objectives are in the interest of all Canadians and, more importantly, the reconciliation of aboriginal societies with the rest of Canadian society may well depend on their successful attainment."[40] Just as proving a particular claim of Aboriginal title or Aboriginal rights depends on the evidence in the particular case, infringing on Aboriginal rights may also depend on the facts of the case.

In *Sparrow,* the Court also stated that to establish any policy affecting their rights, the Crown had to consult with the First Nations affected by the infringement. Justice McEachern considered the scope of this duty to consult in his trial-level decision in *Delgamuukw* (1991). He said that there should be "reasonable consultation so that the plaintiffs will know the extent to which their use might be terminated or disturbed."[41] The right to be consulted does not include the power to veto or the requirement of consent, but the courts desired some type of agreement.

The B.C. Court of Appeal has recently discussed the extent of the Crown's duty to consult in a series of cases: *R. v. Jack, R. v. Sampson, and R. v. Little.*[42] In these cases, the Court considered the Crown's duty to consult a number of First Nations on Vancouver Island about implementing conservation measures that affected their treaty fishing rights. Although the courts upheld Justice McEachern's finding that the duty to consult does not give the First Nations the right to veto or to demand their consent, their decisions make clear that consultation must be meaningful. Members of the First Nation affected must be fully informed of any measure that might affect their rights.[43]

How Do Aboriginal Rights Affect Third-Party Interests?

One question that always comes up in a discussion of Aboriginal rights is: How do Aboriginal rights affect the interests of third parties, such as forest and mining companies, and commercial and sports fishers? Unfortunately, there is no clear answer. The decision in *Delgamuukw,* which recognized that the First Nations have non-exclusive Aboriginal rights in the claimed territory, left it to the parties involved to define exactly what those rights were. By leaving this question open, the majority of the court expressed its desire, and indeed its confidence, in having the parties resolve these issues themselves. In his concluding remarks, Justice Macfarlane said:

> During the course of these proceedings it became apparent that there are two schools of thought. The first is an "all or nothing approach," which says that the Indian nations were here first, that they have exclusive ownership and control of all the land and resources and may deal with them as they see fit. The second is a co-extensive approach, which says that Indian interest and other interests can co-exist to a large extent, and that consultation and reconciliation is the process by which the Indian culture can be preserved and by which other Canadians may be assured that their interests, developed over 125 years of nationhood, can also be respected. The Indian plaintiffs have taken the first step in recognizing the importance of other vested interests by not making a claim to lands within the territory held by others under a fee simple title.
>
> I favour the second approach.[44]

By leaving open the issue of what the Gitksan and Wet'suwet'en's specific rights are for the parties to work out, the Court of Appeal also endorsed Justice MacFarlane's second approach. This is emphasized by the finding that the Gitksan and Wet'suwet'en's rights are "non-exclusive," meaning that they must consider the interests of others.

The Case for Negotiating Settlements

British Columbia's historical departure from the treaty process

The history of the practices and policies that have defined the Crown's relationship to Canada's First Nations shows that treaties are the way colonial objectives and Aboriginal interests have traditionally been reconciled. Treaties were the means by which the Crown got the First Nations to give up their interests in the land to clear the way for settlement. Treaty-making advanced with European settlement, from eastern to western Canada. They left intact any Aboriginal rights that they did not specifically extinguish. They also contained specific agreements to certain benefits, and the rights to continue hunting and fishing.

In B.C., the original treaty-making process stopped in 1899 with Treaty 8. This cleared the way for gold miners passing through Aboriginal territory in the northeast corner of B.C., and for the settlers that followed in their wake. The colony of British Columbia refused to make treaties throughout the rest of the province, leaving us with a legacy of uncertainty about the existence and effect of Aboriginal rights and title.

The lack of treaties in most of B.C. was not a major obstacle to settling the land. The number of First Nations peoples diminished due to disease and the influx of settlers. Under provincial laws and a federal bureaucracy, Aboriginal people were contained on reserves. Laws limited their access to traditional resources. If Aboriginal title and rights continued to exist, they were invisible to most of the larger population, including legislators.

The Crown's obligation to seek treaties

The courts have not yet been asked to rule on whether the practice of making treaties with Aboriginal peoples is obligatory, or is a condition of valid interference with existing Aboriginal rights. It is, however, settled law that the Crown has a fiduciary duty to protect the interests of First Nations, since they cannot transfer their title to anyone but the Crown.

Reconciling constitutionally protected Aboriginal rights, the Crown's related duties to Aboriginal peoples, and the broader public interest presents a major challenge to Canadian society in general, and to the judiciary in particular. To what extent does section 35 limit the rights and powers of the Crown? Is there a legally enforceable duty to negotiate treaties?

If we start with the premise that Aboriginal title may be defined as the right to use a certain territory, we can argue that the fiduciary duty arising from First Nations' inability to transfer their interest to anyone but the Crown obliges the Crown to seek the surrender of land by treaty in good faith, before anyone attempts to enter the land as subjects of the Crown (for purposes such as resource development). This was the clear intent of the *Royal Proclamation of 1763*. Though the courts have found the Proclamation does not apply in B.C., its terms reflect the general policy of the Crown during the period of colonization.

We may also argue that the Constitution's confirmation of Aboriginal rights means that the Crown is obliged to pursue treaties if it wishes to substantially interfere with existing Aboriginal rights or title to achieve other valid objectives. The Court in *Sparrow* described section 35 as "a solemn commitment that must be given meaningful content," and that incorporates the Crown's fiduciary duty.[45]

The opposing view is that the Crown has no such obligation to negotiate treaties. However, once the Crown decides to seek treaties as a matter of policy, the Crown's honour requires that it negotiate in good faith.

Those who argue that the Crown is not obligated to make treaties before resource development proceeds say that, under the Constitution, only the federal government has the power to make treaties, while the provincial government has ownership and sole legal authority over provincial lands and resources. How, then, can the federal Crown have the duty to negotiate treaties before the development of lands and resources over which it has no direct control? They also say that, even though the provincial Crown must consult with Aboriginal peoples before it makes allocations of lands and resources that may affect Aboriginal rights on those lands, this obligation is not a clear duty to make treaties.

However, at a purely practical level, if the provincial government approves an activity on lands claimed by a First Nation, and the First Nation seeks to prevent the activity from proceeding, the First Nation must prove that it has Aboriginal rights or title, and that its rights have been infringed. If the government cannot justify its infringement, then the First Nation may be entitled to either a legal injunction to stop development, or to damages, depending on the activity and how it affects the Aboriginal rights or title in question.

Even if the Crown does not have a specific legal duty to negotiate treaties, the limits placed by the Constitution on the Crown's power to extinguish Aboriginal rights may leave treaties as the only practical way governments can resolve their objectives with Aboriginal interests.

Making treaties in modern times

In *Sparrow,* the Court emphasized the "importance of context and a case-by-case approach to s. 35(1)."[46] The question of whether the Crown has a legal duty to make treaties has the context of a modern, complex industrial society. The courts are not likely to set conditions for interfering with Aboriginal interests that will paralyze a government's ability to regulate across the wide range of activities that it controls.[47] Neither are they likely to retreat from interpreting section 35 as a "solemn commitment that must be given meaningful content."[48] The Crown's duty will continue to be to impose limits on how governments in Canada use their power. How the courts will provide remedies when they find ongoing failures to uphold the Crown's honour and duty to set limits remains to be seen.

Governments' grants of private rights to use land and resources have, over a long period, eroded the ability of First Nations peoples to sustain their traditional economies. These grants threaten to extinguish First Nations' ability to use their Aboriginal rights, in fact if not in law. Where an existing First Nations' right is threatened, courts may and will intervene to prevent the exercise of Crown-granted rights.[49]

Nevertheless, court decisions, clear though they might be in their definition of rights, are blunt tools when used to establish ground rules for the ongoing relations between diverse cultures. If there is a lesson for governments in the *Saanichton Marina Ltd. v. Claxton* and *Sparrow* cases, it is that the best time to make mutually beneficial agreements is before the courts define constitutionally protected Aboriginal rights. Once such rights are defined, there is much less room for negotiation.

If the Crown's historical practice of treaty-making is to be effective today, all parties will have to resolve disagreements over a broad spectrum of issues. And if settlements are to last, neither side can afford to aim for the type of "victory" that continues to penalize the other. Settlements must benefit both sides, and must enable the parties to move forward certain of their legal rights. As with all complex negotiations, each side weighs its objectives and positions against those of the other side throughout the long process of getting to an agreement.

The roles of government in making treaties

Federal and provincial responsibilities

Under the *Constitution Act, 1867,* the federal parliament has the primary duties and powers concerning Aboriginal peoples.[50] This does not mean that the entire burden of treaty-making must fall on the federal government. The Province's interests in lands and resources is put at risk by the uncertainty of how Aboriginal rights questions will be resolved. Aboriginal rights, even if defined minimally as subsistence rights, may be affected by the use of natural resources. So if First Nations' interests in land and resources are unsettled, the Province's ability to draw on its natural resources may be impaired.

In addition, because the Province has the power to grant land tenures that may interfere with Aboriginal rights, the Province may well have corresponding obligations. Chief Justice Dickson suggests this in his dissenting opinion in *Mitchell v. Peguis Indian Band* (1990):

> It is Canadian society at large which bears the historical burden of the current situation of native peoples and, as a result, the liberal interpretive approach applies to any statute relating to Indians, even if the relationship thereby affected is a private one. Underlying *Nowegijick* is an appreciation of societal responsibility, and a concern with remedying disadvantage, if only in the somewhat marginal context of treaty and statutory interpretation.[51]

The public interest

Under the law, treaties can only be made between the federal Crown and First Nations. As we have noted, the Crown is bound by fiduciary duties to protect the interests of Aboriginal peoples, which are not yet fully defined in the law. But governments of and in Canada must also represent national and provincial interests in negotiations that may result in binding commitments affecting all Canadians.

This responsibility to on the one hand honour the Crown's duty by seeking treaties, and on the other to represent the public interest is not necessarily a conflicting one. Resolving First Nations land title is clearly in the public interest.

It would be naive to think that political parties' need to get re-elected does not affect the progress and outcome of treaty negotiations. But resolving the issues of Aboriginal rights and title has positive consequences for the entire community. The clear advantage to all is that treaties will produce a measure of certainty that does not now exist. That certainly will, in turn, enable all governments, including Aboriginal governments, to act according to their authority, with the confidence that their laws will be upheld. That certainty will also help resolve questions about the rights to use land and resources.

The risks of court action

To decide whether to take legal action on or negotiate a claim of Aboriginal rights or title, any prudent party must carefully weigh the risks of litigation. Some of the questions to consider follow:

- Can the applicant prove that the particular practices, customs, or traditions in question are integral to the distinctive Aboriginal culture?
- If the claim is for Aboriginal title, does the applicant have to prove that their ancestors occupied the particular territory before European contact, or at the time of British sovereignty, or both?
- If the First Nation proves the Aboriginal right, has federal or provincial legislation infringed on it?
- If there is an infringement, will the Crown be able to justify that infringement? What particular facts will be relevant to the case?

- Does the Supreme Court of Canada's principle of continuity (as stated in *Van der Peet*) allow modern-day evolution of Aboriginal rights? That is, are First Nations allowed to do traditional activities such as fishing using modern methods and for modern purposes?
- Does Aboriginal title include Aboriginal rights of self-government? If so, the applicant must meet the same "integral to the distinctive culture" test that applies to any other aboriginal right. Is there evidence to support such a claim?
- What consequences will judicial decisions have for negotiations? Initially, as in *Calder* and *Sparrow,* by confirming the existence of Aboriginal rights, decisions have prompted negotiations. However, as the body of case law develops, it may limit the bargaining room of the parties.

For example, if a First Nation lost a case where it claimed an Aboriginal right to harvest timber commercially, its ability to get commercial timber rights at the treaty table would be slim. Conversely, if a court found that provincial laws on resource use unjustifiably infringed on the Aboriginal rights of a particular First Nation, that decision might undermine the government's ability to negotiate treaty terms that adequately protected not only the Aboriginal interest, but also the broader public interest in resource development on Crown lands.

The challenge of reconciling objectives

In theory, First Nations could insist that all non-aboriginal people stop using Aboriginal lands and that Aboriginal peoples are subject only to Aboriginal government. Federal and provincial governments could also declare that all Aboriginal interests have been extinguished, or that the government has the power to act as it pleases, regardless of Aboriginal interests. Commitment to a process of treaty makes such untenable positions highly unlikely, for the opposite side could not possibly accept them.

All parties must face an important fact when they decide how to achieve what they want. Settling Aboriginal rights and title issues means re-allocating government powers, land, money, and other resources. When treaties take these resources away from current users, disputes will occur. Those disputes will become public, and may either block or limit what the treaties can achieve. When the consequence is an impasse over a particular issue, any party should be able to seek a court decision on that issue, without abandoning negotiations over other issues.

But even through complex negotiations over certain issues, resolution can be reached if the parties can find a way to reconcile their objectives. First Nations' objectives are often to achieve self-government in their traditional territories, and access to the land and resources within them. The government surely seeks the certainty of a clear definition of Aboriginal self-government and Crown rights to land and resources. These objectives are clearly compatible and within reach.

Why are treaties in the interests of British Columbians?

Treaties are how governments can resolve their objectives and duties with existing Aboriginal rights. Because all Canadians depend on the economic use of natural resources, many First Nations and the federal and provincial governments have begun a new treaty process in British Columbia. Without treaties, the ability of governments of and in Canada to permit activities that interfere with Aboriginal rights will be doubtful. And the existence of doubt is not in the public interest.

The British Columbia Claims Task Force was established in December 1990, representing the First Nations, Canada, and the Province. On June 28, 1991, the Task Force presented its report and recommendations (which appear at the end of this chapter). The key recommendation, accepted by all parties, was to establish a commission to oversee a six-stage process of treaty negotiation. The parties have made a formal agreement on this recommendation.

Through their participation in the Task Force and the creation of the Treaty Commission, the First Nations in B.C. have stated their desire to make modern treaties. Now the responsibility to show good faith lies with the federal and provincial governments by doing all they reasonably can to enable First Nations to negotiate.

If these governments do their duties reasonably and in good faith, it is in the interest of all First Nations peoples to have their governments do the same. Why? The Supreme Court of Canada has plainly stated that in a 20th-century society, dependent on the land and its resources to keep pace in the international economy, not even constitutionally protected Aboriginal rights will be absolute (*Sparrow*).

The powers of the Crown to interfere with Aboriginal rights will continue to depend on its ability to justify such interference. If governments of and in Canada show their sincerity in seeking treaties, it will likely support this justification, particularly in any future case where a First Nation seeks compensation against incremental erosion of its Aboriginal rights as a result of actions under the Crown's authority.

Treaties are clearly in the interests of all people in British Columbia, Aboriginal or not. Issues between Aboriginal and non-aboriginal communities are unlikely to ever be fully resolved in court. As Chief Justice Dickson said in *Kruger and Manuel v. The Queen* (1977):

> Claims of aboriginal title are woven with history, legend, politics and moral obligations. If the claim of any Band in respect of any particular land is to be decided as a justiciable issue and not a political issue, it should be so considered on the facts pertinent to that Band and to that land, and not on any global basis.[52]

The recent decisions of the Supreme Court of Canada in *Van der Peet, Gladstone,* and *N.T.C. Smokehouse* each emphasize the highly specific application of Aboriginal rights cases to their specific facts. So does the Court's new test to define Aboriginal rights, which we re-state here for convenience:

> [I]n order to be an aboriginal right, an activity must be an element of a practice, custom or tradition integral to the distinctive culture of the aboriginal group claiming the right.[53]

The public announcements of those involved in the traditional fishing industry tell us a great deal about the impact of the Supreme Court's decision in *Sparrow*. The price of going to the wall on a legal issue is that one side or the other has its future options limited by the result. The question for all of us is whether we want to resolve Aboriginal claims issues through negotiation, compromise, and consensus, or whether we wish to run the legal risks of a case-by-case definition of constitutionally protected rights, or the political risks of failing to address legitimate and deeply felt grievances.

In *MacMillan Bloedel Limited v. Mullin,* and *Martin v. B.C.* (1985), Justice Macfarlane stated:

> The fact that there is an issue between the Indians and the province based upon aboriginal claims should not come as a surprise to anyone. Those claims have been advanced by the Indians for many years. . . . I think it fair to say that, in the end, the public anticipates that the claims will be resolved by negotiation and by settlement. This judicial proceeding is but a small part of the whole of a process which will ultimately find its solution in a reasonable exchange between governments and the Indian nations.[54]

Negotiation can deal with the full range of issues. Only negotiation reveals the concerns and objectives of the parties in such a way that, through mutual compromise, a solution may be found.

Notes

1. *Delgamuukw v. British Columbia*, [1993] 5 W.W.R. 97 (B.C.C.A.).

2. *Van der Peet v. The Queen*, [1996] 9 W.W.R. 1.

3. *Van der Peet*, at p. 27.

4. *Gladstone v. The Queen*, [1996] 9 W.W.R. 149.

5. *N.T.C. Smokehouse v. The Queen*, [1996] 9 W.W.R. 114.

6. Brian Slattery, "Understanding Aboriginal Rights" (1987), 66 *Can. Bar Rev.* 727.

7. *Van der Peet*, at p. 21.

8. *Calder v. British Columbia (Attorney General)*, [1973] S.C.R. 313, [1973] 4 W.W.R. 1.

9. *Johnson v. M'Intosh* (1823), 8 Wheat. 543, 5 L. Ed. 681, at pp. 573–4.

10. *Worcester v. Georgia* (1832), 315 U.S. 515 (U.S.S.C.), at p. 516.

11. *Guerin v. The Queen* (1984), 13 D.L.R. (4th) 321, at pp. 334, 336, and 340.

12. *Mabo v. Queensland* (1992), 107 A.L.R. 1, 175 C.L.R. 1.

13. *Delgamuukw* (1993), at p. 126.

14. *Delgamuukw* (1993), at p. 143.

15. *R. v. Sparrow* (1990), 70 D.L.R. (4th) 385, [1990] 1 S.C.R. 1075, at p. 411.

16. *Paul v. Canadian Pacific Ltd.* (1989), 53 D.L.R. (4th) 487 (S.C.C.).

17. *Hamlet of Baker Lake et al. v. Minister of Indian Affairs and Northern Development et al.*, [1980] 1 F.C. 518, [1980] 5 W.W.R. 193, [1979] 3 C.N.L.R. 17.

18. *Van der Peet*, at p. 17.

19. *Van der Peet*, at p. 26.

20. *Van der Peet*, at p. 26.

21. *Van der Peet*, at p. 27.

22. *Van der Peet*, at pp. 29–30.

23. *Van der Peet*, at p. 30.

24. *Van der Peet*, at p. 31.

25. *Pamajewon and Jones v. Her Majesty the Queen*, [1996] 4 C.N.L.R. 164, 27 O.R. (3d) 95 (S.C.C.).

26. *Pamajewon*, at p. 171.

27. *Stein v. The Ship "Kathy"* (1976) 2 S.C.R. 802.

28. *Van der Peet*, at p. 31.

29. *Van der Peet*, at p. 33.

30. *Van der Peet*, at p. 32.

31. *Van der Peet*, at p. 33.

32. *Van der Peet*, at p. 40.

33. *Delgamuukw* (1993), at p. 22.

34. *Delgamuukw* (1993), at p. 22.

35. *Guerin*, at p. 334.

36. *Sparrow*, at p. 408.

37. *Sparrow*, at p. 401.

38. *Sparrow*, at p. 410.

39. *Sparrow*, at p. 410.

40. *Gladstone*, at p. 51.

41. *Delgamuukw* (1991), at p. 423.

42. *R. v. Jack* (1996), 16 B.C.L.R. (3d) 201; *R. v. Sampson* (1996), 16 B.C.L.R. (3d) 226; and *R. v. Little* (1996), 16 B.C.L.R. (3d) 201.

43. *Jack*, at p. 222.

44. *Delgamuukw* (1991), at p. 179.

45. *Sparrow*, at p. 408.

46. *Sparrow*, at p. 410.

47. *Sparrow*, at p. 410.

48. *Sparrow*, at p. 408.

49. *Saanichton Marina Ltd. v. Claxton* (1989), 36 B.C.L.R. (2d) 79 (B.C.C.A.).

50. See *R. v. White and Bob* (1964), 50 D.L.R. (2d) 613 (B.C.C.A.), per Norris J.A., at p. 638; and also *Mitchell v. Peguis Indian Band*, [1990] 3 C.N.L.R. 46 (S.C.C.), at p. 83.

51. *Mitchell v. Peguis Indian Band*, at p. 76.

52. *Kruger and Manuel v. The Queen* (1977), 75 D.L.R. (3d) 434, at p. 437.

53. *Van der Peet*, at p. 27.

54. *MacMillan Bloedel Limited v. Mullin* and *Martin v. B.C.* (1985), 61 B.C.L.R. 145 (B.C.C.A.), at pp. 172–73.

References

Cases

Calder v. British Columbia (Attorney General), [1973] S.C.R. 313, [1973] 4 W.W.R. 1, 34 D.L.R (3d) 145.

Delgamuukw v. British Columbia, [1991] 3 W.W.R. 97 (B.C.S.C.).

Delgamuukw v. British Columbia, [1993] 5 W.W.R. 97 (B.C.C.A).

Gladstone v. The Queen, [1996] 9 W.W.R. 149.

Guerin v. The Queen (1984), 13 D.L.R. (4th) 321.

Hamlet of Baker Lake et al. v. Minister of Indian Affairs and Northern Development et al., [1980] 1 F.C. 518, [1980] 5 W.W.R. 193, [1979] 3 C.N.L.R. 17.

Johnson v. M'Intosh (1823), 8 Wheat. 543, 5 L. Ed. 681.

Kruger and Manuel v. The Queen (1977), 75 D.L.R. (3d) 434.

Mabo v. Queensland (1992), 107 A.L.R. 1, 175 C.L.R. 1.

MacMillan Bloedel Limited v. Mullin; Martin v. B.C. (1985), 61 B.C.L.R. 145.

Mitchell v. Peguis Indian Band, [1990] 3 C.N.L.R. 46.

Nowegejick v. R., [1983] 1 S.C.R. 29, 144 D.L.R. (3d) 193.

N.T.C. Smokehouse v. The Queen, [1996] 9 W.W.R. 114.

Ontario Mining Co. v. Seybold (1900), 31 O.R. 386.

Pamajewon and Jones v. Her Majesty the Queen, [1996] 4 C.N.L.R. 164, 27 O.R. (3d) 95.

Paul v. Canadian Pacific Ltd. (1989), 53 D.L.R. (4th) 487.

R. v. Jack (1996), 16 B.C.L.R. (3d) 201.

R. v. Little (1996), 16 B.C.L.R. (3d) 253.

R. v. Sampson (1996), 16 B.C.L.R. (3d) 226.

R. v. Sparrow (1990), 70 D.L.R. (4th) 385, [1990] 1 S.C.R. 1075.

R. v. Taylor and Williams (1981), 62 C.C.C. (2d) 227, 34 O.R. (2d) 360 (C.A.).

R. v. White and Bob (1964), 50 D.L.R. (2d) 613.

Saanichton Marina Ltd. v. Claxton (1989), 36 B.C.L.R. (2d) 79.

St. Catherine's Milling & Lumber Co. v. The Queen (1888), 14 App. Cas. 46.

Stein v. The Ship "Kathy" (1976) 2 S.C.R. 802.

Van der Peet v. The Queen, [1996] 9 W.W.R. 1.

Worcester v. Georgia (1832), 314 U.S. 515.

Articles

Slattery, Brian. "Understanding Aboriginal Rights" (1987), 66 *Can. Bar Rev. at p. 727.*

Appendix: Recommendations of the British Columbia Claims Task Force

The Task Force recommends that:

1. The First Nations, Canada, and British Columbia establish a new relationship based on mutual trust, respect, and understanding—through political negotiations.

2. Each of the parties be at liberty to introduce any issue at the negotiation table which it views as significant to the new relationship.

3. A British Columbia Treaty Commission be established by agreement among the First Nations, Canada, and British Columbia to facilitate the process of negotiations.

4. The Commission consist of a full-time chairperson and four commissioners—of whom two are appointed by the First Nations, and one each by the federal and provincial governments.

5. A six-stage process be followed in negotiating treaties.

6. The treaty negotiation process be open to all First Nations in British Columbia.

7. The organization of First Nations for the negotiations is a decision to be made by each First Nation.

8. First Nations resolve issues related to overlapping traditional territories among themselves.

9. Federal and provincial governments start negotiations as soon as First Nations are ready.

10. Non-aboriginal interests be represented at the negotiating table by the federal and provincial governments.

11. The First Nation, Canadian, and British Columbian negotiating teams be sufficiently funded to meet the requirements of the negotiations.

12. The commission be responsible for allocating funds to the First Nations.

13. The parties develop ratification procedures which are confirmed in the Framework Agreement and in the Agreement-in-Principle.

14. The commission provide advice and assistance in dispute resolution as agreed by the parties.

15. The parties select skilled negotiators and provide them with a clear mandate, and training as required.

16. The parties negotiate interim measures agreements before or during the treaty negotiations when an interest is being affected which could undermine the process.

17. Canada, British Columbia, and the First Nations jointly undertake public education and information programs.

18. The parties in each negotiation jointly undertake a public information program.

19. British Columbia, Canada, and the First Nations request the First Nations Education Secretariat, and various educational organizations in British Columbia, to prepare resource materials for use in the schools and by the public.

3

Land and Resource Tenure:

First Nations Traditional Territories and Self-Governance

By Greg Poelzer

The existence and well-being of any community depends on the land it holds and occupies — its territory.[1] First Nations societies in British Columbia enjoy particularly rich relationships with the land. Their relationship to the territory they occupy determines many facets of their culture, from their economy, social structure, and religion to their politics. And because the First Nations' relationship to the land is so different from that of other Canadians, First Nations' concepts of community, government, and territoriality (controlling territories in order to influence others) are very different from those of the larger Canadian society. These differences have proven to be persistent sources of conflict and misunderstanding. If the land settlement process in B.C. is to lead to all British Columbians living together in peace, we must recognize and reconcile them.

This chapter contends that the question of how we control land and resources is fundamentally a political one, inseparably linked to the question of self-government. It

- discusses the concepts of political community, government, territoriality, and land tenure (the conditions under which we hold land)

- outlines the traditional practices of political community and land tenure of First Nations communities in B.C.
- compares First Nations practices with those of the larger Canadian society
- explores current approaches to reconciling differences between First Nations political communities and the federal and provincial governments.

Two important arguments arise from this discussion. First, because First Nations political organizations and cultures are very diverse, we need a variety of approaches to land tenure and self-government. Second, integrating First Nations political communities through the B.C. treaty process will lead to the creation of a third order of government in Canada, in addition to federal and provincial governments.

How Territorial Practices Create Political Differences

Politics are the events and power relationships that arise when the public makes decisions about the internal and external affairs of a political community.[2] They involve struggle and conflict, cooperation and accommodation. A political community is a social group that inhabits a specific territory, shares a common way of life, and is prepared to defend its way of life over that territory.[3] How different political communities make decisions and control territories to achieve their political purposes varies considerably.

Differences between formal and informal government

Many but not all communities organize politics through the institution of government, which is the body that makes authoritative and binding decisions for a political community.[4] Government has three special characteristics. First, it is an institution, which means it behaves in "stable, valued, [and] recurring patterns."[5] The party in power may change, but the nature of that power does not. Second, government makes *authoritative* decisions. It does not have power because it can influence members of a community. Nor does its power come solely from its ability to enforce its will. The government can make decisions simply because it has the right of command. Third, government makes binding decisions. Unlike other organizations, all members of a community must obey the decisions that government makes.

However, it is a common misconception that politics can *only* exist where there is government. As Paul Tennant correctly points out, "Peoples can have politics whether or not they have formal governments."[6] Government is merely one way to organize public decision-making. "In many societies," writes Ted Lewellen, "government simply does not exist."[7]

In contrast to state societies, for instance, where government is the focal point of politics, in band and tribal societies, kinship is the basis of politics.[8] Bands and tribes, nomadic political communities with small populations composed of extended families, and networks of extended families have little need of formal institutions of government. Kinship defines membership in the community and can be significant in leadership selection. Kinship also plays an important role in determining who gets access to group resources. Typically, decisions made in bands and tribes are neither authoritative nor binding. Chiefs are leaders, not rulers. Instead, decisions must be made by consensus and are, in the end, voluntary. Social penalties for disobedience help ensure public decisions are followed. When a group fails to agree, the discord and conflict continue, or the dissatisfied people leave the group to join another community or to establish a separate one.[9] Nevertheless, there is one important similarity between political communities based on formal government and those based on kinship. The way each organizes its decision-making depends directly on its beliefs and practices about territoriality and land tenure.

Differences created by concepts of territoriality and land tenure

"Territoriality" is when a group tries to achieve political influence by asserting control over a specific area of land.[10] By their very nature as social groups that inhabit a specific territory, and defend their way of life on it, all political communities practise territoriality. If they did not, they would cease to be political communities. We often associate political territoriality with modern states, which maintain precisely marked boundaries. But nomadic groups such as small hunter-gatherer bands practise territoriality as well. As Anthony Giddens notes, "nomadic societies occupy definite, if only diffusely bounded, social spaces which they lay claim to, even if only in a temporary way."[11] And, while hunter-gatherer bands "may lack fixed settlements . . . they do typically lay claim to the legitimate control of a domain as their 'territory of operation.'"[12] He concludes that if we define "territoriality" to mean a legitimate occupation of an area of land, then it applies to less permanent types of settlements than villages or cities.[13]

This sociological understanding of territoriality moves us away from legal conceptions of land that imply that land can be owned as an entity or commodity.[14] It does include political communities like nation-states, which claim not only domination, but also actual tangible ownership of territory. But it also includes those indigenous peoples who make no claim to actual ownership of land, but do claim exclusive occupation of it. These different concepts of territoriality remain a major source of conflict between First Nations peoples and the larger Canadian society.

Whereas "territoriality" here means the territorial relationships *between* political communities, land tenure is "the system of land ownership and title to its use"[15] *within* the territory of a political community. Land and resource tenure are the rights and obligations that regulate how we possess and use land and natural resources. Gail Osherenko identifies four sets of rights associated with land and resource tenure:

- "proprietary rights," which allow the holder ownership
- "exclusionary rights," which allow the holder to exclude others from using land or resources
- "disposition rights," which allow the owner to transfer ownership (though these rights may be restricted)
- "usufructory rights," which allow the holder to use particular land or resources for specific purposes (and possibly for limited periods of time).[16]

The different patterns of First Nations land tenure systems and how they connect to their political organizations are examined below.

Kinship: Concepts of Government and Territoriality in First Nations Societies

First Nations' concepts and practices of government and territoriality differ widely not only from those of Europeans who settled in British Columbia, but also among First Nations themselves. Paul Tennant observes that the "rank societies" of First Nations Coastal groups are organized very differently from the "band egalitarian societies" of the Interior groups.[17] Since a number of Interior groups who were in close contact with Coastal peoples adopted important elements of the Coastal rank societies, this basic distinction needs to be qualified to some degree.[18] As well, the hierarchies vary among societies with ranking systems as one moves from the southern to the northern Coastal regions. Fundamental differences also exist in the mobility of First Nations political communities. The band societies of the northeast part of B.C. maintained a highly nomadic way of life in which territorial boundaries were less firm, whereas the rank societies along the Coast were far more sedentary. Their territorial boundaries were more fixed, and land tenure systems more complex.

The following section examines this diversity of political organization and territoriality across the three major cultural areas of British Columbia: the Western Sub-Arctic, the Plateau, and the Northwest Coast.

Western Sub-Arctic Nations

The existence of chiefdoms is one of the things that make First Nations political communities in British Columbia different from those in the rest of Canada. East of the Rockies, bands and tribes are the most common forms of Aboriginal political organization. Chiefdoms don't exist. However, in the Western Sub-Arctic region of northern B.C., a number of Athabaskan-speaking peoples, especially in the northeastern part of the province, do fit the pattern that exists across the rest of Canada. But even here, important elements of Coastal rank societies become increasingly prominent as one moves from east to west.

In northeastern B.C., nomadic movements, fewer people, and methods of subsistence based on hunting and gathering account for band-level organization to a significant degree, especially among the Beaver,

Sekani, and, to a certain extent, eastern Carrier peoples. The Beaver and Sekani, in particular, historically occupy the river systems which flow to the Arctic, and therefore do not have access to salmon resources. They hunt large game such as caribou and moose, fish trout and char, and gather berries and other plant foods. As a result, the Beaver and Sekani fit much closer to the pattern of northern Athabaskan band organization found in northern Canada than other Athabaskan peoples in B.C. Ken Coates has noted the connection between northern Athabaskans' methods of subsistence and their social organization. He writes:

> The extensive mobility required by such hunting, fishing, and gathering determined the nature of aboriginal social organization. A band system evolved, based on the annual summer gatherings, but even these groups had limited structural significance.[19]

Methods of public decision-making were determined by band organization. Decisions were accomplished by consensus and typically on an informal basis.[20] Leadership was neither institutionalized, nor authoritative. Among the Sekani, Diamond Jenness observes:

> Each band had a leader, who was neither hereditary nor elected, but acquired his position through force of character, skill in hunting, and sane judgement. His authority, therefore, was merely nominal; he was a leader, not a chief, and if he presumed to issue orders, he had no means of enforcing them.[21]

This distinction between authority and influence in politics is crucial. Communities where decisions are made with authority, and thus are binding, have government. Communities where decisions are made by consensus and influence, and thus are voluntary, do not.

Public decision-making by consensus, combined with nomadic movements and band organization, shaped ideas of land tenure among the Sekani and Beaver. They consider a particular territorial area to be a band's domain, but no single person or institution within their political community regulates land use. Hugh Broady argues, for instance, that for the Beaver, land use is based on the principles of "freedom of access, flexible use, and rotational conservation."[22] (Rotational conservation is the practice of rotating areas where resources are harvested so that they do not become depleted.) Reinforcing this flexibility of land use is a sense of group stewardship over the band's territory. As Broady notes:

> Because everyone has depended on a collectively high level of harvesting and on sharing of meat, there is a widespread feeling of dependence upon lands that lie beyond any single individual's area of land use.[23]

According to Jenness, the closely related Sekani have a similar approach to land tenure:

> [T]he Sekani were divided into bands, each of which possessed its own hunting territory. Sometimes the individual families scattered and hunted separately, sometimes they wandered in groups of two or three; yet just as frequently, perhaps, they held together for mutual support and moved as a unit from one place to another within their domain. There were no family hunting grounds, no districts of which a family or small group of families claimed exclusive possession. Family rights to special hunting grounds have come only in recent times. . . . Since every family was coequal with every other, and often depended on its neighbours for support, it was necessary to consider all food as common property whenever two or more families lived side by side.[24]

While land tenure systems and boundaries may be flexible, the band as a political community has a history of actively defending its territory. Between the Sekani and Gitxsan, for example, there were territorial conflicts at Bear Lake in the first half of the 19th century which resulted in the loss of life:

> Although they [Long Grass Sekani] married frequently with the Gitxsan, from whom they were separated by Klappan mountains, any member of one tribe who hunted in the territory of the other was killed without pity. Five Long Grass Indians and several Gitxsan were killed in a fight about 1865.[25]

These territorial disputes were eventually settled peacefully. However, they do emphasize the fact that even the most decentralized and nomadic peoples are self-determining political communities with a sharp sense of territoriality.

Not all Athabaskan peoples of the Western Sub-Arctic were as egalitarian as the Beaver and Sekani, nor were their systems of land tenure as flexible. The Alkatcho Carrier of the eastern slopes of the Coast Mountains and the Wet'suwet'en of the Bulkley Valley, for example, display a number of important elements found in the rank societies of the Northwest Coast.

True to their Athabaskan roots, neither the Wet'suwet'en nor the Alkatcho Carrier are sedentary peoples. The Wet'suwet'en, for instance, unlike their Tsimshian-speaking Gitxsan neighbours, annually abandoned their summer fishing sites at what is now Moricetown, and dispersed throughout their expansive territory for the winter villages. In the spring, they moved to lakes for fishing before returning to their salmon fishing sites. At the same time, both peoples adopted the clan and crest systems of their Coastal neighbours, and both had ranking systems within their communities. Irving Goldman suggests that in the case of the Alkatcho Carrier:

> Property concepts changed relatively little under Northwest Coast influence. The extended family, equivalent to the Athabascan band, hunted over a common territory and shared the proceeds. It appears, however, that the crest group, which as we have seen was an honorific society cutting across family lines, also had hunting and fishing rights in common.[26]

The Wet'suwet'en were influenced much more by Coastal societies. They had developed strong relations with the Gitxsan, and adopted a similar matrilineal clan and house system. (This adoption goes back possibly thousands of years.) It is through the house system that the Wet'suwet'en practise land and resource tenure. Each house has a chief and subchiefs who govern the fishing sites and outlying territories. Rights to use the territory of another house can be obtained through marriage ties or permission of the house chief. Trespassing could lead to the offender's death. Alan McMillan argues, however, "While these 'chiefs' had great prestige and were accorded respect, they lack real political authority; the basic individual autonomy of the Athabaskans was retained."[27] Nevertheless, compared to the Beaver and Sekani, Wet'suwet'en political organization and land tenure is far more structured and complex.[28]

Perhaps Tonia Mills best sums up the situation of the Wet'suwet'en and other Athabaskan peoples who neighbour the rank societies of the Coast:

> Wet'suwet'en society has responded to all the changes it has experienced over the centuries through its own unique adaptation of the coastal, prerogative-oriented system of rank titles associated with control of access to fishing spots and hunting territories, as well as through its Athabaskan flexibility and appreciation of individually acquired spiritual prowess. . . . That culture owes as much to the headwater Athabaskan origins as to its downriver coastal neighbours.[29]

Plateau Nations

The Plateau culture area is located in the southern Interior of British Columbia. Although Athabaskan- and Kutenai-speaking peoples are represented here, by far the largest language group is the Interior Salish (Okanagan, Shuswap, Thompson, and Upper Lillooet peoples). Salmon is a key resource in the Plateau economies, except for in Kutenai and Chilcotin, which have no salmon. As we move upstream, dependence on salmon decreases, as other food resources, especially deer, become more important. The Plateau economy is thus marked by a seasonal variety of fishing, hunting, and gathering activities.

For the most part, the Plateau peoples have had a nomadic or semi-nomadic way of life based on seasonal subsistence patterns. The band is the primary form of political organization, with the winter village community as the largest unit. Beyond the village community, political organization is limited, since "no mechanism existed to link the various communities speaking the same language."[30] Nevertheless, marriage created ties among bands of neighbouring winter villages. Even though the Plateau Nations had more people per territory than those of the Western Sub-Arctic, migration between winter villages and spring and summer fishing sites helped make formal institutions of government unnecessary. "The informality of daily living and the required seasonal movements" among Okanagan fishers and hunters prevented the creation of formal power structures. "A chief was followed because of his attributes and did not have power to force people to do his will."[31]

Although the methods the Interior Salish use to make decisions are relatively informal, like those of the northeastern Athabaskan peoples, their concepts of land and resource tenure are more complex and less flexible. At the same time, however, the way they use land and resources is not nearly as fixed and regulated as the peoples of the Northwest Coast. This distinctiveness of Plateau land tenure is especially evident in the way the Interior Salish manage fishing, hunting, and gathering resources.

The Lillooet, for instance, have three types of ownership for salmon fishing sites: individual, band, and public. Individuals own rocks where they build fishing platforms every year. Who owns which rock is well known within a community, and the owners are entitled to transfer their sites to members of their extended families.[32] At the community level, each band has collective resource rights to the stretch of river associated with it. Rights to use the band's stretch of water can be obtained through marriage.[33] Finally, there are public fishing rights. Some fishing sites at falls or river mouths within a band's traditional territory are understood not to be "owned" by anyone. In fact, even Shuswap and Okanagan bands have visited the fishing sites within Lillooet territory. In return, the Lillooet bands shared in the trout fishing in Shuswap territory.[34]

Plateau cultures appear to use hunting and gathering sites in a way similar to the Beaver and Sekani of the Western Sub-Arctic. One study found that "All *Xaxli'p* and *Ts'kw'aylaxw* elders indicated that, within bands, there was no ownership of hunting or plant gathering sites and that access was free to all band members."[35] Diana Alexander contends that access rights to trapping, hunting, and plant gathering extend beyond the band associated with a particular territory to other related bands, but not to "strangers."[36] Access to resources on a band's lands was flexible, but specific families recognized their responsibility to manage particular sites. She suggests that "the lands may be seen as the common property of the tribe, while specific locations were still 'regulated,' though not 'owned,' by individual families."[37]

Finally, like the Athabaskan peoples of the Western Sub-Arctic, the Interior Salish peoples have a clear sense of territoriality that defines the lands of their communities from those of others. Peter Carstens argues that the territoriality of the Okanagan peoples, for instance (and perhaps for other Plateau groups), can be divided into four components:

"the location of permanent and less permanent villages, the terrain used for hunting, fishing, gathering, and similar activities, their own perception of their territory, and the perception that other people had of Okanagan territory."[38] Those who did not have access to the territory of a band or, where it existed, the tribe (a network of bands that have some degree of political allegiance), were repulsed or killed.

Northwest Coast Nations

The First Nations of the Northwest Coast stand out in contrast to other Aboriginal peoples in British Columbia, and especially in the rest of Canada.[39] Their social system of "chiefdoms" differs from the egalitarian social organizations of bands and tribes in several important ways. Chiefdoms are marked by clear social and political inequality, on the basis of status. They also had a relatively permanent method to regulate the community's economic activities in the form of the potlatch.[40] Even when outlawed, these large gatherings obliged the host to give extravagant gifts to all of his guests.

The position of chief is typically hereditary, and carries with it the right of command. The degree and the scope of this authority varies. In some communities, the chief's power is quite extensive, including the power of life or death over community members. In others, the power of a chief is much more limited.

The chiefdoms of the Northwest Coast share similar features with others around the world, such as those found in the South Pacific. However, the Northwest Coast chiefdoms also share many features with neighbouring bands and tribes. The Northwest Coast societies are based on rank, and these ranks give certain privileges to chiefs or "nobles" not shared by others. But the number of people who hold high rank is often large. Among the Kwagiulth at one time, for instance, for "a population of about 1,500 people, there were 650 named titles or positions, and some of these were held by more than one person at a time."[41] Without question, the highest-ranking chief of a village has some authority not enjoyed by others. But this authority is not total. Social control often takes the form of various social penalties for disobedience, as practised in bands and tribes. Finally, potlatch-givers depended heavily upon their kin to help provide the goods to be distributed—no one was wealthy enough to hold a potlatch by themselves. Those invited were expected to return the favour. The potlatch "suggests a system of reciprocity, common to bands and tribes, rather than the centralized redistribution that supposedly defines the quality of chiefdoms."[42]

Even so, the Northwest Coast political communities are not egalitarian. The degree of their hierarchies varies, with the most hierarchical in the northwest part of the province. Not surprisingly, public decision-making and land tenure systems are complex. The access an individual has to land and resources depends on that individual's rank. As Harold Barclay points out, "among the Nootka [Nuu-chah-nulth] the chief or senior 'noble' of several local settlements had certain prior rights to the salmon streams and ocean waters for fish and sea mammals. . . ."[43]

Invariably, kinship is the foundation of the Northwest Coast peoples' land tenure systems. Among the Gitxsan, as with the Wet'suwet'en, land and resource tenure continues to be organized along a matrilineal house system: "Since all resources are owned by Houses which are controlled by dominant lineages within them, a person's primary access to resources depends on his relationship to the dominant lineage within the House to which he is ascribed by birth."[44] This pattern varies among the Coastal Salish, as lines of descent and corresponding resources can be traced on both sides of the family. But in either case, the house system of kinship regulates how the community owns and uses land and resources.

Nationalism: Concepts of Government and Territoriality in Modern States

How First Nations societies organize their politics and land use is so very different from how the larger Canadian state does so, that the many years of misunderstanding and conflict between the two is not surprising. In contrast to First Nations political communities, modern Euro-Canadian states organize their decision-making in a very formal, hierarchical, and impersonal way. Territories are precise and fixed. The basis of what we shall call the "modern state" system of government and territoriality is outlined below.

Nationalism and the "modern state" society

Nationalism and universal citizenship are crucial to defining political community in the modern European state. Benedict Anderson observes that nationalism is not really an ideology like liberalism or fascism, but is rather like a form of kinship and religion.[45] "Nationalism" comes, of course, from the concept of "nation," which Anderson defines as "an imagined political community—and imagined as both inherently limited and sovereign."[46] The nation is therefore very different from the much more personal First Nations political communities. It is also very different from political communities in feudal and absolutist states:

> The earlier, dynastic states in Europe placed few demands on the majority of their citizens, and they did not require cultural uniformity in society. It did not matter that serfs spoke a different language from that of the rulers, or that the serfs in one region spoke a different language from those in another region.[47]

The advent of nationalism changed all of this, turning "peasants into Frenchmen."[48] The concept of nationalism offered at least the ideal of shared identity and belonging, regardless of social inequalities. At the same time, the nation demanded that all its members be uniform and give their universal commitment, including the ultimate sacrifice of their lives for the nation's good.

The notion of universal citizenship has always been attached to the idea of nationalism. Citizenship describes the rights and obligations that members have in order to be associated with the social unit of the nation.[49] So while universal citizenship entitles members to certain universal benefits, it also demands that they all participate in the political community. The benefits vary significantly according to the particular regime. Liberal democracies promote political and civil rights, for example, where socialist regimes promote economic rights "in combination with the severe curtailment of political and civil rights."[50] The rigidity and abstractness of modern state societies such as Canada is in complete contrast with the flexibility and concrete nature of kin ties in many First Nations political communities.

Territoriality in the "modern state"

How "modern states" own and use land and resources is based on
the notions of sovereignty, borders, and "internal pacification" (the
ability to police its people). Sovereignty means a political group's
command over a territory. That authority is impersonal and ultimate.
Carl Schmitt describes the sovereign as "he who decides on the exception."[51] For Schmitt, the exception is a condition of emergency in which
the sovereign acts with unlimited authority, unconstrained by law, in
order to preserve its rule: "In such a situation it is clear that the state
remains, whereas law recedes."[52] According to this view, sovereignty
does not come from law; it comes before law.[53] To be sovereign is to
be able to decide on political action beyond the legal order itself, and
to decide when the legal order can and must be suspended to maintain
rule.

The achievement of state sovereignty is very modern, "an outstanding characteristic of the constitutional state of the nineteenth century."[54]
For our purposes, it is important to note that for a modern state, the
existence of other self-governing political communities threatens its
internal sovereignty.

Not surprisingly, modern states have borders rather than frontiers.
This distinction is crucial. The boundaries of frontiers can be internal
or external (to separate them from another state). Geographical demar-
cations are poorly defined, and so are the political and social structures.
In frontier areas, the political authority of the centre is thinly spread.
By contrast, borders are precisely marked boundaries—geographical,
social, and political. The territory they enclose is closely watched and
policed by the political administration. The ideal modern state is one
without internal borders: federal states represent a major deviation from
this rule.[55]

The modern state also possesses a high degree of control in the form
of "internal pacification"—the ability to police activities across the
entire territory to both control violence and to monitor all the social
activities within the state.[56] This ability is possible because of rapid
advancements in communication and transportation technologies and
the development of modern bureaucracy. As a result, it is "a political
and administrative machine run by civil servants recruited on an impersonal basis according to meritocratic criteria."[57]

The modern bureaucracy is unprecedented in terms of organizational power and efficiency. It can maintain almost unlimited information on virtually all relevant social, economic, and political activities. Internal pacification and bureaucracy help create the foundation for a more centralized, autonomous, modern state.

With a critical exception, the larger Canadian political community follows the pattern of the modern state. The critical exception is its federal organization. It divides sovereignty between national and subnational political orders. As a result, a political culture has developed that allows certain communities to have political autonomy based on their territory and ethnic culture. Quebec is an example (though likely a controversial one). This political culture suggests that it is possible to reconcile First Nations' aspirations for territorial self-government within the Canadian federal system.

How Can First Nations and Euro-Canadian States Coexist in Peace?

"'Politics,'" Paul Tennant correctly argues, "is the first and final word pertaining to the land use question."[58] When Europeans first contacted them, First Nations societies in British Columbia represented a diversity of self-determining political communities. Ever since, the politics of relations between communities and the larger Canadian state have been marked by First Nations' struggles to exist equally with the larger British Columbian and Canadian political communities. Today's treaty process asks a number of important questions. What are possible ways to accommodate everyone? Can we make a variety of different self-government agreements and land title settlements to reflect the diversity of First Nations traditional practices? Is a high degree of uniformity more likely? What lessons can we learn from other federal states?

If we believe it is necessary and important to settle First Nations aspirations for land, treaties, and self-government, then we must begin by recognizing the fact that First Nations political communities remain distinct from the larger British Columbian and Canadian political communities within which they exist. It is equally important to recognize that these political communities have varying forms of traditional government and land tenure. These differences are crucial to understand the

First Nations' varied approaches to land tenure and self-government, and to challenge approaches to treaty negotiations that insist on one uniform agreement.

It is impossible to discuss the cases of all First Nations societies in B.C., but two underscore the problem of unitary approaches: the Nisga'a Agreement-in-Principle based on traditional land selection and the Gitxsan-Wet'suwet'en proposals for co-management with house ownership of lands. The federal and provincial governments' basic position in negotiations with British Columbia First Nations is based on the principle of land selection, where each First Nation chooses a single land base, then negotiates the size of that territory. In the case of the Nisga'a, the Nisga'a Tribal Council was able to secure 10% of the original land they claimed. In this case, the traditional land selection model was less problematic, for a number of reasons. Two are that there are relatively few non-Nisga'a residents living in the Nass Valley (the territory the Nisga'a chose), and the Nisga'a are the principal First Nation who occupy the Nass River system. At the same time, although last year's vote on the Agreement-in-Principle showed the Nisga'a First Nation supported the deal overwhelmingly as a whole, some members have expressed reservations over the Agreement because their traditional house lands fall outside the area of the negotiated land settlement.

The Gitxsan-Wet'suwet'en are pursuing a different course of action. Instead of seeking a small percentage of their traditional land bases, they want jurisdiction (legal authority) over their entire traditional territory, with land ownership of individual territories based along house lines. The scope of jurisdiction would be determined by negotiation, but the Wet'suwet'en in particular are seeking some form of co-management, similar to the Gwich'in land claim in the Northwest Territories. This approach is reflected in the Gitxsan, Wet'suwet'en, and Gitanyow Community- Based Governance Agreement-in-Principle of January 1995.[59] However, neither the federal nor the provincial negotiators have the authority to negotiate any other form of land settlement than the traditional land selection model. As a result, constructive negotiations are on hold until the outcome of a court action is known. In the foreseeable future, the prospects for fruitful negotiations are not very good without the flexibility to accommodate the diversity of traditional land tenure practices.

What are possible alternatives? The success of the Gwich'in land claim in the Northwest Territories shows that, where appropriate, co-management arrangements between the provincial and First Nations governments are worth exploring. However, in areas where the non-aboriginal population is very high, or where there is significant agricultural, industrial, or resource development, such a solution may not be very realistic.

Another possibility can be found in the recent experiences of the Russian Federation. With the dramatic changes in the former Soviet Union, aboriginal peoples in Russia have been seeking land settlement and self-government. One of the emerging arrangements in Russia today is a *rodovaya obshchina* (clan commune) where an individual family or extended family has the title to part or all of their clan's traditional lands. If B.C. used this approach, it could mean, for example, that individual houses (of rank societies) or extended families (of egalitarian societies) would obtain the title to part or all of their traditional lands, assuming that such land was available. The actual bundle of rights associated with that land and the actual powers of self-government would be determined by negotiation.

One final point. If the current treaty process is successful, it will lead to the accommodation of First Nations political communities *within* the federal political order. Contrary to the mistaken view that non-aboriginal Canada is built on the principles of "One Country, One People, One Law," the federal political order is very much a collection of political communities, some with very distinct cultures, joined together by a "treaty" called the Constitution. The creation of another order of territory-based government within the Canadian federation would be an extension of an already-existing practice, one that promotes integration and accommodation. What we require now is some imagination to make it work for both Aboriginal and non-aboriginal British Columbians.

Notes

1. I would like to thank the Laurier Institution for supporting the research for this paper. I would also like to thank the following individuals: Sally Nyce, Edith Munroe, Edna Way, Sharlena Clayton, Kym Guno, Tanya Adams, Don Ryan, Marvin George, Ken Coates, and especially Tom Hutton, Tonia Mills, and Gail Fondahl. None of these people, of course, is responsible for any errors or shortcomings in this chapter.

2. Marc J. Swartz defines politics as those "events which are involved in the determination and implementation of public goals and/or the differential distribution and use of power within the group or groups concerned with the goals being considered."

While many scholars view politics "vertically," in terms of "haves" and "have-nots," Carl Schmitt offers one of the most poignant, "horizontal" definitions of politics as the struggle between political communities: "The specific political distinction to which political actions and motives can be reduced is that between friend and enemy," (*The Concept of the Political,* p. 26). For Schmitt, the friend-enemy distinction is an existential, not a symbolic, one. The enemy is a real social group that threatens one's existence as a community: "Each participant [exclusively] is in a position to judge whether the adversary intends to negate his opponent's way of life and therefore must be repulsed or fought in order to preserve one's own form of existence" (p. 27). This understanding of politics may more accurately describe conflicts between First Nations communities and the larger society that, for example, result in roadblocks on traditional lands.

3. This follows Max Weber's definition: "a separate 'political' community exists where we find (1) a 'territory'; (2) the availability of physical force for its domination; and (3) social action which is not restricted exclusively to the satisfaction of common economic needs in the frame of a communal economy, but regulates more generally the interrelation of the inhabitants of the territory," (*Economy and Society,* p. 902).

4. See Dickerson and Flanan, p. 5; and Ranney, p. 23.

5. Huntington, p. 12.

6. Tennant, p. xii.

7. Lewellen, p. 1.

8. Service, p. 111. For other important discussions of politics in band and tribal societies, see *Politics and History in Band Societies,* eds. Eleanor Leacock and Richard Lee (Cambridge: Cambridge University Press, 1982); Harold Barclay, *People Without Government* (London: Kahn & Averill, 1982); Morton H. Fried, *The Evolution of Political Society: An Essay in Political Anthropology* (New York: Random House Inc., 1967); *Tribes Without Rulers: Studies in African Segmentary Systems,* eds. John Middleton and David Tait (London: Routledge & Kegan Paul Ltd., 1958); Max Gluckman, *Politics, Law and Ritual in Tribal Society* (Chicago: Aldine Publishing Company, 1965); *Politics and Society: Studies in Comparative Political Sociology,* ed. Eric A. Nordlinger (Englewood Cliffs, N.J.: Prentice-Hall, Inc., 1970); Pierre Clastres, *Society Against the State,* trans. Robert Hurley (New York: Zone Books, 1987).

9. The absence of government does imply social disorder or chaos. In anarchical political communities, order is achieved through non-authoritative means, notably through diffuse social sanctions. See Barclay, pp. 16–27.

10. Sack, p.3.

11. Giddens, *A Contemporary Critique,* p. 45.

12. Giddens, *A Contemporary Critique,* p. 92.

13. Giddens, *A Contemporary Critique.*

14. The United States' purchase of Alaska from Russia is a good example.

15. Small and Witherick, p. 136.

16. Osherenko, pp. 1086–87.

17. Tennant, p. 6.

18. See, for example, Mills, *Eagle Down is Our Law,* and McMillan, pp. 241–247.

19. Coates, p. 6.

20. Substantial evidence suggests most Aboriginal peoples did make decisions by consensus. First, records of the Jesuits' first encounters with Aboriginal peoples indicate they did not have chiefs with authoritative powers. Second, a number of Aboriginal languages do not have a word for "government." Third, my own research among the Métis of northern Alberta included discussions with Aboriginal elders about decision-making processes. They invariably stated that community decision-making was rare, and that most of the time the specific people involved made decisions through mutual understanding. For example, the question of who fished and hunted where was often decided by mutual consideration and family tradition, not by the broader community. Moreover, most of the year, many Aboriginal peoples travelled in groups of one or two families, and did not need formal decision-making mechanisms.

21. Jenness, p. 44.

22. Broady, p. 87.

23. Broady, p. 163.

24. Jenness, p. 44.

25. Jenness, p. 18.

26. Goldman, "The Alkatcho Carrier: Historical Background of Crest Prerogatives," p. 401; and "The Alkatcho Carrier of British Columbia."

27. McMillan, p. 245.

28. See Ray for a discussion of Hudson Bay trader accounts in the early 19th century of Babine and Wet'suwet'en land tenure systems.

29. Mills, p. 42.

30. McMillan, p. 172.

31. Hudson, p. 452.

32. Romanoff, p. 242–44.

33. Romanoff, p. 245.

34. Kennedy and Bouchard, p. 314.

35. Tyhurst, p. 398.

36. Alexander, pp. 142–143.

37. Alexander, p. 143.

38. Carstens, p. 6.

39. Dickason, p. 66.

40. Service, p. 144; Lewellen, p. 37.

41. Lewellen, p. 39.

42. Lewellen, p. 40.

43. Barclay, p. 49.

44. Adams, p. 25.

45. Anderson, p. 5.

46. Anderson, p. 6.

47. Eriksen, p. 104.

48. Eriksen.

49. Dahrendorf, p. 31.

50. Giddens, *The Nation-State and Violence,* p. 309.

51. Carl Schmitt, *Political Theology.*

52. Carl Schmitt, *Political Theology,* p. 12.

53. There are clearly different views on the question of law and sovereignty. Some argue that law, temporally and logically, precedes sovereignty. Others argue that law and sovereignty are two sides of the same coin, in that one presupposes the existence of the other. My view is that sovereignty and law are analytically distinct, although related. Law literally precedes sovereignty by thousands of years. However, as the foundation of ultimate decision-making power within the modern state, sovereignty has precedence over law. This view is consistent with the universalizing political logic of the modern state.

54. Poggi, *The Development of the Modern State*, p. 102.

55. Poggi, *The Modern State,* p. 23. There are only 17 federal states in the world; unitary states account for 90% of independent nation-states (Guy, pp. 142–45).

56. However, the existence of everyday violence in the ghettos of major American cities, for example, demonstrates that the modern state is not omnipotent.

57. Badie and Birnbaum, p. 105.

58. Tennant, p. xii.

59. *Gitxsan, Wet'suwet'en and Gitanyow Community-Based Governance Agreement-in-Principle.*

References

Adams, John W. *The Gitksan Potlatch: Population Flux, Resource Ownership and Reciprocity.* Toronto: Holt, Rinehart and Winston, 1973.

Alexander, Diana. "A Reconstruction of Prehistoric Land Use in the Mid-Fraser River Area Based on Ethnographic Data." In *A Complex Culture of the British Columbia Plateau,* ed. Brian Hayden. Vancouver: UBC Press, 1992.

Anderson, Benedict. *Imagined Communities: Reflections on the Origin and Spread of Nationalism.* Rev. ed. London: Verso, 1991.

Badie, Bertrand, and Pierre Birnbaum. *The Sociology of the State.* Trans. Arthur Goldhammer. Chicago: University of Chicago Press, 1983.

Barclay, Harold. *People Without Government.* London: Kahn & Averill, 1982.

Broady, Hugh. *Maps and Dreams.* New York: Pantheon Books, 1981.

Carstens, Peter. *The Queen's People: A Study of Hegemony, Coercion, and Accommodation among the Okanagan of Canada.* Toronto: University of Toronto Press, 1991.

Coates, Ken S. *Best Left as Indians: Native-White Relations in the Yukon Territory, 1840–1973*. Montreal: McGill-Queen's University Press, 1991.

Dahrendorf, Ralf. *The Modern Social Conflict: An Essay on the Politics of Liberty*. Berkeley: University of California Press, 1988.

Dickason, Patricia G. *Canada's First Nations: A History of Founding Peoples from Earliest Times*. Toronto: McClelland & Stewart Inc., 1993.

Dickerson, Mark O. and Thomas Flanan. *An Introduction to Government and Politics: A Conceptual Approach*. 4th ed. Scarborough, Ont.: Nelson Canada, 1994.

Eriksen, Thomas Hylland. *Ethnicity and Nationalism: Anthropological Perspectives*. London: Pluto Press, 1993.

Giddens, Anthony. *A Contemporary Critique of Historical Materialism*. Berkeley: University of California Press, 1981.

———. *The Nation-State and Violence*. Berkeley: University of California Press, 1987.

Gitxsan, Wet'suwet'en and Gitanyow Community-Based Governance Agreement-In-Principle, 24 January 1995.

Goldman, Irving. "The Alkatcho Carrier: Historical Background of Crest Prerogatives." *American Anthropologist,* vol. 41 (1943).

———. "The Alkatcho Carrier of British Columbia." In *Acculturation in Seven American Indian Tribes,* ed. Ralph Linton. New York: Appleton-Century, 1940.

Guy, James John. *People, Politics & Government*. 3rd ed. Scarborough, Ont.: Prentice Hall, 1995.

Hudson, Douglas. "The Okanagan Indians." In *The Native Peoples: The Canadian Experience,* eds. Bruce Morrison and C. Roderick Wilson. Toronto: McClelland & Stewart, 1986.

Huntington, Samuel P. *Political Order in Changing Societies*. New Haven: Yale University Press, 1968.

Jenness, Diamond. *The Sekani Indians of British Columbia*. Ottawa: J. O. Patenaude, I.S.O., 1937.

Kennedy, Dorothy I.D., and Randy Bouchard. *"Stl'atl'imx* (Fraser River Lillooet) Fishing." In *A Complex Culture of the British Columbia Plateau,* ed. Brian Hayden. Vancouver: UBC Press, 1992.

Lewellen, Ted. *Political Anthropology: An Introduction*. 2nd ed. Westport, Conn.: Bergin & Garvey, 1992.

McMillan, Alan D. *Native Peoples and Cultures of Canada*. 2nd ed. Vancouver: Douglas & McIntyre, 1995.

Mills, Antonia. *Eagle Down is Our Law: Witsuwit'en Law, Feasts, and Land Claims*. Vancouver: UBC Press, 1994.

Osherenko, Gail. "Property Rights and Transformation in Russia: Institutional Change in the Far North." *Europe-Asia Studies,* vol. 47, no. 7 (1995).

Poggi, Gianfranco. *The Development of the Modern State: A Sociological Introduction*. Stanford: Stanford University Press, 1978.

―――. *The Modern State: Its Nature, Development and Prospects*. Stanford: Stanford University Press, 1990.

Ranney, Austin. *The Governing of Men*. Rev. ed. New York: Holt, Rinehart and Winston, 1966.

Ray, Arthur J. "Fur Trade History and the Gitksan-Wet'suwet'en Comprehensive Claim: Men of Property and the Exercise of Title." In *Aboriginal Resource Use in Canada: Historical and Legal Aspects,* eds. Kerry Abel and Jean Friesen. Winnipeg: University of Manitoba Press, 1991.

Romanoff, Steven. "Fraser Lillooet Salmon Fishing." In *A Complex Culture of the British Columbia Plateau,* ed. Brian Hayden. Vancouver: UBC Press, 1992.

Sack, David Robert. *Human Territoriality: Its Theory and History*. Cambridge: Cambridge University Press, 1986. As quoted in R. J. Johnston, *A Question of Place: Exploring the Practice of Human Geography* (Oxford: Blackwell, 1991), p. 188.

Schmitt, Carl. *The Concept of the Political.* Trans. George Schwab. New Brunswick, NJ: Rutgers University Press, 1976.

———. *Political Theology.* Cambridge, Mass.: MIT Press, 1985.

Service, Elman R. *Primitive Social Organization: An Evolutionary Perspective.* New York: Random House, 1962.

Small, John, and Michael Witherick. *A Modern Dictionary of Geography.* 3rd ed. London: Edward Arnold, 1995.

Swartz, Marc J. "Introduction." In *Local-Level Politics,* ed. Marc J. Swartz. Chicago: Aldine, 1968.

Tennant, Paul. *Aboriginal Peoples and Politics: The Indian Land Question in British Columbia, 1849–1989.* Vancouver: UBC Press, 1990.

Tyhurst, Robert. "Traditional and Contemporary Land and Resource Use by the *Xaxli'p* and *Ts'kw'aylaxw* Bands." In *A Complex Culture of the British Columbia Plateau,* ed. Brian Hayden. Vancouver: UBC Press, 1992.

Weber, Max. *Economy and Society.* Vol. 2. Eds. Guenther Roth and Claus Wittich. Berkeley: University of California Press, 1978.

4

How Settlements Will Affect Access to Natural Resources

By Paul Mitchell-Banks

This chapter examines what effects treaty settlement in British Columbia will have on access to and use of resources. The province's overall economy, as well as that of First Nations communities, has of course relied heavily on natural resources in the past. Changes in who owns them and who will have rights to use them will have a profound impact on all B.C. residents. Questions to be answered include:

- who will control access to resources?
- who will profit from their development?
- who will get jobs to bring the resources to market?
- who will be responsible for maintaining and renewing scarce resources?
- what roles will First Nations communities, private businesses, and the government play?

Until the early 1990s, British Columbia refused to recognize the concept of Aboriginal title, and consequently made little progress towards settlement.[1] The resulting uncertainty and confusion about what form settlements might take became clearer with the successful negotiation of the Sechelt Self-government Agreement and the Nisga'a Agreement-in-Principle. The Sechelt Nation obtained self-government in 1986, and in 1989 released a proposal for title settlements. The Nisga'a Agreement-in-Principle was reached February 15, 1996. The B.C. government has suggested that it will be a standard for any future treaties within the province. There are striking similarities between the two. While the Sechelt are now at stage four of the six-stage treaty process and are negotiating an Agreement-in-Principle,[2] their current government structure already closely reflects what the Nisga'a Agreement-in-Principle proposes.

With most of B.C. facing negotiations for numerous settlements, it is useful to analyze the examples of the Sechelt Self-government Agreement and the Nisga'a Agreement-in-Principle to discover what their implications are for future settlement. We will examine the details of the Nisga'a Agreement particularly closely, also drawing on examples of settlements from other parts of Canada and the world. These include

- *Aboriginal Lands Rights (Northern Territory) Act,* 1976 (Australia)
- *Western Arctic (Inuvialuit) Claims Settlement Act*, 1984 (Inuvialuit Final Agreement)
- the Waikato-Tainui Deed of Settlement, 1995 (New Zealand)
- the Council for Yukon Indians Umbrella Final Agreement, 1993
- *Alaska Native Claims Settlement Act,* 1971
- the James Bay and Northern Quebec Agreement, 1976.

Sechelt Nation Self-Government and Treaty Negotiations

The Sechelt approach to self-government and treaty settlements has been based on the "good neighbour" principle. The Sechelt will continue to contribute to the larger community; they will not seek to diminish the rights and interests of their neighbours.[3]

The Sechelt have actually been practising this principle for over 30 years. They have also long been known for their initiative and for their desire to manage their own affairs. Before achieving self-government, the band took on all powers allowed under the *Indian Act,* including managing the band's money, increasing local authority (including local taxation), and managing both reserve and surrendered lands. However, the Sechelt Nation still felt constrained. In 1971, the Department of Indian and Northern Affairs encouraged them to seek self-government.[4] In 1984, after a long period of preparation, negotiations began.

Four specific acts were passed to establish self-government.[5] The federal *Sechelt Indian Band Self-Government Act* of 1986 is an enabling statute, creating the Sechelt Band, and giving it the powers and responsibilities of self-government. Section 37, which states that "all federal laws of general application in force in Canada are applicable to the band, its members and its lands," limits the powers of the Sechelt government and indicates that it is not a sovereign state.

The other three acts were passed by the B.C. government:

• *Sechelt Indian Government District Enabling Act* (1987)
• *Land Title Amendment Act, 1988*
• *Sechelt Indian Government Home Owner Grant Act* (1988).

The *Sechelt Indian Government District Enabling Act* complements the federal act of the previous year. It

• recognizes the Sechelt Indian Government District
• gives the Sechelt government certain provincial powers
• creates an appointed advisory council
• applies provincial laws, and grants provincial benefits to the band
• suspends the province's ability to collect direct property taxes
• enables the province to delegate certain responsibilities to the band.

The *Land Title Amendment Act, 1988* registers lands that the Sechelt hold "in fee simple" (as proprietary owners) under the *Land Title Act*. Interestingly, even though the Sechelt initiated this amendment, any other First Nations group in the province can use it to register their land under the Torrens land registration system. The *Sechelt Indian Government Home Owner Grant Act* simply enables Sechelt Band members to be eligible for the Provincial Home Owners Grant. In the past, First Nations people living on reserves did not qualify, even though non-aboriginals living on band lands did. The statute now ensures that all people living on Sechelt Band lands are equally eligible.

The Sechelt Nation model for self-government gives the Nation a number of legal powers, including the following:

• accessing and living on Sechelt Band lands
• zoning and land use
• expropriation of lands for community purposes
• building regulation

- assessing and collecting tax
- managing band lands
- preserving and managing natural resources
- managing fish and wildlife
- maintaining public order and safety
- regulating businesses and professions
- setting fines
- adopting any law of the Province of British Columbia as its own law
- exercising any power that the Province gives it.[6]

Along with their proposal to share the royalties and other payments earned from natural resource extraction on the Sechelt Traditional Territory equally with the Province, these legislative powers give the Sechelt a strong voice in determining access to and use of resources on their lands. Because the Sechelt control so many access points, their share of the royalties from development would bring them new wealth.[7]

The Sechelt treaty settlement process is occurring in three stages:

- Phase One: achieving self-government
- Phase Two: settling land claims
- Phase Three: having the Sechelt Nation take their rightful place as a contributing people within the Canadian Confederation.

Phase One is of course successfully completed. Phase Two is underway, undoubtedly influenced by the precedent of the Nisga'a Agreement-in-Principle.

The Nisga'a Agreement-in-Principle

The Nisga'a Agreement-in-Principle was reached February 15, 1996. As we pointed out earlier, the B.C. government has stated that it will likely serve as a template for any future treaties within the province. Indeed, it is hard to imagine the first modern-day treaty in British Columbia not serving as a precedent, particularly given the number of pending and forthcoming claims.

The Agreement is in fact the basis of a final settlement, which "will be a treaty for the purposes of sections 25 and 35 of the *Constitution*

Act, 1982." [8] The final treaty that will be negotiated over the next few years will likely closely follow the Agreement's structure. The similarity of the powers it proposes to those of the Sechelt Nation further supports that at least the future legislative frameworks will be similar. We can therefore use the Nisga'a Agreement as a tool to analyze the effects of treaty settlements in general on access to and use of resources.

The Agreement covers a broad range of issues and concerns directly related to access to resources. Here are some of its relevant general provisions:

- The final treaty will not affect the constitutional division of powers between Canada and British Columbia.
- The Nisga'a Nation will gain its full powers of jurisdiction and self-government gradually over time. In those areas where the Nisga'a government does not have legal authority, general federal and provincial laws will apply.
- If the final treaty is not consistent with federal and provincial laws, then the federal and provincial laws will apply on those points of inconsistency.
- The final treaty will be the entire agreement. Unless the parties agree otherwise before signing the final treaty, no other representation, warranty, collateral agreement, or condition will affect the final treaty.
- The final treaty will clearly set out
  - ownership and use of land and resources in the Nass Area
  - application of laws in the Nass area
  - the Nisga'a Nation's rights under section 35 of the *Constitution Act, 1982.*
- The final treaty will be a full and final settlement. It will completely define the Aboriginal title, rights, and interests of the Nisga'a people to resources in Canada. It will also clearly define the extent and geographic area of all the Nisga'a's treaty rights, including all jurisdictions, rights, and obligations of the Nisga'a government.
- Eventually, the *Indian Act* will no longer apply to the Nisga'a Nation and its people, except to determine whether a person is an "Indian." The final treaty will set out steps for transition from the *Indian Act* to full self-government.

- The rights of the Nisga'a Nation set out in the final treaty will not be affected by any treaties with other First Nations (*Agreement-in-Principle,* pp. 6–8).

In the following sections, we will review each of these provisions in the context of specific resources.

Nisga'a lands

On the date that the final treaty takes effect, the Nisga'a will own two types of lands: Nisga'a lands and fee-simple lands. Nisga'a lands are one large continuous area within the traditional territory. The Nisga'a Nation will own them communally, with title vested in the Nisga'a government. Existing reserves now inside this area will cease to be reserves and will become Nisga'a lands. Reserve lands *not* located within the Nisga'a lands area will become fee-simple lands, owned by the Nisga'a government and subject to provincial laws. These lands are essentially identical to private property held by non-aboriginal people and corporations in B.C.

Nisga'a lands will not include lands now owned by others, or land under agriculture leases and wood lot licences. Other third-party interests such as rights of way, fishing licences, guiding and outfitter licences, and traplines will continue on the terms they were first established under (*Agreement-in-Principle,* p. 12). The Nisga'a government will be able to set conditions on any new land and resource uses they grant in the future. This is consistent with the ARA Consulting Group's 1995 study of the social and economic impacts of a number of Aboriginal treaty settlements. In none of the six case studies were privately owned lands or leased lands transferred to First Nations groups as a result of treaty settlements. In the Yukon, land was actually "frozen" until the treaty was settled. In all six cases, transfers of land and resources were based exclusively on Crown properties (state, federal, or commonwealth).[9]

The Nisga'a government will be able to create or transfer holdings in Nisga'a lands without the consent of Canada or British Columbia. The only limitations on transfer will be whatever conditions of ownership are set out in the Nisga'a Constitution and the final treaty. Powers are similar to those given to the Sechelt Nation in its Constitution, which sets out exactly how the Sechelt lands are held for the band and members, with procedures for buying and selling land, and transferring rights.

Overlapping claims present a particular challenge, especially in the North Coast area.[10] The Nisga'a Agreement addresses these problems by stating Nisga'a land boundaries will not be finalized until the Nisga'a and Tsimshian Tribal Councils can resolve the issue. Discussions are already under way.

Future treaties may create similar lands and use similar strategies to address overlapping claims. In fact, the *1991 Report of the British Columbia Claims Task Force* recommended that First Nations are best qualified to resolve the overlapping Traditional Territories among themselves. Boundaries cannot be set until all parties with claims are included in negotiations. The Nisga'a Agreement may well be the spur for these negotiations to begin. However, boundary definitions are a highly sensitive issue for First Nations, and negotiations throughout the rest of the province may be more complex for a number of reasons.

The first possible complication may arise from other First Nations being less organized and united than the Nisga'a have been in their settlement process. Each of the bands within the nation seeking settlement must first organize its members, and cooperate with other bands. Only then can the nation as a whole organize to deal with boundary disputes. Some First Nations in B.C. are still struggling with internal disputes and politics that are preventing them from even filing a comprehensive claim for settlement, much less following up on it to negotiate with other First Nations.

A second boundary problem can arise from the conflict of band reserve lands and traditional territory with transportation corridors and residential or industrial development. The Nisga'a live in a fairly remote part of the province, with few non-aboriginal residents and limited industrial development in the area. Reserves are located fairly close to each other within the Nisga'a Traditional Territory. More populated or developed areas, such as the Okanagan, the Kootenays, the Cariboo, the Fraser Valley, and the Fraser Canyon, will create a bigger challenge, setting aside settlement lands that do not include lands held by other private owners, or lands that impinge on other First Nations' traditional territories.

Subsurface resources

The Nisga'a government will own all mineral resources on or under Nisga'a lands, including

- precious and base metals
- coal, petroleum, natural gases, and geothermal resources
- earth, soil, peat, and marl (deposits of clay and calcium carbonate)
- sand, gravel, rock, and stone (*Agreement-in-Principle,* pp. 10–11).

The property rights associated with these resources can be held, traded, or sold, just as the provincial and federal governments do to produce revenue. First Nations groups were granted similar subsurface rights in the Northern Territory (Australia) and Yukon land claim settlements, and in the Inuvialuit Agreement.[11] However, none were given in the Waikato-Tainui, James Bay, and Northern Quebec settlements. The Nisga'a Nation will also own those mineral rights on or under the Nisga'a reserves located outside the Nisga'a lands. In addition to these reserve lands, the Nisga'a Nation will own 15 additional fee-simple interests—but the Province will own the mineral resources on or under the Nisga'a's 15 other fee-simple holdings.

Uranium gets special consideration as a resource in the Nisga'a Agreement-in-Principle. Federal laws on prospecting, refining, and handling will apply (*Agreement-in-Principle,* p. 11). This is clearly due to concerns for health, safety, and the environment that the material presents, and of course the need to closely monitor any use of the substance potentially available for production of nuclear power and weapons.

The Nisga'a and B.C. governments will have the option of making agreements to use provincial administrative systems to register claims, record and inspect resource exploration and development, and even possibly to collect royalties. Since the provincial government has already established such systems, and it would be costly and time-consuming for the Nisga'a to do so, these agreements would benefit both parties. The provincial government could collect administration fees for such services, and could ensure efficient operations continue, to accommodate industry interests. Subsurface development would also generate additional employment and tax revenue for both parties.

The Nisga'a Agreement-in-Principle addresses the issue of subsurface mineral rights effectively and clearly, with the Nation holding most of the subsurface rights for the land that they will own. This approach will be easy to implement and monitor, and would be an excellent precedent for subsequent treaties. Clearly defined mineral ownership is critical for successful mining development and administration.

Mining and hydrocarbon development requires exploration, development, and management expertise, as well as access to large pools of capital. First Nations currently face not only a capacity shortage of trained and experienced band members, but also limited access to funds. Banks and other financial institutions have not been particularly effective in funding First Nations' development, with uncertainty over legal status (a primary consideration for a conservative lender) being a major impediment. There has also been a mutual lack of understanding and awareness of the cultural and social norms within which both First Nations and lending institutions exist and operate.

First Nations are able to use a number of means to address the lack of experience, training, and capital that they face. Joint ventures, partnerships, concessions, or other vehicles are able to be employed. There is also the possibility of having a company develop an operation and over time, revert the ownership and control back to the Aboriginal government, as band members obtained the education and experience to take over management and operational functions. If the First Nations choose to develop the subsurface resources themselves, they can bring in any one of a number of mining and petroleum consulting companies, and can also tap into the expertise of the larger accounting and management consulting firms.

Forest resources

The Nisga'a government will own all forest resources on Nisga'a lands. It will also have the right to set rules and standards to regulate forest practices on these lands, as long as the rules and standards meet or exceed provincial standards such as those under the *Forest Practices Code of British Columbia Act* for timber harvesting, silviculture, and road construction. The Nisga'a government can also establish harvesting and conservation practices for non-timber resources that meet or exceed the relevant federal and provincial legislation for private lands.

This is very similar to the Sechelt's powers to make environmental laws that meet or exceed the federal or provincial statutes.[12] The Nisga'a final treaty must provide an objective way to evaluate whether Nisga'a forest regulations meet the required standards (*Agreement-in-Principle,* p. 19).

The Nisga'a and the Provincial Governments may negotiate agreements that determine when timber resources on Nisga'a lands can be harvested. The Nisga'a are able to set a limit on how much timber is cut. This will give the Nisga'a greater flexibility in how they manage forest resources.

First Nations resource management is often considered to be more holistic, and historically has not been driven by large-scale industrial development.[13] Only in the last 20 years have First Nations groups begun to regain some of their use and management rights over their traditional lands, and they may want to bring a new approach of using resources (rather than "exploiting" them) to the management of their lands. This will likely take some time to evolve, and could incorporate traditional elements of management as well as some aspects of conventional industrial forestry.[14] In the Merritt area, the Nicola Tribal Association's Forestry staff and Fish and Wildlife staff ask the elders for their input every year at Natural Resources and Land Use Workshops. The Association has adjusted its management practices to reflect the elders' concerns.

Currently, private or fee-simple lands in British Columbia do not come under forestry laws, especially the *Forest Practices Code of British Columbia Act,* unless they are "Schedule A" lands within a "Tree Farm License." The only standards that might apply to timber harvesting on private lands would be under the *Fisheries Act,* prohibiting the discharge of pollutants into fish-bearing waters. The Nisga'a's agreement to subject their privately owned forest land to rules that meet or exceed current provincial standards will increase their harvesting, road-building, and silviculture costs considerably.

Timber from Nisga'a lands will also have to meet provincial policies and rules of manufacturing (*Agreement-in-Principle,* p. 19). Only timber harvested from Crown or "Schedule A lands" must now obey similar laws. This again is a significant concession on the part of the Nisga'a. Log exports can be very lucrative, and do not require the very high investments in capital and skills that a processing facility requires. They could be the Nisga'a's highest producer of revenue. The Nisga'a could then re-invest in additional forestry development, other industries, education, training, and infrastructure. In fact, concern over the possible resulting displacement of local manufacturers is what likely led to the request for the concession.

Timber licences in the area will certainly influence the transitional provisions for forest resources. The final treaty settlement will include details to ensure an orderly and efficient transition of timber harvesting and management from Crown control to Nisga'a control. In the period between the Agreement-in-Principle and the final treaty, the B.C. government will consult with the Nisga'a Tribal Council on all timber harvesting and management activities on Nisga'a lands, including existing Forest Development Plans and any changes to them (*Agreement-in-Principle,* p. 20). This common-sense approach will ensure the Nisga'a are not being left lands that were aggressively managed and harvested just before they took them over. How effective this provision is will depend on the level of goodwill and the degree of communication and co-operation between the two governments. Professional forestry consultants may have to help the Nisga'a remedy any shortcomings.

Beginning three years after the treaty is effective, and lasting for the next five years, the Nisga'a Tribal Council and the Province will then negotiate a schedule of Annual Allowable Cuts to permit a smooth transition to the harvest levels the Nisga'a have determined to be acceptable. They will also prepare a plan to help offset unemployment, reductions in fibre flow, and any other difficulties arising from the transition that both governments decide are necessary to address before the treaty goes into effect. Once again, goodwill, co-operation, and available staff will determine how successfully the transition is negotiated and implemented. At the end of the five-year period, forest development plans will have to meet the Nisga'a Forest Practices Codes and be under Nisga'a management.

The Nisga'a Agreement-in-Principle states that the Nisga'a will not establish a primary timber-processing facility for ten years after the treaty date, but allows them to build facilities to meet domestic lumber requirements or "value-added" facilities (secondary processing facilities). Similarly, the Nisga'a government can enter into any partnership or joint venture with an existing timber-processing facility (*Agreement-in-Principle,* p. 21). This permits the Nisga'a to develop smaller-scale processing that could serve as a training base for larger-scale facilities. Creating employment for band members is a concern of First Nations across Canada, especially in more remote areas.[15]

British Columbia has also agreed in principle to the Nisga'a purchasing forest tenures with a total volume of up to 150,000 cubic metres. As required under the *Forest Act,* they would first need the permission of the Minister of Forests. Any timber on the land would be regulated by provincial legislation and regulation like the *Forest Practices Code.*

Most future treaty agreements will have to address the same forest resources issues as the Nisga'a Agreement-in-Principle, including:

- transferring ownership of a large area of forested land from the Crown to the First Nations government
- accommodating the tenure and forestry rights of current licence-holders
- dealing with effects on employment and fibre flow
- ensuring First Nations have the financial and administrative skills to take over the management of the forest resources.

There may be slight differences in management arrangements, but most future treaty settlements will need to include similar provisions. Recognizing the legal rights of the existing licence-holders and creating a transition period to adjust forest operations sets a standard that the forest industry will strenuously work to maintain in future treaties. This is a particular concern in light of the large capital investments involved and the high demand for harvesting rights, which limits possibilities for relocation.

In other parts of British Columbia, the numbers of forestry companies, and types of rights to be allocated for such activities as trapping, guiding, and recreation will be higher, increasing the complexity of the settlement process. The same settlement approach will likely apply, but to a number of smaller and separate land areas rather than the large continuous land base held by the Nisga'a.

In the Alaska settlement, forestry activities have continued under joint venture arrangements in the Sealaska region. In the James Bay area, the forestry activities by non-Cree contract developers around Cree lands have not been significantly affected by the settlement.[16] And in B.C., there are numerous examples of successful partnerships between First Nations and the forest sector around the province, including the Weyerhaeuser Cooperative Agreement with five bands in the Merritt area, Qwa'eet Forest Products and Nicola Pacific Forest Products (both joint ventures in the Merritt area), Burns Lake Specialty Woods, and the Interfor Agreement with the Sechelt.

As KPMG's consultants have identified, First Nations face serious capacity challenges in the large-scale commercial management of their resources, particularly if they will have to meet a requirement under the *Forest Practices Code*.[17] While many First Nations members have worked within the forest sector, most have been in harvesting, and very few in technical and especially professional management roles. Institutions such as the Nicola Valley Institute of Technology have been established to remedy such shortfalls. Progress is being made, but it is slow. There are now less than ten First Nations Registered Professional Foresters (RPFs) in British Columbia, and the settlement of large commercial forested areas will require dozens of RPFs and many more forest technicians. First Nations will likely want to provide band members with employment in the forest industry, but it will be some years before they can staff a significant number of management positions. In the interim, professional consultants, management contracts, or joint ventures could help First Nations to get involved in commercial forest management and to develop local expertise as effectively and efficiently as possible.

Access

As owners of the Nisga'a lands, the Nisga'a Nation will have the same rights and obligations as the owners of real property (property under fee-simple title), except for any modifications made in the final treaty. They will also have the same liabilities as the Crown for unoccupied lands (*Agreement-in-Principle,* p. 26).

The Nisga'a Agreement-in-Principle states that the Nisga'a will provide reasonable access to their public lands for temporary non-commercial and recreational uses. People may harvest or extract resources only with the Nisga'a government's authorization. They cannot cause damage to Nisga'a lands or resources, cause mischief, or interfere with previously authorized activities (*Agreement-in-Principle,* p. 26). The Nisga'a will also give the public reasonable opportunities to hunt and fish on their public lands, subject to any regulations they set for public access, and for measures to protect wildlife in the final treaty. Considering that private landowners are generally very protective of privacy and concerned about trespassing, the reasonable public access offered by the Nisga'a (similar to Scandinavia's "everyman's access" tradition), is a significant property rights concession.

Land settlement areas will likely be smaller in the southern and more heavily populated parts of the province, due to greater proportions of privately owned lands, larger residential developments, a higher percentage of non-aboriginal people, hydroelectric reservoirs, and valley bottom loss. Rights of public access in these other settlement areas is difficult to predict, since the land parcels will likely be smaller but more numerous, which creates different access problems than in the Nisga'a's large and sparsely populated area. Demographic, geographic, and industrial development will determine whether these settlement areas offer the same degree of access to non-aboriginal people.

Indeed, the area of the future Nisga'a landholdings is so large that to prevent the public from having reasonable access to it would cause great resentment and interfere with freedom of movement. This is reflected in the Agreement's provisions for public access, and in its provisions for roads through traditional territories.

The "Nisga'a highway" will allow public access into and through the Nisga'a lands, and will be the main form of access to Nisga'a villages. On the date the treaty becomes effective, the highway will be under provincial legislation, and will include the road from Terrace north to Nass Camp, and the road from New Aiyansh to Greenville, including the road to Gitwinksihlkw. It will later include the Kincolith extension and the road from Nass Camp to Highway 97 (*Agreement-in-Principle,* p. 27). Highways or major transport corridors passing through future treaty settlement would likely have to be similarly made public, since relocating or decommissioning highways would add huge costs to any treaty settlement.

The Sechelt addressed the highway question in their settlement proposal by arguing that reserve land taken up by Highway 101 was given in fee-simple title to the province by the Department of Indian and Northern Affairs without the band's consent. They propose that the B.C. government give the Sechelt back the title to this land when the status of the road is eventually downgraded to a secondary highway, and it is no longer used as the main route to the Sechelt Peninsula.[18] The Sechelt solution imposes no cost on the parties (other than transfer fees), elegantly solving both the access and ownership issues.

"Crown roads" will be identified in the Nisga'a treaty. These roads will provide access to resources and recreational areas, and may include existing Forest Service and other roads, depending on what the Nisga'a and the provincial government agree to. British Columbia will be responsible to maintain and repair these roads, and will be liable for them. The Nisga'a and provincial governments may agree to temporarily close these roads for a variety of reasons, including to protect Nisga'a rights (*Agreement-in-Principle*, p. 27).

Even though the Nisga'a Nation will own all roads within their lands, the Province will hold a permanent, exclusive right-of-way for the Nisga'a highway and Crown roads, equal to the standard road width for each type of road found elsewhere in the province, with terms that ensure the Province can build, maintain, and repair the roads (*Agreement-in-Principle*, p. 28). Again, this solution solves the access and ownership issues in a non-confrontational way. Future treaties will likely follow the same course of action, particularly in the more populated areas of the province where highways have been established for a long time, and relocating or rebuilding them would be far too expensive.

Fisheries

Conserving fish stocks is one of the Agreement's main concerns, as it would reasonably be in any future treaty. The Ministry of Fisheries and Oceans and the Province will retain overall responsibility to conserve and manage the fisheries and fish habitat, according to their particular legal authorities. International treaties (related to anadromous species that travel upriver to spawn, like salmon) and the constitutional division of powers (sections 91 and 92 of the *Constitution Act, 1982*) clearly define what fisheries responsibilities the federal and provincial governments have. Historically, they have been unwilling to give up overall control, so they won't be liable for failing to meet treaty and legislative requirements.

The Nisga'a will manage their harvest through a fisheries trust, which will fund the Nisga'a stewardship of Nass river fisheries (*Agreement-in-Principle in Brief*, p. 4). The three governments will also establish a "Joint Fisheries Management Committee (JFMC)," to plan and manage fisheries co-operatively, to regulate Nisga'a fishing, and to enhance fisheries in the Nass region. Some of the JFMC's duties include having to

- share information about both existing and proposed fisheries that might affect Nisga'a fisheries
- arrange to collect and exchange fisheries data
- give advice about setting "escapement" levels and making in-season adjustments to fishing plans
- give recommendations to the Minister of Fisheries and Oceans and the Nisga'a government about any other conservation needs and resource management, according to the final treaty
- give advice to the three governments on what basic entitlements the Nisga'a have to species other than salmon in the Nass region
- make recommendations to the Fisheries Minister and Nisga'a government on how the Nisga'a should harvest their entitlements and how to monitor that harvest according to the final treaty, including an annual fishing plan
- make recommendations on research and salmon enhancement projects to the Minister of Fisheries and Oceans and the Nisga'a government
- carry out other responsibilities delegated to it by the three levels of government (*Agreement-in-Principle*, pp. 43–44).

The JFMC will be made up of six members, two from each of the federal, provincial, and Nisga'a governments. The Nisga'a and federal representatives will be responsible for fisheries managed by Canada, and the Nisga'a and provincial representatives will handle those managed by British Columbia.

The Agreement also specifies the Nisga'a's entitlement to fish: on average, being 18% of the Canadian Nass River total allowable catch per year. The Nisga'a will also receive a percentage of sockeye and pink salmon for commercial purposes under a separate harvesting agreement. They will be able to market their salmon, but must do so under general federal and provincial laws. The Nisga'a can harvest species other than salmon (such as halibut, oolichan, and shellfish) for domestic consumption only; they cannot sell them commercially. All of these entitlements will be held communally. The Nisga'a cannot transfer them to individuals or to corporate bodies (*Agreement-in-Principle,* p. 34).

The Nisga'a Agreement also specifies that the Nisga'a will receive $11.5 million to purchase vessels and licences in the coastal commercial fishery. However, they cannot establish large fish-processing facilities for 12 years after the treaty date (*Agreement-in-Principle,* pp. 47–48). This will allow industry time to adjust. No mention is made of potential joint ventures or partnerships with existing fish processors, but nothing suggests that such an arrangement could not be made during this 12-year period. (Remember the similar arrangement to refrain from forestry processing for ten years.)

First Nations have long fished for subsistence or commercial purposes. A review of the location of First Nations communities illustrates the importance of fishing in their livelihood and culture. This drives a strong desire to be involved in federal fisheries management policies such as the Federal Aboriginal Fisheries Strategy, or regional policies like those of the Nicola Watershed Stewardship Fisheries Authority administered by the Nicola Tribal Association.

Constitutional restrictions on the division of powers will limit the federal and provincial governments' flexibility on fisheries issues for future treaty settlements. This lack of flexibility, plus the implications of fisheries management, run-off, and factors like erosion (both natural and artificially caused)[19] that often extend far beyond Traditional Territory borders, forces fisheries and resource management to be integrated—something the Canadian federal system attempts to do. The occasional conflict between the provincial and federal governments on resource management would be complicated to an impossible degree if each treaty settlement created significantly different resource laws and regulations.

Treaty settlements must also consider the technical difficulties in managing fish stocks. Taking inventories, gathering biological or habitat data, and monitoring fish population and health is a complex business. Tracking and managing sea-going species is particularly challenging, especially if they are of a high economic value, under heavy harvesting pressure, and cross many legal boundaries. These challenges further support a co-operative approach among regions.

Fisheries agreements in treaty settlements for the more populated areas of the province—particularly along the Fraser, Thompson, and Skeena Rivers—will be even more complicated. The First Nations have possible conflicts over fisheries control, intensified by the different concerns of "up-river" and "down-river" bands. For some years, up-river bands have criticized fishing practices of both the commercial and Aboriginal bands down-river, closer to the ocean. Salmon have to pass through their nets, fishery traps, and fishing spears on their way to the spawning grounds. Salmon has played a central role in the culture of most First Nations in British Columbia from time immemorial. Its importance fuels strong opinions on management and desires for increased control, made even stronger by declining fish populations and the resulting economic and environmental concerns. These tensions could lead to confrontation.

Wildlife

The Nisga'a Agreement-in-Principle outlines a "Wildlife Management Area" that encompasses most of the Traditional Territory. In this area, the Nisga'a will be entitled to hunt wildlife for their own purposes, limited by conservation needs (*Agreement-in-Principle,* p. 51). A wildlife committee with equal representation from the Nisga'a and the Province will recommend how to manage preservation and Nisga'a hunting.

The Nisga'a will also develop a yearly management plan for the hunt, which will require provincial government approval. They will be able to hunt moose and certain other species, up to a specified percentage of the total number of animals in the area. Percentages will change to reflect the total number of the species to be harvested (*Agreement-in-Principle,* p. 51). Nisga'a citizens hunting wildlife outside the management area will do so under provincial laws. They may hunt migratory birds according to international conventions and general federal and provincial laws (*Agreement-in-Brief,* p. 4).

The Nisga'a Agreement states that the Nisga'a will not be able to sell wildlife, but may trade or barter among themselves or with other

Aboriginal people. A similar provision applies to the harvesting of fish. First Nations have always traded heavily in wildlife and fish, which undoubtedly drove this provision. Tracking this trade in wildlife and fish will be extremely difficult to monitor and even more difficult to enforce, as evident from the difficulties now experienced by the Department of Fisheries and Oceans (federal) and the Fish and Wildlife Department (provincial). It remains to be seen how effectively or aggressively this trade will be monitored and enforced.

As is the case with fisheries, wide-ranging movements of wildlife, and the complexities created by different natural and artificial impacts (like disease, fire, air pollution, large-scale timber harvesting, and hydro-electric development) strongly support a co-operative approach among regions. One way to implement this is by sharing management with the provincial and federal governments. Responsibilities for wildlife management are clearly outlined under the Constitution. Such co-management of wildlife resources has already been successful in the Sechelt and James Bay Cree arrangements.[20] One criticism of the James Bay co-management arrangements, however, is that they are effective at dealing with specific species, but do not address the environment as a whole.[21] But like all other management systems, co-management arrangements can evolve and respond to new challenges and lead to new understanding of the issues that come up.

One particular strength of co-management is that it can incorporate the traditional ecological knowledge of the Aboriginal people. The marriage of rich, qualitative, traditional knowledge with the scientific and quantitative information of conventional systems can lead to more effective wildlife management.[22] Co-management also gives all parties the chance to develop relationships, which reduces conflict.

Co-management of fish and wildlife resources among provincial, federal, and First Nations governments will likely occur throughout the other settlement areas. Indeed, there is already a large degree of co-operation between the provincial Fish and Wildlife Department and those of many Tribal or Band Councils, evident in how they share information and data, and form research partnerships.

Environmental assessment and protection

Recognizing how complex it is to assess and protect the environment across a multitude of separate jurisdictions, the Agreement tries to co-ordinate requirements for environmental assessment among the Nisga'a, B.C., and federal governments. This would avoid duplicating assessments for single projects (*Agreement-in-Principle,* p. 61). All parties must

- receive timely notice of and relevant information on any project that could cause environmental damage to lands or resources
- be consulted about the environmental effects of the proposed project
- have an opportunity to participate in the environmental assessment process.

As with forestry-harvesting regulations, the Nisga'a may set environmental protection standards on Nisga'a lands, as long as they meet or exceed those set by the federal or provincial governments (*Agreement-in-Principle,* p. 64). In fact, any province is permitted to set an environmental standard equal to or higher than the federal law on that environmental issue.

After the treaty takes effect, the British Columbia and Nisga'a governments will negotiate an agreement about which provincial environmental duties the Nisga'a will take on in designated areas. Any agreement will consider the technical and administrative skills and the resources the Nisga'a have to carry out environmental protection according to provincial standards (*Agreement-in-Principle,* p. 64). This consideration has wide-ranging implications for the Nisga'a treaty and for any future treaties, which we will examine in the following section on self-government.

Self-government

Funding the Nisga'a government will be a shared responsibility for the Nisga'a and the B.C. and federal governments. It will include the costs necessary to establish and operate Nisga'a government institutions, public services, and programs, considering location, accessibility, and exactly which government services the Nisga'a will provide (*Agreement-in-Principle,* pp. 94–96).

However, the Agreement does not thoroughly document the challenges the Nisga'a face in establishing their own expertise in these matters. Creating smaller jurisdictions and sharing government powers and duties can result in a need for more people and resources to administer the area. The Nisga'a settlement covers approximately 2,000 sq. km of land that they will own either communally (Nisga'a lands) or hold in fee simple, plus the Wildlife Management Area, which appears to be over 10,000 sq. km. This is a large land area to manage. Any efforts to staff it entirely by citizens of the Nisga'a Nation are unrealistic given their shortages in the necessary skills. A more likely strategy will be some combination of the following:

- hiring qualified Nisga'a residents, then qualified non-Nisga'a people (both Aboriginal and others)
- contracting government services to outside providers
- working with provincial and federal agencies to gradually transfer powers and duties as the Nisga'a Nations' ability to handle them develops.

The challenges of assuming government will be onerous. Having to meet or exceed the standard of existing government rules and regulations will mean First Nations must provide services that are at least equal to those currently offered.

Many of these challenges stem from the disruption of First Nations societies caused by past federal policies on assimilating First Nations people into the larger surrounding community (Williams, 1996). Loss of language and traditional knowledge, uncompleted educations in an alien cultural system, and difficulties in getting and keeping jobs in that system have left many First Nations people caught between cultures. Aboriginal communities are now trying to recapture traditional languages and knowledge, through conducting Traditional Use Studies, studying customs, making audio recordings of threatened languages, and creating written languages. Elders are being asked to pass on their knowledge. Not only band schools, but post-secondary institutions such as the Nicola Valley Institute of Technology have built programs centred on the needs of First Nations students and communities. The construction of the First Nations Long House at the University of British Columbia to assist First Nations students, and the staffing of Aboriginal counsellors in faculties, are other attempts to encourage First Nations students to go to university and to successfully graduate.

Self-government will also require technical experts to manage the use of and access to resources. Fisheries, wildlife, and forestry biologists, and professional foresters, engineers, biologists, and geologists will be needed, as well as experts in such areas as hydrology, entomology, pathology, and soils. The supply of non-aboriginal consultants currently providing these services is far greater than that of First Nations people in the same line of work. As previously mentioned, there are now only a handful of Aboriginal Registered Professional Foresters in the province, and they are already in high demand. While more First Nations students are now being educated in professional fields, there won't be enough to help manage even a few treaties the size of the Nisga'a settlement, let alone treaties throughout the province.

Along with professional resource managers and technicians, First Nations will also need support staff in secretarial, administrative, accounting, legal, and consulting positions. Band and tribal administrations are taking on more responsibilities every year, but with the exception of the Sechelt and the Nisga'a, these do not approach the level required for assuming government under a treaty. The Sechelt have assumed government over the land they own, which covers about 25 sq. km. This comes nowhere close to the 2,000 sq. km that the Nisga'a will own and must administer.

Transferring government and resource administration successfully will take time. Hiring resource management professionals may be difficult due to the already high demand for them, particularly in forestry. As it is, numerous companies and government offices have had trouble hiring qualified staff since the implementation of the *Forest Practices Code*. Additional demands resulting from treaty settlements will only increase the difficulties.

Given these challenges, the transfer of powers will likely be gradual and controlled, to avoid inconsistencies. The Nisga'a Agreement addresses this obliquely, saying that each party is expected to "enforce its environmental laws in a fair, impartial and effective manner, through appropriate governmental action, consistent with prosecutorial discretion" (*Agreement-in- Principle,* p. 64). It specifies that "no party should relax its environmental standards for the purpose of providing an encouragement to the establishment, acquisition, expansion or retention of an investment" (*Agreement-in- Principle,* p. 64). The requirement for the Nisga'a and Sechelt to set standards that meet or exceed those of current laws will be a challenge for them to fulfil. Since existing governments are struggling with financial restraints and limited resources (in staff, equipment, and facilities) to meet their obligations, it would be unrealistic to expect First Nations governments to have it easier.

Summary

The Nisga'a Agreement-in-Principle presents some common-sense approaches to treaty settlement that offer a number of opportunities for economic gain for both Aboriginal and non-aboriginal peoples. Since potential investors in resource development are heavily influenced by perceived risk, certainty of ownership and sound administrative systems will give investors greater security. Partnerships between industry and First Nations peoples could provide another avenue for success. As in every business, the quality of relationships, feasibility, and economics will play key roles. Market forces will limit levels of royalties or rents. The challenge is to successfully manage and develop First Nations lands and resources. Co-operation with both the provincial and federal governments will be critical.

Joseph Kalt suggests that the relatively successful aboriginal groups in the United States have three ingredients in common: (1) sovereignty, (2) capable government, and (3) a match between the Tribe's type of government and their cultural beliefs about what constitutes legitimate political power. [23] By sovereignty, Kalt means genuine decision-making control over how tribal affairs and resources are run. The Nisga'a and Sechelt agreements provide this, as do the Inuvialuit and Yukon settlements.

Kalt's second ingredient, capable government, is met by putting formal governing institutions in place that perform three basic tasks. They "1) efficiently make and carry out strategic choices and policies; 2) provide a political environment in which investors—large or small, tribal members or non-members—feel secure; and 3) mobilize and sustain the tribal community's support for its institutions and for particular development strategies" (pp. 4–5). Kalt also argues that politics must be separate from day-to-day management; powers must be limited and discrete (p. 8). The Nisga'a Agreement-in-Principle seems to set the groundwork for the first two conditions. Time will reveal whether the third comes about. Evidence from the Sechelt, the Yukon, and the Inuvialuit settlements suggests that self-government has been successfully established.

The third component, the cultural match between the people and their form of government, will also take some time to reveal itself. Again, the Sechelt, the Yukon, and the Inuvialuit seem to be pleased with their government structures. It is highly unlikely that the Nisga'a would be a party to a negotiated government that they did not believe in.

Notes

1. Cassidy and Dale, p. 12.

2. Government of British Columbia, p. 11.

3. Sechelt Indian Band Council, *A Practical Proposal,* p. 3.

4. Indian and Northern Affairs Canada *Information Sheet No. 20, Self-Government Sechelt Style,* p. 2.

5. Taylor and Paget, p. 311.

6. Allen, pp. 10-11.

7. Sechelt Indian Band Council, *A Practical Proposal,* p. 17.

8. Government of Canada, et al., *Nisga'a Treaty Negotiations, Agreement-in-Principle,* p. 6. Because they are numerous, all other references to this publication will appear in the text, as will references to the following related publication: Government of Canada et al., *Nisga'a Treaty Negotiations, Agreement-in-Principle in Brief.*

9. The ARA Consulting Group Inc., p. 18.

10. Indian and Northern Affairs Canada, *British Columbian Indian Comprehensive Claims,* map.

11. The ARA Consulting Group Inc., p. 7; McDonald and Hasselfield, p. 62.

12. Mitchell-Banks, p. 2.

13. Notzke, p. 1.

14. First Nations Forestry Council, p. 11.

15. McMillan, p. 300.

16. The ARA Consulting Group Inc., p. 16.

17. KPMG Management Consulting, p. 5.

18. Sechelt Indian Band Council, *A Practical Proposal,* p. 18.

19. Notzke, p. 50.

20. Taylor and Paget, p. 336; and Birkes et al., p. 15.

21. ARA Consulting Group Inc., p. 17.

22. Birkes et al., p. 12.

23. Kalt, p. 3.

References

Allen, Graham. "Forms of Self-Government, Sechelt Indian Self-Government." The Self-Government Project: First Nations' Government Structures and Powers Conference, University of British Columbia, Vancouver B.C., May 5–6, 1988.

ARA Consulting Group Inc. *Social and Economic Impacts of Aboriginal Land Claim Settlements: A Case Study Analysis, Final Report.* For the Ministry of Aboriginal Affairs, Province of British Columbia, and the Federal Treaty Negotiation Office. Vancouver: ARA Consulting Group Inc., December 1995.

Birkes, Fikret, Peter George, and Richard J. Preston. "Co-management, the Evolution in Theory and Practice of the Joint Administration of Living Resources." *Alternatives,* Vol. 18, No. 2, 1991.

British Columbia Claims Task Force. *The Report of the British Columbia Claims Task Force.* Vancouver: British Columbia Claims Task Force, June 1991.

Cassidy, Frank, and Norman Dale. *After Native Claims?* Lantzville, B.C.: Oolichan Books, 1988.

First Nations Forestry Council. *First Nations Forestry Council Strategic Plan.* Victoria: Queen's Printer, 1995.

Government of British Columbia. *Treaty Status Report.* Victoria: Queen's Printer, 1996.

Government of Canada, Province of British Columbia, and Nisga'a Tribal Council. *Nisga'a Treaty Negotiations, Agreement-in-Principle.* Victoria: Queen's Printer, 15 February 1966.

————. *Nisga'a Treaty Negotiations, Agreement-in-Principle in Brief.* Victoria: Queen's Printer, 1966.

Indian and Northern Affairs Canada. *Information Sheet No. 20, Self-Government Sechelt Style.* Ottawa: Government of Canada, 1991.

————. *British Columbia Indian Comprehensive Claims,* Revised Map 1991 Ottawa: Government of Canada, 1996.

Kalt, Joseph P. "Statement of Prof. Joseph P. Kalt, Harvard Project on American Indian Economic Development." John F. Kennedy School of Government, Harvard University, before the United States Senate Committee on Indian Affairs, 17 September 1996.

KPMG Management Consulting. *First Nations Forestry Council, Aboriginal Participation in the Forest Sector.* Victoria: KPMG (no date).

McDonald, Neil, and Ginny Hasselfield. *The McDonald Summary of Aboriginal Issues Today.* Winnipeg: Cross Cultural Communications, 1994.

McMillan, Alan D. *Native Peoples and Cultures of Canada.* Vancouver: Douglas and McIntyre, 1988.

Mitchell-Banks, Paul J. "Indigenous People's Environmental Monitoring and Enforcement: A Case Study with the Sechelt Indian Band using Fisheries Co-Management as a Means to Establish the Band's Own Environmental Monitoring and Enforcement Program." Unpublished Master's Thesis. University of Toronto, Program in Planning, 1992.

Notzke, Claudia. *Aboriginal Peoples and Natural Resources in Canada.* North York, Ont: Captus University Publications, 1994.

Sechelt Indian Band Council. *A Practical Proposal for Resolving the Indian Land Claim in British Columbia as it Affects the Sechelt Indian Band.* Sechelt: Sechelt Band, 1989.

————. *Constitution.* Sechelt: Sechelt Band, 1989.

Taylor, John P., and Gary Paget. "Federal/Provincial Responsibility and the Sechelt." For the National Conference on Federal and Provincial Governments and Aboriginal Peoples, Carleton University, Ottawa, October 1988.

Williams, Allison. "Native Urbanization in Ontario: History, Processes and Problems." Unpublished Masters Thesis. University of Toronto, Department of Geography, 1996.

5

Investment and Capital Productivity

By Steven Globerman

This chapter considers how settling First Nations treaties may affect the investment and use of capital in British Columbia.[1] It focuses mainly on the possible consequences to financial investment, but also pays attention to the effects treaty settlements may have on economic factors like the availability of technical expertise, a skilled labour force, and modern transportation facilities.

Why are these factors important? The quality and availability of "complementary assets" like "human capital" and social infrastructure will determine both how willing the private sector is to invest financial capital, and how productive that financial capital ends up being. And it is the level of capital investment and its productivity that will in turn be an important influence on how much real income or spending power British Columbians will have in the future.

The conclusions this study draws are admittedly speculative. We know far too few aspects of the relevant environment, including the precise nature of future treaty settlements themselves, to offer any firm forecasts of their future impacts. In addition, further developments in the British Columbia economy (such as government policies affecting timber harvesting and mining exploration and development) will also influence the economic impact of land claims settlements. This increases the difficulty of making confident predictions. Nevertheless, critical analysis of the information we do have is more useful than uneasy guesswork.

This study tries to improve on existing evaluations of the consequences of First Nations treaty settlements to capital investment in two ways. First, it identifies the nature of the possible consequences in a more comprehensive way. Current studies tend to focus on one or two possible effects, such as reductions in investors' uncertainty once land claims disputes are settled "once and for all."[2] But in fact, quite a few factors have the potential to affect how treaty settlements will influence investment and capital productivity.

Second, this study integrates the arguments surrounding treaty settlements into the research on foreign direct investment. Because treaty settlements may result in a wide variety of political regulatory systems in B.C., analyzing future assessment patterns in the context of international investment, where the conditions are similar, is very useful. Information on foreign investment offers some valuable insights into the dynamics of property rights regimes and investment flows.[3]

Here is an overview of the discussion that follows:

- The first section is a non-technical discussion of the factors that are likely to determine investment and capital productivity, highlighting those that are particularly sensitive to treaty settlements.
- The second section is a more detailed analysis of how treaty settlements may affect returns to capital and incentives to invest.
- The third section reviews a number of case studies and other related evidence that shows how past settlements have influenced returns to capital and incentives to invest.
- The fourth section summarizes the main arguments and offers some conclusions on policy.

Factors Likely to Determine Investment: A Conceptual Framework

The First Nations treaty settlement process has been criticized or defended on a variety of legal, political, and economic grounds.[4] The issues of primary importance to this study are those related to how treaty settlements may affect capital investment and productivity in B.C. The tangible and intangible capital available to the provincial labour force, and how productively they use that capital, will strongly influence British Columbians' average real incomes.

Increased investment does not always result in greater economic benefits for society. Some profitable investments may have social costs that are greater than their social benefits. For example, a heavily polluting pulp mill might have a negative overall impact on the welfare of British Columbians, even though it creates income and profits for some residents. The costs to provincial taxpayers of large financial subsidies to a new manufacturing facility might outweigh the benefits of the employment income it produces. Therefore, when I support increased investment as a policy goal, either by outright statement or by implication, I mean investment that creates positive net social benefits for the province.

The discounted net present value (NPV) rule

The main economic argument supporting First Nations treaty settlements is that they will reduce the uncertainty about how resources on Crown lands can be used, and that this uncertainty is a significant barrier to increased investment. Opponents, arguing from how treaty settlements have been carried out so far, have countered that negotiations only add to the uncertainty about the future. They say that, among other things, negotiations raise expectations of large and unpredictable changes in systems of land tenure and ownership, and in conditions attached to using property rights in the affected areas.

Risk and uncertainty are certainly relevant issues to investors. However, other factors are also relevant, and should be incorporated in any overall analysis of investment behaviour. One standard framework for assessing value and making investment decisions that incorporates these relevant factors is the discounted net present value (NPV) rule.[5]

The NPV rule subtracts operating costs from operating revenues in each time period, and discounts the net values by an appropriate interest rate. It also discounts capital costs (primarily those of depreciation and amortization), interest payments, and tax liabilities by an appropriate interest rate, then subtracts them from the net operating income. Any revenues from other sources, such as government grants, are also discounted over time, and included in the NPV calculation.

In principle, the NPV rule states that, as long as they have adequate financing, investors should undertake all projects that have positive expected NPV values (revenues are expected to be greater than costs).

If their financing is limited, investors should rank projects by their NPV values.

What determines the NPV?

From the previous discussion, we can conclude that potential investors will be encouraged to invest by higher expected profits and lower expected risks. Because the risks associated with any investment are reflected in the interest rate that the investor must pay (directly or indirectly) to raise financial capital, we can say that the level of risk is one of the factors that determines financing costs. So if all other things are constant, an investment will become more attractive if the expected revenues increase and the expected costs decrease.

Figure 5.1 below lists the general factors that can influence both operating costs and financial costs. Before we discuss it, we should recognize that the costs of any activity depend on two factors:

- the prices of the resources, materials, and energy used
- how efficiently these inputs are used.

If prices for resources are lower, and they are used with greater efficiency, the activity will cost less.

Take an activity like producing minerals from a mine. A variety of resources must be combined with the natural resource of the ore body to produce a commercially valuable product. These complementary resources (or "complementary inputs") include the services of managers and employees, who have various degrees of skills and training, and the services of physical capital like earth-moving equipment. If all other things are constant, the greater the supply of these resources, the lower their prices will be, and in turn, the less the activity will cost.

How efficiently these resources are used will depend on both the mix and the quality of the resources. The best possible mix is being used when it's impossible to increase production without also increasing costs. In this case, the producer is thus using neither too much nor too little of any particular resource. Determining the precise quality of any resource, especially people, is often impossible. But we can determine quality in a general way. Some people may be better than others at organizing and carrying out certain jobs, for example, and thus will be more productive. If the producer can obtain resources (including human resources) of such above-average quality at average market prices, overall efficiency will improve. As Figure 5.1 shows, operating costs will be influenced by the cost and quality of resources like management and labour skills and physical infrastructures (such as roads).

In short, if management policies make it possible to get more and better-quality resources, costs of production will decrease, all other things being constant. Investment flows will increase, and the productivity of accumulated capital stock should also improve. The reverse is also true. If management policies have the effect of decreasing the number and quality of resources available, productivity will decrease.

Figure 5.1: Factors That Generally Influence Costs

Factors Influencing Operating Costs

- Availability and quality of resources ("complementary inputs")
    - skills of management and labour
    - physical infrastructure (such as roads)
- Government policies
    - environmental laws and regulations
    - other business regulations
    - taxes and subsidies
- Competition

Factors Influencing Financing Costs

- Uncertainty surrounding property rights
- Ability to hedge risks
- Access to competitively priced capital

Figure 5.1 also identifies that government policies are another factor affecting operating costs. More stringent and comprehensive environmental standards and other business regulations generally increase costs of private-sector activities, although they can also result in lower social costs. (Activities not directly regulated by certain laws may benefit from them indirectly.)[6] Highly regulated businesses will see an increase in costs for at least two reasons:

- They will have to spend money to satisfy the regulations, which will increase the overall costs of doing business.
- They may not be able to use the most economic technologies available, or to operate efficiently without violating the regulations.

As a result, stricter and wider-reaching environmental and other business regulations will likely discourage investment in the private sector.[7]

Higher taxes are also an added cost of doing business. If business can't recover higher taxes by increasing prices for consumers, or through saving money on other factors of production, profits will decrease, which will discourage investment. On the other hand, if the government uses the revenues to improve the business environment directly or indirectly, say by financing the construction of new port or rail facilities, the overall impact may be to encourage private investment. In theory, what matters to investors is the net impact of the government's financial activities. This is supported by practical evidence from studies of foreign investment.[8]

Competition certainly influences operating costs, but how it influences investors is not clear. On one hand, a market that is open to competition is likely to have access to the best technology and highest-quality resources. This by itself should encourage new investment and higher productivity. Higher income in a region should also invite investment. But, on the other hand, competition reduces what are called "economic rents." These are the profits that investors might get above and beyond the amounts that provide a rate of return sufficient to keep capital from leaving the activity in question. Competition ensures that investors will not earn economic rent.

We now move to the factors that influence financing costs. One of these is risk. To understand the effect risk has on investors, we need to distinguish between diversifiable and non-diversifiable risk.

Investors can protect themselves from diversifiable risk in one activity by also putting money into other activities that have different cash-flow schedules. They can't protect themselves from non-diversifiable risk in this way, so they expect to get higher returns on such investments as compensation for taking that risk. Diversifiable risk is usually associated with activities in the normal business cycle.

For example, the profits of the telephone industry don't vary much with economic expansions and contractions, while the profits of the forestry industry vary quite a bit. By investing in telephone companies, investors who also own forestry assets can reduce the variability of their earnings over the course of business expansions and contractions. Non-diversifiable risk is usually associated with the consequences of government policies, especially those that affect the investor's property rights.

Finally, costs of financing investments will be affected by the investor's access to financial capital. Those who have above-average information about alternative sources of financing are likely to obtain it at better rates than those who do not. Similarly, investors with above-average credit ratings and good collateral will likely pay less for financing than those who do not.

What determines capital productivity?

The factors in Figure 5.1 also generally determine how productive the capital stock is. In particular, "social capital"—physical structures like roads and other transportation facilities, and social assets like respect for the law—affects how productive privately owned assets are.[9]

Clearly, government policies and regulations strongly influence social capital. They can also affect how productive capital is in other ways. For example, regulations can limit how investors use their resources, or limit their ability to obtain other complementary resources. (Again, these government restrictions may justly serve broader social interests.) Conversely, taxes can fund improvements in social capital, like education to improve the skills of workers.

Greater competition also improves capital productivity. Among other things, it encourages producers to use the most economical assets in the best possible ways. It also prompts them to adopt new technologies and management practices more quickly, to save money, and to enhance quality. The virtual collapse of the highly protected Japanese economy in the 1990s has helped disillusion those who argue that we must protect domestic producers, especially those in industries relying heavily on technology. The stronger emerging view is that a nation's ability to compete in international markets is strengthened by highly competitive domestic markets.

Finally, uncertainty about property rights will likely reduce productivity. If investors are worried about their assets being expropriated by the government or confiscated through taxes, they won't invest as much money in vulnerable activities. This may in turn result in production facilities being smaller than they should be for optimum efficiency. Uncertainty about property rights may also cause investors to economize on some resources such as physical capital, and invest more money in assets such as labour. This may upset the mix of assets most effective for production.

How do treaty settlements affect this?

Arguments have been put forward on both sides about how treaty settlements will affect investment and capital productivity. This subsection brings together the major ones, which will be evaluated and analyzed in the next section.

Changes to environmental and business regulations

As we noted earlier, stricter environmental and business regulations will likely increase costs of resource-based activities like forestry, mining, and oil and gas production. (At the same time, reduced environmental damage might lower the costs or improve the profits of other activities like fishing and tourism.) Because resource-based industries are so important to the B.C. economy (see Table 5.1 below), any significant changes in government regulations, especially environmental ones, may affect investors' incentives to invest in the province, and also affect how productive the capital stock in these industries is.

One argument contends that First Nations treaty settlements will lead to changes in environmental laws and regulations that will in turn increase costs. It is based on three assumptions. The first is that First Nations have a "preservationist bias" that will make investing in the resource sector less attractive, and will reduce the productivity of capital in that sector. The second is the fear of much higher administrative costs to monitor and enforce private sector compliance with any new regulations. The last is that conflicting laws and regulations will mean

Table 5.1: Share of British Columbia Gross Domestic Product in 1994, by Industry

Sector	Share
Primary (agriculture, fishing, logging, mining)	6.4%
Manufacturing (sawmills, factories, smelting)	12.3%
Construction, utilities, etc.	9.3%
Services	72.0%

Source: Province of British Columbia, *British Columbia Financial and Economic Review* (Victoria: B.C. Stats, 1995).

costly and lengthy delays in the investment-planning process, especially for investments like pipelines, which will cross numerous political boundaries.[10]

The opposite argument is based on the premise that a stronger role for First Nations in the process of government (including self-government) may lead to environmental regulations more favourable to investors. Why? First Nations groups would have more authority to create the regulations governing industrial and commercial development within their territories. Those First Nations wishing to promote economic development could use their regulatory authority to promote the kinds of industrial and commercial activities they desire within their own jurisdictions.[11]

Reductions in tax revenues

Some of those opposing First Nations treaty settlements have argued that transferring ownership of income-producing assets to First Nations investors will reduce the tax revenues the provincial government gets from these assets. Their primary concern is that under current tax laws, First Nations are exempt from paying such taxes.[12]

The effect treaty settlements will have on the finances of the B.C. government will in turn affect investors' willingness to invest in the province, both directly and indirectly. For example, if treaty settlements erode the provincial government's financial status, they could result in higher taxes or a decrease in government spending. Higher taxes would of course directly discourage investors. Decreased government spending would reduce investment more indirectly, by causing a deterioration in the social capital supplied by government.

Changes to risk and uncertainty

The possible effect of First Nations treaty settlements on risk, especially politically related non-diversifiable risk, has created perhaps the greatest controversy. One theory is that resolving disputes will reduce the uncertainty of who holds property rights on Crown lands, which will then reduce the risks and uncertainties of investing in resource-based activities. The implication is that settlements may encourage investments now postponed by investors afraid of the risk. Another theory is that the uncertain status of sites affected by treaties has only a small effect on investment decisions made by the private sector. The view here is that settlements themselves may introduce new uncertainties that will create additional and perhaps greater risks for investors.

A Closer Look at the Possible Effects of Treaty Settlements

In this section, we consider in more detail how treaty settlements may affect incentives to invest and capital productivity. First, however, we should discuss a more basic issue.

Transfers of property ownership

Do transfers of property ownership affect how the transferred property is used? Many of the arguments against treaty settlements are based on the assumption that once control over certain resources (such as rights to fisheries) shifts, how those resources are used will change. And, as a result, the financial benefits that the residents of B.C. get from those resources will also change.

This perception may not be true. The most widely quoted economics study of all time, written by the Nobel Laureate Ronald Coase, makes the following point: If the transaction costs are relatively low, private exchange will ensure that an asset is used in the activity where it is most highly valued. Transferring control of land will not necessarily change how that land is used.[13]

For example, if logging is a more commercially valuable activity than tourism, investors who have a competitive advantage in logging activities are presumably able and willing to bid the use of the land away from those who would use the land for tourism activities. However, changing who owns the underlying resources will of course also change who gets the money from them.

The key stipulation behind Coase's theory is that the costs of making the transactions must be relatively low. Transactions costs depend on a number of factors. One is the number of people who are interested in the bargaining process. The larger the number, the higher the costs of the transaction. Some are concerned that the bargaining process will be quite costly after treaties have been settled because resource-based companies not owned by First Nations will have to negotiate with individual tribes or band councils, many of which may have different rules and arrangements for investors. This process will be more complex than negotiating with a provincial government department or ministry.

The costs of transactions can also be affected by cultural differences. These may increase the difficulties that the most well-intentioned negotiators must deal with in seeking agreements. If more direct negotiations between First Nations and other groups are necessary to create an efficient way to operate resource-based activities, transaction costs may become a greater obstacle to investing and using capital efficiently. On the other hand, giving a more formal and integrated role to First Nations in making decisions about allocating resources might actually reduce transactions costs from what they are now. Consider the social costs alone of First Nations' protests such as the long and expensive dispute over roadblocks to the Apex ski resort in the Okanagan Valley.

Environmental and business regulations

We discussed concerns about changes in environmental and other business regulations causing higher costs of administration and compliance in the first section. However, we can't assume that First Nations will have a greater influence on environmental matters after treaties are settled than they do now. Aboriginal communities have a substantial influence on resource development through legal and non-legal means. One example is the pressure local First Nations groups have exerted on Inco. They forced the mining company to request a full environmental approval process for its planned Voisey Bay mining development, a process which is expected to delay Inco's production.[14] Another is our previous example of roadblocks set up by a local band in the Okanagan Valley that prevented access to the Apex ski resort.

Extending Aboriginal self-government through treaty settlements also does not necessarily lead to more unwieldy laws and regulations. Governments have a strong interest in controlling conflicts in regulations and administrative systems between jurisdictions simply because they discourage investment across different jurisdictions. The new legislation planned for the Northwest Territories that creates a hybrid legislature of First Nations bands and publicly elected MLAs is a case in point. It will give Aboriginal bands and Métis groups the right to sit as a separate assembly within the legislature, and will guarantee them representation by two members in a six-member cabinet.[15] Supporters of the proposed legislation argue that it may be the only way to keep the western Northwest Territories united after the territory of Nunavut is created in 1999, taking with it about one-third of the population.

Finally, giving greater practical as well as legal control to First Nations over environmental policies could introduce more efficient ways of conserving natural resources, and have the associated benefit of increasing long-term investment in activities involving renewable resources. In fact, some experts argue that First Nations fishery practices are more environmentally-sound than those used by other commercial fisheries.[16]

The concern that settling First Nations treaties will significantly increase the costs of complying with new regulations may thus be unfounded. First Nations can and do have great influence on environmental practices in B.C now. The ability to compete among themselves for outside capital investment might actually weaken their "preserva-tionist" stance. (However, treaty settlements may limit their ability to change environmental regulations and standards for the purpose of at-tracting investment. The Nisga'a Agreement-in-Principle, for example, requires them to "meet or exceed" provincial standards.) In any case, studies of international business show that, with the exception of a few activities like mining, the influence of environmental standards on in-vestors' decisions has been insignificant. Even in the case of the min-ing industry, the availability of low-cost ore is a much more important factor in deciding location than the costs of complying with environ-mental regulations.[17]

Taxes and subsidies

In principle, the redistribution of income brought about by treaty settlements could affect provincial tax revenues by changing the tax rate on that income. If income is redirected to taxpayers with smaller in-comes, the average tax rate will decrease, given a progressive tax struc-ture (and all other things held constant). This effect will clearly be even more pronounced if the new recipients are exempt from paying income taxes and other taxes, as First Nations groups are. However, their tax status may well change over time, partly as a result of land claims set-tlements. The Nisga'a Agreement, for instance, states that the Nisga'a must pay taxes.

Some observers have suggested that the impact of treaty settlements will actually have very little effect on the provincial government's fi-nances, for several reasons. One is that the cash payments involved in settlements are likely to be small in comparison to the value of lands to be transferred.[18] For example, when ratified, the Agreement-in-Prin-ciple with the Nisga'a tribe will give the Nisga'a $190 million and just over 1,900 sq. km of land. The taxes generated from economic activ-ity on the transferred land may change a great deal over time, depend-ing on who owns it. But the immediate financial consequences for the government will involve the transfer of cash, which is likely to be a small part of the overall transfer.

A second reason for downplaying the financial consequences of treaty settlements is the expectation that the federal government will provide the bulk of the cash payment required, under cost-sharing agreements between the federal and provincial governments. One study argues that the total financial benefit of these federal government transfers to B.C. (most of which will go to First Nations), after subtracting the provincial government's share of cash, the costs of negotiations, and the federal costs that British Columbians pay through taxes, is between $3.9 billion and $5.3 billion (in 1995 constant dollars).[19]

The key assumption supporting this estimate is that the federal government will not reduce other cash transfers to British Columbia as a result of treaty settlement, which is certainly questionable. Owen Lippert contends that Ottawa will try to bury some of the costs of land claims settlements by reducing federal transfers to B.C.[20] Another assumption is that treaty settlements will not affect government costs, also questionable. Mel Smith, for example, has argued that forming new governments and staffing new bureaucracies will create small and inefficient administrative units in the province, which will result in higher costs.[21] Transfers from the federal government may not cover these higher costs, possibly requiring higher taxes or reductions in other types of government spending.

As the example of the Northwest Territories suggests, innovations in legislation and administrative structures can possibly ease the costs of creating many independent First Nations political jurisdictions. And if the federal government can reduce the Indian Affairs bureaucracy after treaty settlements come into effect, they may save a good deal of money. Treaty settlements may also allow First Nations people to earn higher incomes. This would reduce the burden on taxpayers to fund income support payments.

Given the uncertainty of future government structures and exactly how income will be redistributed to First Nations, we can only speculate about the exact financial consequences of treaty settlements. Nevertheless, we cannot deny that redistributing assets to owners who pay different tax rates can have an important influence on the provincial government's financial position.

The calculations outlined in Figure 5.2 below illustrate this point. They are based on KPMG's estimation that British Columbia will get about $14 billion from the federal government as part of the settlement process. They also assume that a transfer of provincial land will take place for up to $10 billion. So provincial treaty settlements may involve transfers of $14 billion in assets to First Nations.[22]

Figure 5.2: Returns to Capital and Tax Yields

Case 1
Let's say investors generally expect to earn a 10% return on assets of $14 billion, and their tax rate is 30%. The real value of annual tax payments on the income from the $14 billion in assets will be $420 million.
Tax revenue = $14 billion x .10 x .30 = $420 million

Case 2
First Nations investors pay taxes of 20%. To get the same annual tax revenue on income they would earn on $14 billion of assets, they would need to earn a 15% return on their investments.
$420 million = $14 billion x .20 x .15

Let's assume that non-native investors could always expect to earn a 10% real rate of return on the assets, so they would get $1.4 billion a year. Let's also assume that the investors would have to pay a 30% tax rate on this income. They would then have to pay $420 million a year in taxes.

In comparison, if the tax rate for First Nations people is 20%, they would need to earn a higher return on the assets—15% versus 10%—in order to keep tax revenues at the same $420 million a year.

These calculations illustrate the point that we should pay some attention to the financial implications of transferring assets. (First Nations could pass on the benefits of their tax status in the form of joint ventures in which they have controlling ownership.)[23]

Productivity of capital: the quality of complementary assets

As we discussed earlier, physical capital is more productive if the stock of complementary inputs is larger, and the quality of complementary assets like managerial and technical expertise, skilled labour, and social infrastructure (such as transportation facilities) is higher. The more productive capital is expected to be, the more attractive further investment in it is. Studies of international investment show that the availability of a skilled domestic labour force and modern infrastructure like transportation are strong inducements to foreign investment.[24]

Many First Nations people have shown that they possess substantial business and management skills.[25] However, experts generally recognize that as a group, First Nations people have lower levels of professional and technical skills, and less formal education, than the general population. Add to this the factor that a variety of difficulties in getting financial capital continues to prevent First Nations from making their own investments in physical infrastructure (like roads and other public works). It follows that if treaty settlements lead to First Nations managers and workers replacing current management and staff, physical capital will likely be less productive. As a result, activities owned and managed by First Nations groups may attract less investment from outside communities.

One question that often arises is how much First Nations groups would insist on using First Nations peoples to manage and staff their business activities. Another is whether First Nations groups will ask non-native businesses to employ First Nations people as a condition of being allowed to own and operate enterprises on First Nations lands. Studies of international investment suggest that both of these events would discourage both foreign investment and investment from the outside community. But we also should recognize that the B.C. government has often emphasized creating local jobs at the expense of economic efficiency. Any similar First Nations policy might not be a dramatic difference from the way things are now.

Past cases have shown that First Nations groups are in fact likely to emphasize creating jobs for Aboriginal people in businesses that operate in First Nations communities. BHP Diamonds, the owner and operator of a planned diamond mine in the Northwest Territories, has apparently agreed to hire two-thirds of its workforce from the North. Half of the workers will be First Nations people. BHP Diamonds has also agreed to make other commitments, including paying the air fare of workers from communities from as far away as the Arctic coast, and offering training and apprenticeship programs.

Clearly, First Nations groups could overcome many of these obstacles by hiring others to work for them. The market for such technical and managerial staff is fairly competitive, so First Nations owners may be able to hang on to many of the "economic rents" that they would get from natural resource activities on their lands. Over time, using some of these rents to provide education and training programs for First Nations people would close their current gaps in business and technical expertise.

First Nations groups might also compensate for shortages of certain assets by doing activities that don't require as many of them. They could more easily manage and staff tourism and other service activities, for example, than they could activities that involve extracting and processing natural resources. If the rates of return on investments are lower for service-related activities than for resource extraction and processing, total capital investment might also be lower. However, the overall welfare of British Columbians might actually improve. Service-related activities such as tourism tend to damage the environment far less.

Altogether, if First Nations groups insist that the economic activities carried out on their lands employ mostly First Nations people, and if those people have lower levels of skills, then returns to capital invested in those economic activities will decrease. This in turn will likely reduce investment on Aboriginal lands, unless investors find lower returns acceptable.[26] The resulting availability of a "pool" of workers displaced by this employment policy might prompt others in the larger community to create new activities on non-aboriginal lands. However, many of the available workers may move to other parts of North America, contributing to an overall reduction in the number of skilled workers and managers in B.C.

If First Nations groups make employment and social policy part of their investment policies, returns to capital investment may well decrease significantly, discouraging future capital investment in the related businesses. We can expect strong pressures from the First Nations community to integrate social and economic policies in this way. However, provincial and municipal governments are also under the same pressure. And there are advantages to using First Nations workers on local projects that could moderate any negative effects, especially in more remote areas. Because they are familiar with the area, First Nations workers will be more likely to remain settled there. Investors may save on the high transportation and settlement costs of bringing a workforce to a new site.

Productivity of capital: competition

As we noted earlier, increased competition can affect investors' incentives in contradictory ways. It can improve how efficiently producers use their resources, which should make the capital more productive and stimulate investment. On the other hand, increased competition could also reduce the profits that would ordinarily attract new producers and investors—narrow the field, so to speak.

But the real issue that arises here is whether First Nations groups will try to protect their businesses from competition with non-aboriginal businesses. If federal laws protecting market competition continue to apply to First Nations' lands and activities, they will ease this concern. However, they won't eliminate it. First Nations policy-makers could use means like restrictive licensing arrangements and zoning regulations to protect certain suppliers.

However, First Nations groups already have power to indirectly influence investors' decisions to create or expand new ventures through such means as zoning. The practical effect of treaty settlements may then be simply to extend this power over a wider area. And in the past, First Nations groups have tended to align their zoning processes with the municipality's.

Whether First Nations groups would protect favoured suppliers more than other governments tend to do is unclear. (After all, the B.C. government is apparently willing to accept a reduction in competition in the airline industry to support Canadian airlines.) If First Nations leaders are pressured by their constituencies to create the maximum amount of jobs for First Nations people, policies to restrict investment by outsiders might be unpopular and hard to sustain. These types of considerations again highlight how important the type of political environment that emerges after treaties are settled will be. Particularly crucial is the question of whether the influence of special-interest groups will be strengthened or weakened by the changes in government structure.

Perceived risks

Many believe that the uncertainty surrounding treaty settlements has dampened investors' willingness to invest in provincial resource-based activities. The assumption is that investors cannot easily protect themselves from the risks involved. Price Waterhouse tried to pinpoint exactly how significant the uncertainties around treaty settlements were by surveying companies in B.C.'s forest products, mining, and oil and gas industries. Companies identified the following factors as creating the most uncertainty:

- unsettled rights of access to land and resources
- the possibility that production or shipment would be disrupted, which would affect the company's reliability as a supplier
- the possibility of unsatisfactory financial compensation if a treaty settlement affected a company's interests.

Most of those who participated in the survey said that while treaty settlements did create uncertainty, they did not adjust "investment premiums" to reflect this uncertainty. Specifically, none of the forest products manufacturers had cancelled or delayed capital projects because comprehensive land claims existed. Few expected such cancellations or delays in the near future. Mining exploration companies and oil and gas companies also said that comprehensive land claims did not significantly affect their activities.

The situation was different for mining companies at the development stage. Four of 11 survey participants who had possible mining projects expected difficulties from unsettled land claims. Together, these four projects represented $680 million in capital. By projecting these results and calculating expected impacts, the researchers estimated that mining investments of about $100 million a year would likely be affected by uncertainties of unsettled treaties. The survey results suggested that about half of the projects would be delayed by about three years, the other half cancelled.[27]

It is dangerous to draw conclusions from a single survey, where participants may have tended to overstate the uncertainties surrounding unsettled treaties. The survey did not ask whether other types of risk might arise from the settlement agreements themselves. Nevertheless, it is not far-fetched to conclude that the uncertainty of whether and how treaties will be settled is discouraging some investment in B.C., though how much is difficult to say.[28]

Many agree that federal government policies that make it difficult for First Nations groups to establish collateral for loans or to hold mortgages also create obstacles for First Nations investment. New banking and financing arrangements will help solve some of the problems with poor credit ratings that plague First Nations businesses. However, some of these new arrangements appear to be set up to benefit from the fact that First Nations businesses are exempt from paying taxes. If First Nations investors can hold land and other assets with a clear title, and use these assets as collateral, they should be able to get capital more cheaply, and thus invest more easily.

What Can We Learn from Past Cases?

Because so much depends on the actions of First Nations groups after treaties are settled, we can't pinpoint exactly how these settlements will affect investment decisions and the productivity of investment capital. At one extreme, if the arguments against treaty settlements all come to pass, investors could have very little encouragement to support new ventures. At the other, First Nations groups could make policies that moderate potentially negative effects like political fragmentation. In fact, the resulting competition among First Nations for private investment could improve capital investment and employment throughout the province.

To get a clearer picture of what may happen, it is useful to examine what has happened as a result of treaty settlements so far. Such settlements are few, and each has unique circumstances that limit our ability to make generalizations from them. Nevertheless, they will show at least some of the possible consequences for treaty settlements in British Columbia.

The Australian experience

The *Aboriginal Land Rights (Northern Territory) Act* of 1976 is an interesting case study for treaty settlements in B.C. The Act created

- land trusts for Aboriginal land
- Aboriginal land councils to manage the use and development of land and resources
- a system to distribute royalties earned from land.

It did not provide a cash settlement to Aboriginal people.

Under the Act, minerals on Aboriginal land remained the Crown's property. Northern Territory laws controlled exploration and mining both on Aboriginal land and in the rest of the Territory. The Act stated that investors could obtain exploration and mining interests on Aboriginal land only with the consent of the Minister and the relevant land council—unless the commonwealth government decided that exploration or mining was required in the national interest. Mining companies that applied for mineral lease or oil permits before the Act did not need Aboriginal consent.

Land councils had the role of managing Aboriginal land. They co-ordinated and assisted negotiations on land use among traditional Aboriginal owners, the government, and third-party interests. From 1976 to 1987 there was a period of marked uncertainty around natural resource development. After 1987, the atmosphere was more secure (but by no means confident) as a result of changes made by the *Amendment Act* of 1987.

The main problems before 1987 were the lack of effective time limits to approve applications for exploration licences (ELAs), the lack of clear answers either in favour of or against ELAs, and traditional Aboriginal owners' inconsistent application of their right to veto the ELAs. Potential investors found the veto option especially troublesome, since it meant both uncertainty and long delays in implementing business plans.

The *Amendment Act* was introduced to make it easier for land councils (on behalf of traditional Aboriginal owners) and mining companies to reach agreement. It set out the rights and obligations of each party, plus clear procedures and timetables for agreements. It gave clear guidelines on granting "once only" consent at the exploration stage, and on negotiating (and if necessary arbitrating) the terms and conditions at both exploration and mining stages. The Act also allowed a land council to make binding arrangements on behalf of Aboriginal owners for exploration or mining activities on lands under claim, which reduced delays in finalizing agreements.

The Act did seem to improve investment on Aboriginal lands. From 1976 to 1987, only one ELA was granted. After 1987, 53 ELAs got approved. But the 53 approved ELAs were only about 12% of the proposals made to land councils. In contrast, around 2,000 ELAs have been approved on non-aboriginal lands since 1987. ARA Consulting Group Inc. notes that the higher approval rate for non-aboriginal lands was partly due to the fact that they had more abundant mineral resources.[30]

Nevertheless, the Northern Territory's experience is a caution against assuming that granting title to land will by itself significantly reduce the risks and delays investors experience in getting satisfactory property rights. Investors are very concerned about how Aboriginal land is governed. Exploration expenditures have apparently held firm in the Northern Territory, but offshore expenditures by Australian mining companies doubled over the same period. This suggests that procedural delays in getting ELAs on Aboriginal lands caused exploration companies to seek markets with less obstruction and greater certainty to investment.

Property rights arrangements among Aboriginal peoples also appeared to deter development. Traditional Aboriginal owners shared royalty payments from resource developments with other Aboriginal people living in the affected areas, even if these residents didn't have title to the land. As a result, owners had little interest in promoting development on their lands.

The western Arctic (Inuvialuit) settlement

The Inuvialuit Final Agreement (IFA) took effect on July 25, 1984. Under the IFA, the Inuvialuit received clear title (fee-simple title) to about 91,000 sq. km in the western Arctic, with rights to the surface and subsurface resources of about 13,000 sq. km of that area. They also received a cash payment of $152 million, plus payments of $10 million for an "economic enhancement fund" and $7.5 million for social development. The Inuvialuit also got the exclusive right to harvest certain animals in the entire settlement territory. And the IFA guaranteed that developers would pay compensation to Inuvialuit harvesters for any losses caused by developments in the settlement territory.

The IFA is an example of comprehensive co-management of resources and economic development shared among First Nations, the provincial government, and the federal government. It has no provision for First Nations self-government. Given the isolation of Inuvialuit lands, issues of development and access are arguably less complex than for other cases with more diverse geography. The main commercial resource-based activity has been in oil and gas, but little development is actually taking place in the settlement territory. There are also few conflicts over the use of non-commercial lands, because of the region's isolation and a dominant First Nations population.

Government observers have argued that the IFA either has not had a material effect on economic development, or has led to a more positive attitude in the business community by reducing uncertainty. Representatives of Shell Oil and Imperial Oil have commented that land access is controlled by a large but consistent bureaucratic system. Its processes and procedures can be long, but they hold no surprises for investors. They stressed that the limited oil explorations in the region are due to the high costs of finding oil rather than to the treaty settlement.

There are other positive signs. Some investment has occurred in tourism and service industries, and Inuvialuit contractors have successfully completed government contracts for national defence work. Recognizing a shortage of First Nations expertise, Inuvialuit businesses have hired non-aboriginal people for senior positions. A fairly comprehensive set of training programs aims to improve skill levels.

The Tainui settlement (New Zealand)

Under their 1995 settlement agreement, nearly 18,000 hectares of land will eventually be returned to the Tainui Maori. The most common observation about this agreement appears to be that it is too soon to assess the stewardship of the transferred lands and money. The Tainui seem to have emphasized tourism as a method of economic development, and the Maori have demonstrated significant skill at it. At the same time, the non-aboriginal business community has been relatively neutral toward the settlement. There appear to be no early increases or reductions in capital investment.

The Alaska Native claims settlement

The *Alaska Native Claims Settlement Act* of 1971 established 13 regional Native corporations, set up according to negotiated territorial boundaries. First Nations groups showed a clear interest in developing the resource base of their lands. However, the experiences of each corporation have differed. Some have had great success and continue to invest in commercial enterprises. Others had bad business experiences, and have concentrated their following investments in financial assets.

The James Bay and northern Quebec agreement

Under the James Bay and Northern Quebec Agreement of 1975, the James Bay Cree and northern Quebec Inuit received both cash payments and lands, some of which their councils and boards could administer for their exclusive use. The Agreement created a vast administrative structure which led to overlaps in jurisdiction, and resulted in complications. The Inuit responded by proposing a new form of regional government. The proposed Nunavik government differs from self-government in that it would be an extension of the provincial government serving both First Nations groups and other communities in the area.

Environmental co-management with the federal and provincial governments has been contentious. Economic developments in transportation, fisheries, tourism, and agriculture have gone forward. But in both the Inuit and Cree regions, few substantial commercial resources exist. Where they do, they are expensive to develop. One complaint is that the administrative bureaucracy has grown substantially.

What do these cases tell us?

Our review of the available case studies emphasizes how different they are. There are too few to discern general patterns or draw relationships, but we can make several tentative conclusions.

First, we can expect different regions to have different economic experiences according to their wealth of resources. Second, a lack of clear and straightforward administrative procedures will seriously handicap the efforts of First Nations to promote economic development.

These conclusions suggest that First Nations groups should have the flexibility to choose the economic development strategies that they prefer, since the competitive advantages of each group will differ. They also suggest that the administrative structures governing any new political systems that result from treaty settlements should be easy to understand and efficient to operate.

Conclusions

Any evaluation of the possible economic effects of treaty settlements must be realistic about the alternatives. We must acknowledge that many factors quite apart from unsettled treaties now discourage investment in British Columbia. These include uncertainty about future government policies on the environment and on economic development, and bitter conflicts between environmental groups and resource companies. We can't compare the potential difficulties of settling First Nations treaties with a problem-free investment environment.

We must also acknowledge that increased investment may not always be in the public interest. The quality of that investment is important. We must carefully weigh the social costs of developing natural resources. Giving First Nations groups a more prominent role may improve how we make decisions about resource development. Certainly the dismal state of B.C. fisheries should leave none of us with any illusions about our past management of the province's endowment of natural resources.

The social benefits we realize from settling First Nations treaties will largely depend on how well integrated the resulting new laws and administrative systems are. Changes to policies affecting the tax status of First Nations groups and to property laws are also crucial. Existing tax laws arguably encourage investments that are primarily designed to take advantage of tax savings. At the same time, limited access to capital markets hinders First Nations groups from making efficient investments themselves.

What we need is a careful study of how existing public policies may directly or indirectly discourage investment after treaties are settled. Some of these are even now having a malignant effect on investment incentives in British Columbia. When we balance the possible consequences, we cannot conclude that settling treaties will in itself dramatically change the overall investment environment in the province. Our attention is better directed towards the broader issue of how British Columbia will be able to compete for scarce investment capital in the future, regardless of the share of Crown lands that are ultimately transferred to First Nations.

Notes

1. Many thanks to Marvin Stark for his helpful suggestions, and for providing extensive background on the land claims settlement process. John Helliwell and participants at the Laurier Institution 1996 Conference on the Economic Effects of Aboriginal Treaty Settlements provided many insightful comments on an earlier draft. They share no blame for my analysis and conclusions.

2. For economic impact estimates of treaty settlements in British Columbia, see Price Waterhouse and KPMG.

3. Some might object that the federalist model is more appropriate than the international to assess the impact of self-government by First Nations groups on investment. However, even though we do not know the exact nature of future regulatory systems, we can assume with some confidence that future investment environments in B.C. are likely to be more diverse politically and economically than they are today. These differences support the relevance of capital mobility studies.

4. For some examples, see Smith.

5. There are other rules for making investment decisions, and some are theoretically more applicable to the NPV rule under certain circumstances. However, these are not relevant to our purposes here.

6. For example, environmental regulations limiting the emission of pollutants will save home-owners money by reducing how often they have to paint their houses. They will also improve the health of people who have difficulty breathing.

7. The regulations will improve social welfare only if they create benefits for society that outweigh the costs to those involved in the regulated activities. In certain circumstances, social benefits can certainly outweigh costs to business.

8. For an extensive review of studies on foreign investment, see Globerman, "The Private and Social Interests in Outward Direct Investment."

9. The extent of this influence is unclear. For an overview of some relevant evidence, see Globerman, "The Information Highway and the Economy."

10. These arguments are discussed in Cassidy and Dale.

11. Hill makes this point.

12. For example, see Smith, p. 10.

13. See Coase.

14. See Scoffield.

15. For a fuller description, see Laghi.

16. See Cassidy and Dale, p. 54.

17. For a review of this evidence, see Globerman, "The Environmental Impacts of Trade Liberalization."

18. This argument is critically reviewed in Lippert.

19. See KMPG.

20. Lippert, p. 14.

21. Smith, p. 8.

22. We are not trying to justify KMPG's estimations, but are simply using them to illustrate the point that differences in how assets are used are important from a financial standpoint.

23. Helin, p. 1.

24. Some of this evidence is summarized in Caves and Dunning.

25. See Platiel.

26. Studies of international investment show that obligations such as increased exporting and hiring of local people discourage direct foreign investment. This in turn suggests that international investment is a relatively competitive activity. See, for example, Safarian.

27. See Price Waterhouse.

28. Research on international business highlights the importance that investors place on a clear and relatively stable property rights system.

However, current provincial government policies on setting aside land for parks and wilderness preservation, along with inconsistent policies to compensate private investors, may also be discouraging investment in the province.

29. The cases discussed are summaries of more detailed case studies in the ARA Consulting Group Inc., *Social and Economic Impacts of Aboriginal Land Claim Settlements.*

30. ARA Consulting Group Inc., p. 13.

References

ARA Consulting Group Inc. *Social and Economic Impacts of Aboriginal Land Claim Settlements: A Case Study Analysis, Final Report.* For the Ministry of Aboriginal Affairs, Province of British Columbia, and the Federal Treaty Negotiation Office. Vancouver: ARA Consulting Group Inc., December 1995.

Cassidy, Frank, and Norman Dale. *After Native Claims?* Lantzville, B.C.: Oolichan Books, 1988.

Caves, Richard. *Multinational Enterprise and Economic Analysis.* Cambridge: Cambridge University Press, 1982.

Coase, Ronald. "The Problem of Social Cost." *The Journal of Law and Economics,* Vol. III, October 1960, pp. 1–44.

Dunning, John. *Multinational Enterprises and the Global Economy.* Wokingham, England: Addison-Wesley, 1993.

Globerman, Steven. "The Environmental Impacts of Trade Liberalization." In *NAFTA and the Environment,* ed. Terry Anderson, pp. 27–44. San Francisco: Pacific Research Institute for Public Policy, 1993.

———. "The Private and Social Interests in Outward Direct Investment." In *Canadian-Based Multinationals*, ed. Steven Globerman. Calgary: University of Calgary Press, 1994.

————. "The Information Highway and the Economy." In *Implications of Knowledge-Based Growth for Microeconomic Policies,* ed. Peter Howitt, pp. 417–51. Calgary: University of Calgary Press, 1996.

Helin, Calvin. *Doing Business With Native People Makes Sense.* Victoria: Praxis, 1991.

KPMG. *Benefits and Costs of Treaty Settlements in British Columbia—A Financial and Economic Perspective.* Victoria: project report, 1996.

Laghi, Brian. "New NWT Legislature in Works." *The Globe and Mail,* 17 October 1996, p. A4.

Lippert, Owen. "Questioning the Nisga'a Agreement." *Fraser Forum.* Vancouver: The Fraser Institute, March 1996, pp. 13–15.

Platiel, Rudy. "Native Business Growing in Canada." *The Globe and Mail,* 30 October 1996, p. A8.

Price Waterhouse. *Economic Value of Uncertainty Associated with Native Claims in B.C.* Mimeograph, 1990.

Safarian, A.E. *Multinational Enterprise and Public Policy: A Study of the Industrial Countries.* Aldershot, England: Edward Elgar, 1993.

Scoffield, Heather. "Environmental, Aboriginal Issues Threaten to Delay Voisey Bay's Production." *The Financial Post,* 10 October 1996, p. 18.

Smith, Mel. "What Government Aboriginal Policy Is Doing to Canada." *Fraser Forum.* Vancouver: The Fraser Institute, March 1996, pp. 5–12.

6

The Impact of Aboriginal Title Settlements on Education and Human Capital

By Stephen McBride and Patrick Smith

The demand for Aboriginal people with post-secondary education and professional training far outstrips the numbers available. It will only increase with treaty settlements and self-government. This chapter will look at the demands treaty settlements and self-government will place on Aboriginal education and how this education may affect employment and income levels in First Nations communities. First Nations groups have had considerable success in providing educational services through their own institutions and by entering into partnerships with mainstream institutions, so the chapter will also consider the most effective content and methods for Aboriginal education. The following sections examine

- a brief profile of Aboriginal economic and social conditions, including statistics on employment, income, and education
- self-government as a solution to economic and social problems
- educational strategies such as the "human capital" approach and the "partnership" approach
- changes in the working world and their effect on Canadian workers
- federal strategies to meet the educational needs of Aboriginal peoples, including the Pathways to Success program, the subsequent

National Framework for First Nations Human Resources Development, and the Mi'kmaq and Nisga'a Agreements-in-Principle
- the outlook for First Nations education in B.C., including
  - the types of programs that will best serve the needs of First Nations
  - the language and culture components that should be included
  - whether aboriginal education programs can be completely self-sufficient
  - how First Nations programs may be financed.

A Brief Statistical Profile of Aboriginal Peoples' Economic and Social Conditions

In his last major speech in the House of Commons, Tommy Douglas drew attention to what is now obvious. "Most native people in Canada live in dire poverty. . . ; probably the blackest page in the history of this country is our treatment of native people. We robbed them of their land, we deceived them and we made promises to them which we have not kept."[1] His was a view well known to observers outside Canada. In 1974, for example, a study for the United Kingdom Minority Rights Group noted the "chronic problems of poverty, neglect and cultural and social alienation" that were the by-product of governmental "high-minded paternalism, ruthlessness, sentimentality and self-confidence."[2] It was a theme also well known to Aboriginal peoples[3] (for example, as expressed by Harold Cardinal in *The Unjust Society*).

Most recently, the Royal Commission on Aboriginal Peoples has added its voice to the general condemnation. In its 1996 final report, *People To People, Nation To Nation,* the Commission concluded that "the main policy direction, pursued for more than 150 years, first by colonial then by Canadian governments, has been wrong."[4] The consequences for Aboriginal peoples have been terrible. The movement to settling Aboriginal treaties seeks to redress some of these past wrongs. For Aboriginal peoples, looking back is the first step to gathering strength to restructure their lives.

As First Nations move toward self-government in the 1990s, many of the social and economic problems noted almost 20 years ago remain. A quick profile of Aboriginal peoples' current levels of employment, income, and education helps highlight the circumstances they face as they make ready for the changes to come.[5]

The numbers of people affected are substantial. In the *1991 Aboriginal Peoples Survey,* 388,900 people in Canada reported having Aboriginal identity: 74.14% were Indian, with 35.4% living in settlements or reserves. In British Columbia, 65,650 people (16.9% of Canada's total) identified themselves as Aboriginal: 92.9% with Indian heritage, and 33% living in settlements or reserves.

Employment

According to the *1991 Aboriginal Peoples Survey,* the official unemployment rate for Aboriginal peoples was 24.6% across Canada, and 27.8% in British Columbia. As Table 6.1 below shows, among Indian peoples, unemployment was similar overall (23.4% in Canada and 25.9% in B.C.), but higher for those living on reserves or settlements (30.8% across Canada and 33.8% in B.C.). To put this in context, the unemployment rate in all of Canada for people over 15 at the time was around 10%. An unemployment rate three times higher than the national average is just one problem faced by First Nations as they move toward treaty settlements and self-government. This significant imbalance has continued, with the least amount of people employed living on reserves.

Table 6.1: A Comparison of Unemployment Rates in Canada, 1991[6]

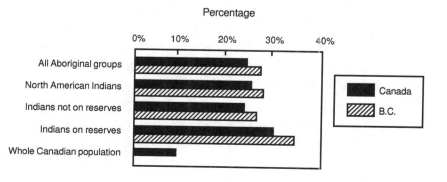

Income

The link between joblessness, underemployment, and poverty amongst First Peoples is clear when we compare levels and patterns of income. The *1991 Aboriginal Peoples Survey* found that over half (54.2%) of all Aboriginal peoples in Canada had an annual income of less than $9,999. A significant 25.2% of all adults over 15 years old had a total income of less than $2,000. Because only 59.6% of those surveyed reported *any* employment income in 1990, four out of ten Aboriginal people had no work, which is considerably above the "official" unemployment rate.

In British Columbia, the pattern was a bit better: 22.9% reported an income of $1,999 or less, and 53.9% had an income of under $10,000. In B.C., more Aboriginal peoples said they received income from employment: just under two-thirds (64.24%), which is 5% higher than for Aboriginal peoples in the country as a whole. Altogether, figures on income reveal a pattern of continuing poverty for Canada's Aboriginal peoples, with those on reserves facing the most significant levels of destitution.

Among Indian peoples, 25% had an income of under $2,000, and 55.3% earned less than $10,000. Forty-two percent reported no employment income at all. In B.C., just under one-quarter (23.4%) reported earning under $2,000. A further 31.34% reported between $2,000 and $9,999.

This pattern of depending on income from other sources leads to life at subsistence levels in many communities. The problem is more acute on reserves. Almost three in ten people living on reserves in Canada (28.7%) had an income of under $2,000 in 1990, with almost two-thirds (64.4%) reporting income of $9,999 or less. Well over half of those living on reserves (53.3%) said they received *no* income from employment. In B.C., over one-quarter (25.7%) got less than $2,000, and 62.6% had an income less than $9,999.

If we compare income earned by other Canadians, the disparities become alarmingly clear. Table 6.2 below shows income patterns according to the 1991 Canadian census and the *1991 Aboriginal Peoples Survey.*

Table 6.2: Income Received by Canadians and British Columbians in 1991

Employment Income in Canada

Percentage

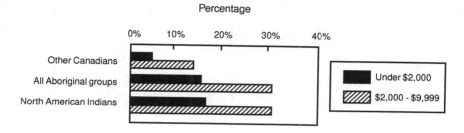

Employment Income in B.C.

Percentage

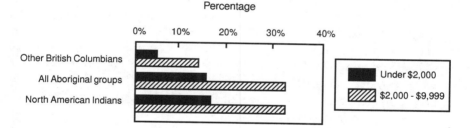

Education

When we next look at education levels, some of the barriers to getting more work and higher incomes become clear. The idea that education is a way out of the social poverty that First Peoples face is a common one. However, education alone will not overcome long-established and deep patterns of disparity, as illustrated by the United Kingdom's Educational Priority Areas (EPA) program in the 1960s and 1970s.

The British found that extra funding for special educational assistance programs in urban working-class areas failed to be enough. Social scientists like A.H. Halsey (who was involved in developing the

EPA program) and interests such as the National Children's Bureau agreed that the initiative had largely failed. Their report, *Born to Fail,* concluded that using educational reforms to remedy significant social problems was simply insufficient to overcome them. Indeed, the Bureau found that such expectations were too much to ask of the educational sector. Any real hope of significant success required broader social and economic action.[7] Similar American experiments over the past several decades, with special educational funding for inner cities and early-start programs to remedy educational imbalances in ethnic populations, produced generally similar conclusions. However, in both countries, educators and the public did note that education and educational reform had a role to play. Depending on it as the key to success was asking too much.

Such conclusions are important because of the current emphasis on education as the cure-all for the social imbalance between Aboriginal peoples and the general population. First Peoples themselves seem clear that education must be only part of an overall strategy for self-sufficiency. Two-thirds (67%) of Canada's Indian population identified joblessness as the key problem in the *1991 Aboriginal Peoples Survey,* ahead of poverty-related ills like alcohol abuse (62%), drug abuse (49%), and family violence (39%). Even on reserves and settlements where poverty has made these last issues greater problems, 78% rated unemployment highest, over alcohol abuse (73%), drug abuse (59%), and family violence (44%).

Aborginals on reserves also have the widest gap in education levels, as Table 6.3 below shows.

However, these figures mask both the changes and successes that First Nations have had in addressing this educational deficit. Between 1986 and 1991, for example, "functional illiteracy" in adult Aboriginal people dropped from 25.9% to 18.4%, the Aboriginal/non-aboriginal literacy "gap" closed from 8.6% to 4.6%. Also, more people graduated from high school, closing the gap between completion rates for Aboriginal and non-aboriginal Canadians.[8]

Apart from the question of whether First Nations can rely on education as the only tool for social change, the issue of cultural survival and control over educational institutions and programs is clearly one of prime importance for Aboriginal peoples. Whether in South

Table 6.3: Levels of Education

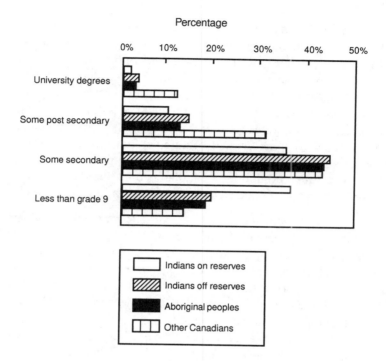

America, the Pacific, or Canada, Aboriginal people have recognized the significance of controlling educational and cultural structures and policies. Given Canada's history on constitutional matters, especially concerning Quebec, this should not come as a surprise.

The issue of control over education is a long-standing one. Twenty-five years ago, the National Indian Brotherhood presented a policy paper that argued that "the present school system is culturally alien to native students. . . . we want education to provide the setting in which our children can develop the fundamental attitudes and values which have an honoured place in Indian tradition and culture."[9] They recommended changes in education from nursery schools to the post-secondary level, in adult education and vocational training, in training programs for teachers, in alcohol and drug education, and in the language of instruction. The 1972 policy paper called on the federal government to:

> adjust its policy and practices to make possible the full participation and partnership of Indian people in all decisions and activities connected with the education of Indian children. . . . Those . . . who have had authority in all that pertained to Indian education have . . . tried various ways of providing education for Indian people. The answer to providing a successful educational experience has not been found. There is one alternative which has not been tried before: in the future, let Indian people control Indian education. . . . If this policy is recognized and implemented . . . then eventually the Indian people themselves will . . . develop an appropriate education program for their children.[10]

Has this call for change borne any fruit? Roger Cobb and Charles Elder's study of "agenda building" in public policy suggests that a process called "incubation" often occurs: "keeping a policy idea alive while the problem to which it is addressed grows."[11] Groups and people who air an important idea, like First Nations' control over their own education, play a key role in advancing such ideas in the public mind. The 1972 argument from the National Indian Brotherhood was not the first, nor would it be the last, to suggest the need to rethink control over all aspects of First Peoples' education. Cobb and Elder also remind us that in many instances of significant policy change, the gestation period between the "perceived need" or idea and the policy to address it can be long. Medicare, first posed in Canada in the 1860s to the 1880s by women who also lobbied for the vote, only arrived on the desks of decision-makers in the 1960s. The shift from relatively tentative policy papers on education by Aboriginal organizations in the 1960s and early 1970s to the more proactive stances of First Nations 25 years later is much shorter in comparison.

Self-Government as a Solution to Economic and Social Problems

Just as control over education has moved from a perceived need to the point of reality, so has the notion of Aboriginal self-government. As the federal government has recognized, "the concept . . . is not new. Aboriginal peoples . . . have long expressed their aspiration to be self-governing, to chart the future of their communities, and to make their own decisions about matters related to the preservation and development of their distinctive cultures."[12]

Section 35 of the *Constitution Act, 1982* recognized existing Aboriginal and treaty rights of the Aboriginal people of Canada. Section 25 of the Charter stated that "any aboriginal, treaty or other rights or freedoms that pertain to . . . aboriginal peoples" could not be abolished. After trying for ten years to formally amend the *Constitution Act, 1982* the new federal government of 1993 shifted to dealing with reforms through negotiations with Aboriginal peoples. The goal was "to implement a process that will allow practical progress to be made, to restore dignity to Aboriginal peoples and empower them to become self-reliant."[13]

Given that commitment, there have been high expectations for the effect self-government will have on social and economic disparities of Aboriginal life. Rick Ponting outlined the following aspirations for the self-government policy direction:

1. greater self-determination and social justice; protection of, and control over, own destiny rather than subordination to political and bureaucratic authorities based outside the ethnic group;
2. economic development to end dependency, poverty and unemployment; economic justice in the sense of a fair distribution of wealth between the Indian and non-Indian populations;
3. protection and retention of Indian culture; and
4. social vitality and development that will overcome such existing social problems as ill health, the housing crisis, irrelevant and demeaning education, and alienation (including its manifest symptoms—interpersonal violence, suicide, and the abuse of drugs and other substances).[14]

Other experts agreed that there were real advantages to explicitly recognizing the special role to be played by Indian communities, and to locate decision-making at the local level.[15] The Canadian government had recognized this by 1993: "Aboriginal governments need to be able to govern in a manner that is responsive to the needs and interests of their people. Implementation of the inherent right to self-government will provide Aboriginal groups with the necessary tools to achieve this objective."[16]

This was clear evidence that the Canadian government had begun to move in the direction of self-government, largely because of the failure to arrive at a constitutional resolution of this issue. Kathy Brock, for example, argues that:

> global forces and domestic interests have constrained the choices available to policy-makers, but within those constraints the Liberals have, in fact, distinguished themselves from their predecessors in the area of Aboriginal policy. The Liberal government has created new opportunities and begun to fundamentally alter the historical relationship between First Nations and the federal government, but it has not been through a radical and abrupt departure from the past. Instead, many of the seeds of the new relationship were sown during the previous administration. While the path is still rocky and filled with resistance, a new direction has been charted.[17]

Similarly, Radha Jhappan has noted that "self-government for land-based Indians has been an emerging reality as more bands take over the administration and sometimes design of services such as health care, resource management, economic development, child welfare and policing."[18] However, non-status, landless Aboriginal people and off-reserve registered Indians are now a majority amongst First Nations peoples, and are far less affected by these moves to self-government. The federal government recognizes this. With Inuit, Métis, and Indian groups that lack a land base, the 1995 *Federal Policy Guide: Aboriginal Self-Government* posed the possibility of developing many different arrangements for self-government, "forms of public government, devolution of programs and services, [and] the development of institutions providing services and arrangements . . . where it is feasible to exercise authority in the absence of a land base." In some instances, the government is even prepared to discuss land grants.[19]

Educational Strategies: The "Human Capital" and "Partnership" Approaches

Though it's certainly not the only answer, education can help to cure the economic deprivation of Aboriginal communities by improving the skills that individuals can bring to the labour market. In the late 1980s the federal government began to devise a labour market strategy that eventually would be extended to Aboriginal peoples. The strategy was based on two core principles: increasing the value of people through education (the "human capital" approach) and creating partnerships between leaders in the labour market (the "partnership" approach).

The human capital theory suggests that in a global economy, one of the ways to be more competitive is through a highly skilled workforce capable of high-quality production. A high level of productivity would make paying high wages possible. At the individual level, the human capital approach simply notes that a person's employability, income, and ability to adapt to a changing economy are linked to the level of education and skills the person has.[20]

The partnership principle allows labour market leaders more power by giving them more decision-making powers or privileged access to decision-makers as advisors. The assumption is that those closest to the labour market, whether at the national, sectoral, or community level, know most about it, and consequently should have a key role in the design and delivery of labour market programs.

These principles have been expressed in various federal reports,[21] in the creation of the Canadian Labour Force Development Board, and through sectoral councils. Many provinces also set up provincial labour force development boards, either in cooperation with the federal government, or on their own.

The two principles are related in that pursuing a strategy of high-quality production and high wages creates a common interest between social partners, who then have a motivation to work together to improve human resources. The tone was set by *Success in the Works*:

> What counts for Canada now are not natural advantages, but the "engineered" advantages we can create through technology, innovation and a skilled workforce. The growth industries today are those which develop the people with skills to harness technology, create a high value-added product, and improve productivity. These are the industries which will determine economic growth for the future.[22]

The report argued that the spread of information technology in particular was creating a "permanent revolution" that required continuing "remolding and upgrading of knowledge and skills."[23] In this situation workers would be faced with the task of upgrading existing skills, acquiring new skills, mastering more skills than ever before, and using them more flexibly. Such adaptability would require higher levels of education, and education that promoted flexibility, adaptation, and continuous learning. With this would go the need for better human interaction and work habits, which would demand that workers have analytical, problem-solving, communication, and interpersonal skills. The report projected that two-thirds of new jobs would require 12 years of formal education, and almost half would need 17 years of education and training. Those who don't have these qualifications will get left behind:

> Many of those who are displaced by the changing demand for some occupations will find it increasingly difficult to move into new jobs without retraining and education. . . . The workers who are most likely to be laid off are those in occupations where job growth is lowest—the jobs which require lower skills. In many cases, their options will be limited to extended unemployment, or jobs for which they lack the necessary skills . . . the probability of permanent lay-off was highest for those with lower levels of education, especially those who had not completed secondary school. Continuing education and training will play an increasingly central role in helping these workers to adjust to change.[24]

How are Aboriginal peoples to prepare themselves? A recent Canadian Labour Force Development Board report concluded that:

> Aboriginal people face a number of obstacles in their attempts to enter the work force for the first time or to return to the workforce after an absence. The social and economic status of aboriginal people is largely determined by three indicators; education, income and occupation. Current data on these three indicators clearly point out that the aboriginal population significantly lags behind the overall Canadian population in all three areas. The problem is exacerbated for the aboriginal youth whose educational level and training skills are not adequate for securing successful employment.[25]

Simply put, the wide gap between the education, occupation, and income levels of Aboriginal peoples and those of the rest of the population will not be easy to close. Overall labour market conditions have deteriorated over the past two decades, and the labour market, like other markets, is insensitive to the cultural aspirations of minorities, unless these are backed by economic power.

Better education or training alone is unlikely to be enough to guarantee a job, and better-educated Aboriginal peoples still experience higher unemployment rates than the general population. But some evidence suggests that improving education seems to increase overall levels of employment for First Nations people.[26]

However, some criticize applying the human capital approach to the labour market problems of Aboriginal peoples. Terry Wotherspoon and Vic Satzewich, for example, warn that it ignores "the underlying features of social reality, including labour market structures, that give rise to social and economic inequalities. These approaches also tend to reduce education to a matter of economic concern, thereby undermining the significance of formal education to character formation and personal development."[27]

Human capital approaches to education and training are not rooted in the cultural aspirations of Aboriginal people. They are based on the logic of the market. They alone will likely not be able to solve the economic problems from which many Aboriginal people suffer. Wotherspoon and Satzewich point out that:

> the availability of a substantial pool of low-cost labour power is crucial to the success of many aboriginal enterprises and on-reserve economic development projects. Whether managed or employed by natives or non-natives, the social and economic circumstances are such that a massive underclass of aboriginal peoples will remain a long-standing reality within the Canadian social landscape.[28]

This view is only reinforced when we consider general labour market conditions in Canada.

General Changes in the Working World and Their Effect on Canadian Workers

The free market economic policies of the 1980s and the process of structural adjustment which accompanied them, together with startling technical advances and profound changes in the world's production and marketing methods, have served effectively to stand the world of work on its collective head.[29]

The Canadian working world has undergone major transformations in the last 20 years. In many ways its condition has deteriorated to levels not seen since the 1930s. Unemployment has risen and shows no signs of diminishing much below 10%. It has now been greater than 9% for six years. The last time that occurred was in the 1930s. During the 1990 to 1993 recession, nearly a third of the labour force was unemployed for some period of time. The result is that even the steadily employed feel insecure about their jobs.[30]

The service sector has expanded as an employer, but manufacturing and primary industries, which traditionally have provided many well-paid jobs, have declined. Over 70% of workers are now employed in service industries.[31] Most new jobs being created pay low wages and are relatively unstable.[32]

Workers have also changed. The workforce is increasingly diverse, yet opportunities for jobs and incomes are unequally distributed by age, sex, region, and ethnic background. Part-time work is skewed toward young people and women.[33]

Production methods have seen radical changes too. Companies are now producing goods "just in time" for distribution, and using more casual, last-minute labour to do so. Non-standard employment—part-time, temporary jobs—has generally increased.[34] Sometimes this is the worker's choice, but often it is a substitute for full-time employment. Meanwhile, a significant number of people with jobs find themselves working longer hours. Real wages are stagnant at best. People are maintaining family incomes by bringing in two salaries and working longer hours.

Economic growth and recovery from recession are no longer creating a parallel growth in employment. All sectors of the workforce, the unemployed, the precariously employed, the fully employed, and those who usually work long hours ("the overemployed") are united by a common factor—stress.[35] Lars Osberg has characterized the situation as a "massive downloading of risk, from employer to employee, as employers have increasingly moved to replace long-term, full-time, full-year jobs with non-standard employment of casual, part-time, and temporary or self-employed workers."[36]

Ironically, unemployment and a demand for workers with specific skills exist side by side. Surveys show that a significant percentage of Canadian manufacturers have production problems because of a shortage of skilled labour.[37] This seems to point to a need for a more skilled workforce. However, other research indicates that, compared to the jobs available, the workforce is overeducated and are not using their existing skills fully enough.[38]

The government is designing social policies to end "dependency" and to increase the number of people working. However, they have been ignoring the larger context of social policy reform. High unemployment is a major problem; slow growth and recovery without the jobs to go with it is working against the success of educational or labour-market programs. The government has failed to answer the question of where substantial numbers of new jobs are going to come from. There is, after all, "a world of difference between being employable and being employed."[39] The Canadian labour market already has a surplus of trained workers. As a result, there is little payoff in adding to this surplus.[40] If anything, doing so will decrease wages even further.

At the same time, government is cutting back social programs and its "interventionist" role in general. It is increasingly confined to making policies that it claims will enable the private sector to create jobs. These are aimed at promoting flexibility and adaptability among the workforce. But another way of describing "flexibility" and "adaptability" is "insecurity." The result of all these trends is widespread unease and uncertainty among Canadian workers.

Federal Strategies to Meet the Educational Needs of Aboriginal Peoples

At first, the government overlooked the concerns of Aboriginal people during the development of a national strategy to develop the Canadian labour force. Once they corrected this omission, "it became apparent that programs and policies aimed at the wider labour market would not be sufficient to respond to the specific and growing needs and aspirations of Aboriginal Canadians."[41] Human Resources Development Canada consulted with six national Aboriginal organizations: the Assembly of First Nations, the Métis National Council, the Inuit Tapirisat of Canada, the Native Women's Association, the Native Council of Canada, and the National Association of Friendship Centres.

The consultations revealed that many Aboriginal people felt that their unique labour market needs were not being addressed.[42]

Aboriginal representatives concluded that earlier programs were ineffective and did not consider cultural differences. Previous analyses had concluded that the solution was to shift the power to make decisions about government programs to Aboriginal people themselves.[43]

The Pathways to Success program

The result was "Pathways to Success," an employment and training initiative begun in 1990 that has been described as "a process, not another new program for Aboriginal people."[44] It was based on the idea of a partnership between Human Resources Development Canada (HRDC) and Aboriginal communities.

HRDC has defined Pathways as "a partnership to co-manage programs and services related to labour market training for all Aboriginal people. The intent of the partnership was to provide a greater access and control over human resources development directed training programs and service." Its overall objectives were "to invest in and develop a trained Aboriginal labour force and to facilitate broader Aboriginal participation in the unique Aboriginal labour markets and the broader Canadian labour market."[45]

Structurally the partnership and co-management principles established through Aboriginal management boards, composed of representatives from HRDC and Aboriginal communities, set the ground rules of this partnership. They were to give a series of local Aboriginal management boards the power to decide how best to educate and train Aboriginal peoples.[46] These boards were also established at the regional and national levels.

Each local Aboriginal management board was made up of local HRDC members and representatives of district Aboriginal organizations, bands, and tribal councils. Each was supposed to have equal numbers of men and women, and where appropriate, of Aboriginal peoples living both on and off reserves. The local board was to set priorities for training and employment, taking into account HRDC program criteria and available resources.

Each regional Aboriginal management board was composed of the regional HRDC official and one Aboriginal representative from each local board in the region. The regional boards discussed how to adapt policies to increase effectiveness of programs and services for Aboriginal groups. They also set regional budgets and evaluated programs in the region.

Regional board representatives, representatives from the six national Aboriginal organizations, senior HRDC officials, and a senior adviser from Employment Equity made up the National Aboriginal Advisory Board. This board's role was to give advice on policy and program development, to approve regional budgets, and to monitor and evaluate program developments overall.

Did Pathways' strategy work? An evaluation conducted for the federal government cautiously concluded that many of the partners felt that Pathways was generally effective, but these tended to be HRDC officials rather than the Aboriginal representatives.[47]

However, board members did feel that the program had some benefits. For example, 79% of local board members thought that Pathways had led to progress in developing a training culture in their communities (though the regional boards were divided on this issue).[48] No hard data exists on the actual effect of Pathways, but the general opinion was that Aboriginal participation in labour programs other than those related to unemployment insurance was increasing. Aboriginal management boards and HRDC seemed to agree that this increased participation was due to local boards making the decisions. That said, more work needed to be done before anyone could judge which programs were most effective in achieving employment.[49]

A number of criticisms of Pathways did emerge as experience with it grew. These led the working group that conducted a structural review to propose a new arrangement that would give priority to transferring authority to the Aboriginal organizations more quickly rather than trying to develop human resources. These were some of the recommended actions:

- The new arrangement must accelerate the transfer of authority, support self-determination, and encourage new ways to deliver services, designed by the Aboriginal representatives.
- Aboriginal representatives must have control at the local, regional, and national levels over budgets and over the design and delivery of programs.
- The new relationship must be flexible enough to adapt to changes in Aboriginal government, in light of treaty settlements.
- The new arrangement must be financially responsible and accountable to the community.[50]

These recommendations hinted at shortcomings in the Pathways model, confirmed in stage two of the structural review. HRDC had kept control over budgets, which it sometimes used without consulting with Aboriginal groups. And even pilot projects like the One Agreement Model, which was designed to give greater responsibility and authority to Aboriginal management boards, did not really allow Aboriginal communities to design their own programs. There were also concerns that Aboriginal management boards had not been accountable to local communities, and had made decisions that sometimes favoured one group over another, regardless of merit.

The National Framework for Aboriginal Human Resources Development

In January 1996, the federal government, the Assembly of First Nations, the Métis National Council, and the Inuit Tapirisat signed an agreement for a new program to replace Pathways for Success: the National Framework for First Nations Human Resources Development. According to the Assembly of First Nations, the major change from the Pathways strategy was that "The federal government recognizes that

First Nations governments can not only determine labour-training strategies according to their needs and the needs of their citizens, but also extends that authority outside the reserve boundaries."[51] The Agreement was designed to ensure First Nations governments were accountable to all their constituents, including women, youth, elders, disabled persons, and urban residents. The Agreement also stated that HRDC and First Nations communities would make regional bilateral agreements. These would cover the design and delivery of programs and services to Aboriginal communities, and where possible, try to make sure skills learned were portable, by having them conform to Canadian standards.

The process of negotiating the new structures has been a long one, but a number are now in place. In early 1996, ten more were on the verge of being announced in B.C. Each will be under the direction of a regional framework agreement with First Nations, which was not foreseen when the new national framework agreement was announced, and points to political complexities within the Aboriginal community. The Regional Framework Agreement will set out a system for allocating funds. Because it will not have to use HRDC terms and conditions, each region will be free to innovate and experiment. Because of B.C.'s experience with the so-called "One Agreement Models" that gave major authority to the Aboriginal management boards under the Pathways process, officials believe that Aboriginal groups are more than able to run their own programs.[52] The effect that negotiated self-government agreements will have on the new program is not clear. However, the Regional Framework Agreement does contain provisions for self-governing communities to opt out.

The Mi'kmaq and Nisga'a Agreements

The strategy of solving education and employment problems by increasing Aboriginal autonomy has also been used in other programs, as shown by the following two examples from Nova Scotia and British Columbia.

The Mi'kmaq Agreement

On May 3, 1996, the Mi'kmaw Nation of Nova Scotia and the Government of Canada (represented by the Minister of Indian Affairs and Northern Development) signed an "Agreement-in-Principle with

Respect to Governance in Education." Indian Affairs Minister Ron
Irwin said:

> this [was] the first time in Canada that all First Nations in a prov-
> ince and the federal government have signed an agreement that
> will ultimately see those First Nations have jurisdictional con-
> trol of the education of their children. [This is an] important step
> toward the restoration of First Nations control of their very fu-
> ture, the education of their children.[53]

The significance that Aboriginal control of education has for their
cultural survival is shared across the country.

The Mi'kmaq Agreement came from joint efforts by the Department
of Indian Affairs and First Nations over much of the previous decade
to increase First Nations' control over "a major portion of the administration and programming for education to First Nation and Inuit governments."[54] It began with a proposal from the Assembly of Nova
Scotia Indian Chiefs to the Department of Indian Affairs in 1991, to
create a Mi'kmaq Education Authority to take control of First Nations
education in Nova Scotia. The following spring, the 13 Mi'kmaw
Chiefs in Nova Scotia signed a framework agreement to negotiate the
transfer of Indian Affairs educational programs to Nova Scotia First
Nations. By June 1993, the Mi'kmaw Chiefs had changed their request
to a full transfer of authority over First Nations education in Nova
Scotia.

Throughout 1994, Minister Irwin met with Mi'kmaw Chiefs, and
signed a formal agreement in November 1994. This Political Accord
committed both the Mi'kmaw and the government of Canada to negotiate the transfer of educational authority to the First Nation. Because
the *Constitution Act, 1982* gave jurisdiction for education to the provinces (section 93), the next two years were taken up with parallel negotiations with the Province of Nova Scotia.

The next step was two months of consultations within the 13
Mi'kmaw First Nations to allow community input on the program. In
February 1996, a draft Agreement-in-Principle was initialed by the 13
Mi'kmaw Chiefs and the federal government, followed by an Agree-
ment-in-Principle later in the year.

Mi'kmaw Grand Chief Ben Sylliboy commented on how significant the Agreement was for cultural survival and enhancement: "my vision for education is to encourage our children, in a safe and supportive environment, to become life-long learners, who respect themselves and others, have pride in their culture, and possess a strong desire to succeed." It was a view shared by the Head of the Mi'kmaw Education Authority (now Mi'kmaw Kina'masuti), Chief Noel Doucette Sr.: "As we go forward towards the 21st century, all Mi'kmaq should be proud to have reached this historic milestone toward taking control of education programs of all our people. . . . We now have the opportunity to make sure that our language, culture and Mi'kmaq values are truly protected in the years to come." Grand Chief Sylliboy added that he saw "this historic agreement as a first step in the process of self-government for our Nation."[55]

The basic elements of this Agreement-in-Principle include areas to be negotiated in the final agreement, such as jurisdiction over primary and secondary education, administration of the Department of Indian Affairs' post-secondary education funding, eligibility for educational services and programs, and the specific duties and structures of the Mi'kmaw Kina'masuti. The Agreement-in-Principle included a clear system for political and financial accountability, and a process to resolve disputes. It also set out several future steps, including the need to negotiate a final agreement that involved Nova Scotia, a separate funding agreement, and a second round of Mi'kmaw community consultations.[56] There are clear parallels here with the 1995 B.C.–Nisga'a Agreement-in-Principle.

The 1996 Mi'kmaq–Canada Agreement-in-Principle also recognized certain standard conditions:

- Section 91(24) of the *Constitution Act, 1982* giving the federal government jurisdiction to make laws relating to Aboriginal peoples still remained in place.
- Federal legislation was an appropriate way to implement the inherent right of self-government.
- Section 93 of the *Constitution Act, 1982* gave exclusive authority over education to the provinces.
- The Mi'kmaq Nation must "consider education a lifelong learning process which includes early childhood education, elementary, secondary, adult and post-secondary education, vocational train-

ing, culture and language as well as labour force training and adjustment."[57]

The Agreement also clearly stated the reservations and intentions of the Mi'kmaq Nation:

- The Mi'kmaq Nation intended to pursue its inherent right to self-government through negotiations leading to a treaty.
- The Agreement-in-Principle must not limit the Mi'kmaq's ability to implement the concept of the inherent right to self-government in the future.
- The Agreement must recognize the long-term intention of the Mi'kmaq Nation to have authority over their education by making future agreements.
- The Agreement "does not constitute nor should it be construed as an endorsement by the Mi'kmaq Nation . . . of Canada's policy on the implementation of the Inherent Right of Self Government." These provisions recognized that the Agreement did not extinguish any of the Mi'kmaw's Aboriginal, treaty, or other rights and freedoms.[58]

One of the Agreement's objectives was to determine exactly how "the specific governance and administrative structures through which the Mi'kmaq communities . . . shall exercise jurisdiction with respect to education. . . . on-reserve" and for post-secondary members not living on reserves. Other Aboriginal members not living on reserves would not be covered by the Agreement. However, people who were not members of the Nation but who lived on its reserves would be covered. The Mi'kmaw Kina'masuti would have overarching authority, but individual band councils would be able "to enact laws in respect to education." They would also be able "to create Community Education Boards and determine their powers, duties and functions." Where bands did not create a board, the band council would itself have those powers.[59]

The Agreement-in-Principle also allowed the Mi'kmaw Kina-masuti broad authority over related areas. They could enter into contracts and intergovernmental agreements for

- health, social, and cultural services that support educational development, such as "Head Start," child care, and special education services

- instructional issues like curriculum development, educational level equivalencies, teaching methods, programs and standards, teacher certification, teacher training and development, and evaluation of the education system
- administration of Department of Indian Affairs programs for post-secondary education
- other "culturally appropriate" educational services covered in the Final Agreement.[60]

The Agreement also set out requirements for fair and understandable processes for selecting board members, for how community education boards were to use their authority, and for appeal procedures. Systems for political, administrative, and financial accountability (such as conflict of interest rules, accounting audits, and administrative reviews) were also to be equitable and clear.

A separate process to resolve disputes was included in the Agreement. It moved from information exchange to mediation after three months, arbitration after an additional three months, and a final referral to the appropriate court if arbitration failed.[61] Funding arrangements were to be determined in the Final Agreement. This recognized the need for separate negotiations with the Province to settle the funding of provincial education responsibilities. The Agreement-in-Principle also included a four-page appendix on funding. It provided for five-year terms (with one-year notice on changes or continuance), and set criteria for budgetary controls, reporting, and other financial matters.[62]

While the Mi'kmaq Agreement-in-Principle was just that—not a legally binding document—it was intended to guide discussions toward a Final Agreement and to support discussions with the Province on harmonizing education laws and providing education services in Nova Scotia.[63] The provincial Liberal Government led by John Savage has so far actively participated in the process. This is important, because a separate agreement with the Province is the most likely subsequent requirement. The Final Agreement requires community approval from each of the 13 Nova Scotia bands parties to the agreement.

Like the Nisga'a Agreement-in-Principle on land, resource use, and self-government in British Columbia, the Mi'kmaq Agreement is important as a first model of new arrangements for education, and for jurisdictional transfer to First Nations. How well First Nations communities themselves receive it, how other societies in the province respond to it, and how the Agreement-in-Principle moves to Final Agreement will be central to its success, and to whether it stands as an example to the rest of the country.

The Nisga'a Agreement

In British Columbia, the Nisga'a Agreement-in-Principle of 1996 recognized the long struggle for a just and equitable settlement of the land question. It had included Nisga'a Chiefs travelling to Victoria to demand title recognition in 1887, the Nisga'a Petition to the Privy Council in 1913, and the lengthy Supreme Court of Canada "land" case, *Calder v. British Columbia (Attorney General),* which in 1973 laid the groundwork for the first modern treaty in British Columbia. Canada and the Nisga'a began negotiations after the *Calder* decision in 1976. With the province of British Columbia joining in 1990, the potential for agreement increased. This direct provincial involvement was distinct from the Nova Scotia Mi'kmaq case, where separate provincial negotiations followed the Agreement.

The primary motivation of the Nisga'a for self-government was not to gain control of education, but to gain clear title to land and resources. Economic development was the primary focus, so administration of justice, financial transfers, and taxation were included in the Agreement. Much of the cultural focus was on heritage and repatriation of Nisga'a artifacts.

Preservation of culture and language was discussed in the context of the Nisga'a legislative powers. Among other related powers, the Agreement gave the Nisga'a the authority to make laws

- to preserve and develop Nisga'a culture and language
- on aspects of Nisga'a culture and their relationship to employment
- to regulate education on Nisga'a lands, from pre-school to grade 12, including the teaching of language and culture
- to regulate post-secondary education on Nisga'a lands, including the establishment of and curriculum for post-secondary institutions, certification of teachers and researchers, and adult education comparable to provincial standards.[64]

There was little in the Agreement specific to training beyond the general matters of authority over education. However, given more than 100 years of focus on getting recognition of Nisga'a rights to land and resources, this was not surprising.

The Outlook for First Nations Education in B.C.

What types of programs will best serve the needs of First Nations?

If the Nisga'a and Mi'kmaq Agreements-in-Principle become models for other agreements and settlements, the trend has already been established for autonomous education programs. First Nations themselves are providing their own answers to the question of what types of educational programs will best prepare them for self-government.

Across the country, Aboriginal peoples have a successful record in effective partnerships with mainstream institutions. In British Columbia, all but one of the community colleges have developed programs for Aboriginal students and on Aboriginal subjects, for example. Many of these are delivered in various Aboriginal communities. All are centred in Aboriginal involvement. Some programs, such as at Northwest College and Malaspina College, are quite extensive.

Each of the five public universities in British Columbia has also developed programs for Aboriginal students and on Aboriginal issues. Like the college sector, most of these have been developed in consultation with various First Nations communities and organizations. Examples include Simon Fraser University's (SFU) Shuswap Program, the University of Victoria's Certificate Program in the Administration of Aboriginal Governments, its Child and Youth Care Diploma (now being piloted with the Meadow Lake Tribal Council in Saskatchewan, with federal funding support), and its Law School Aboriginal Program. The University of British Columbia (UBC) has developed a First Nations House of Learning, and the University of Northern British Columbia (UNBC) has established First Nations Studies Bachelor and Master of Arts programs. As the province's newest and only northern university, the UNBC initiatives have been significant.

In all the public post-secondary institutions, Aboriginal programs have major First Nations definition and involvement. B.C.'s Open

University and Open College offer distance education programs in conjunction with Aboriginal institutions like the Institute of Indigenous Government. These programs focus on skills training often related to areas that First Nations communities have identified as social concerns: alcohol, drug and sexual abuse counselling; child and youth care; community economic development; self-government administration; and broader indigenous studies. Many now include an important language component.

Given the push toward Aboriginal self-government in the 1990s, a parallel trend has been emerging: the creation of separate Aboriginal post-secondary institutions. Whether in Nova Scotia with the Mi'kmaq Agreement-in-Principle, or in B.C. with the Nisga'a model, First Nations are already in the education business. In British Columbia, many new Aboriginal institutions reflect this newer educational structure. Because control of education is a linchpin of cultural support and enhancement, and First Nations have a strong desire and need to ensure culturally sensitive curriculum and structures, issues of controlling education seem likely to magnify.[65]

Both the Nicola Valley Institute of Technology and the Vancouver-centred Institute of Indigenous Government reflect the desire for more direct educational control as a centrepiece of maintaining and enhancing Aboriginal cultures. Both clearly signal that First Nations peoples intend to provide their own answers to the question of what skills they need to better place their people in productive economies. Whether this suggests a shift away from the standards of the larger educational community or from those of the general labour market remains to be seen. Surveys and actual program choices suggest a continuing harmonization of standards. In the short term, this is likely to remain the case. These relatively new post-secondary institutions are initially offering Associate of Arts degrees and diplomas (usually two-year programs). As the programs develop into full degree and postgraduate training, more changes may occur. Because institutions need to give students the benefits of transferability, there will always be a need for broader programming, while still allowing for the development of more community-based programs and training. Given the current education deficit, basic upgrading and skills training will be important goals and needs at present. Though there has been some improvement, for example in basic functional literacy, such changes take time.

At the Nicola Valley Institute of Technology (NVIT), established in 1983, the range of programs is considerable, from basic adult education, Addiction Counselling Certificates, Sex Abuse Worker training, College Preparation and Transition studies, and certificates and diplomas in Natural Resource Technology to diplomas and degrees in Aboriginal Community Economic Development, Academic and Administrative Studies, Fine Arts and Indigenous Studies, and Social Work. Many of NVIT's programs are offered off-campus in communities, and in association with parallel programs at provincial universities and colleges such as SFU's Community Economic Development Program. Begun by five area bands, NVIT became a publicly accredited Aboriginal Provincial Institute in September 1995. With 250 students from 195 First Nations Bands, and over 600 others enrolled in community-based, distance, and extension courses across Canada, NVIT has the legal authority to grant certificates, diplomas, and associate degrees, and the right to set its own curriculum through an Indigenous Education Philosophy. In keeping with the more proactive Aboriginal stance on education and training, NVIT is "dedicated to the assertion of its First Nations identity."[66]

Vancouver's newer Institute of Indigenous Government grew out of a 1991 Union of British Columbia Indian Chiefs initiative, and gained support from HRDC's Pathways strategy. It opened in September 1995 as an Aboriginal Provincial Institute with 15 students. It now has approximately 100 full-time students and aims to have 350 by the year 2000. It is an accredited post-secondary institution controlled by Aboriginal peoples, and offers education programs to develop the educational, social, and economic leadership skills of indigenous students.

Given its support by the Union of British Columbia Indian Chiefs, and their opposition to the Department of Indian Affairs' negotiation process,[67] it is not surprising that the Institute of Indigenous Government was established through the Pathways program. In 1993, B.C.'s Ministry of Skills, Training and Labour funded workshops on First Nations economic development, self-government, administration, land research, and library management. Growing out of these, the Institute's first programs were organized into four core areas of specialization: Political Development and Leadership, Indigenous Government Administration, Economic and Social Development, and International Indigenous Relations. Again seeking "to distance itself from the federal Department of Indian Affairs . . . because of its historical treatment of native people,"[68] government funding for the Institute has been split between the B.C. Ministry of Education, Skills and Training and Human Resource Development Canada. Initial government funding was $1.4 million, growing over three years to $1.88 million.[69]

By 1999 the Institute of Indigenous Government expects to offer a four-year Bachelor of Arts degree in Indigenous Government Studies. By its initial two-year agreement, the Institute's accreditation for its Associate Arts degree is given jointly with B.C.'s Open University, to give students maximum flexibility. With the Aboriginal students' drop-out rate being 60% higher than for other Canadians, the Institute hopes to keep students in school for their full term.

Because Aboriginal control of education has become an integral part of the move to self-government, post-secondary institutions devoted to Aboriginal studies have banded together to support this important goal. The Association of Aboriginal Post Secondary Institutes (APSI) (founded in the late 1980s as the First Nations Association of Post Secondary Institutes) now has 17 members, 16 of whom are "voting members" because of their status as Aboriginal-controlled institutions. Apart from UBC's Native Indian Education Program, Aboriginal institution members come from

- Vancouver Island (Chemainus Native College, Saanich Indian School Board, and Victoria Native Friendship Centre)
- central Vancouver (Sechelt Indian Education, Toll:Lthlet Centre in Mission, and the Vancouver Native Education Centre)
- the Interior (AAPSI Education Resource Centre in Westbank, En'owkin Centre in Penticton, Mestanta Technical Institute in Lytton, Nicola Valley Institute of Technology in Merritt, Secwepema Cultural Education Centre in Kamloops)
- the North (Prince George Native Friendship Centre, Tl'azt'en Nation Learning Centre in Fort St. James, and Wilp Wilxo'oskwhl Nisga'a in New Aiyansh)
- the Coast (North Coast Tribal Council Education Centre in Prince Rupert and Helitsuk College in Waglisla).

The larger urban institutes offer more of their own programming. More remote ones work in partnerships, often with B.C.'s Open University, for many of their programs.

Membership in the Association is open to any institution providing Aboriginal education. Its mission is to provide services to communities and organizations for the development of effective Aboriginal education programs. It directly involves Aboriginal communities in program development, delivery, and evaluation. It also reflects Aboriginal culture, interests, and issues. Many of these new institutions are already under pressure from various First Nations to expand their programs, for example from Associate Arts degrees to Bachelor of Arts and postgraduate degrees, and across a broader range of subject areas.

What components of First Nations languages and culture should be included?

The First Nations themselves, whether in UNBC's First Nations Studies programs or in their own developing programs, say that language and culture are central. This same view is reflected in *People to People, Nation to Nation,* the 1996 report of the Royal Commission on Aboriginal Peoples. All see education as central to protecting culture and heritage, and to healing damage done by past practices.

Canada's Aboriginal peoples are not alone in this view. In Mapuche, Chile, for example, the local community was so worried that tying its elementary school to a national computer would mean the loss of its Aboriginal culture that it disconnected the computer link. Each statement on Aboriginal education and each argument for Aboriginal control centres on cultural and linguistic issues. As Aboriginal communities gain control of their educational systems as part of broader self-government, this focus will only grow. Education here is both an end and a means.

How self-sufficient can Aboriginal programs be?

How much can First Nations provide for their own education? Whether in Nova Scotia or British Columbia, the answer to the question of how self-sufficient First Nations education programs can be appears to be the same: more than we might think. Even if Aboriginal institutions continue to adapt their programs, policies, and administration to better meet the needs of Aboriginal peoples, they will need to cooperate with public post-secondary institutions to allow Aboriginal students access to a broad range of disciplinary studies.

At the core, however, for basic education, community economic development, and self-government administration, First Nations clearly intend to offer their own programs. This will require both government funding and agreements with provincial ministries. Because it is a basic component of self-government, self-education will become the norm.

How will First Nations programs be financed?

The model of the Institute of Indigenous Government is one approach to funding. That is, funding does not have to come from the Department of Indian Affairs and Northern Development, but could come from provincial ministries of education, Human Resource Development Canada, and local communities. The early positive track record of First Nations educational initiatives supports the conclusion that this trend will only increase.

Conclusion: Routes to Success

Various modern routes to agreements, treaties, and self-government exist and are being tried in Canada. To be successful, these new relationships between Aboriginal and non-Aboriginal peoples will need to be based on the four principles identified by the Royal Commission: recognition, respect, sharing, and responsibility.[70]

One clear conclusion is that no one route will work for all. Different circumstances, differing local concerns, and a variety of settlement standings will continue to dictate a diverse approach. The Royal Commission came to a similar conclusion:

> the importance of recognizing diversity for public policy is this: no one answer will do for all Aboriginal people. No one model— be it self-government, healing centre or housing design—will speak to all Aboriginal nations. Just as there are many voices, there must be many responses.[71]

Whatever the approach, on everything from education to self-government, Aboriginal communities must themselves determine the form and content.

Notes

1. Lovick, p. 276.

2. Wilson, p. 23.

3. In this chapter, we use "Aboriginal peoples" or "First Peoples" as an inclusive term, to mean people of Indian, Inuit, and Métis origin. We use "Indian" to refer to people strictly of Indian origin, living on or off reserves. (See *People to People, Nation to Nation.*)

4. Royal Commission on Aboriginal Peoples, "A Word From Commissioners," in *Highlights,* p.1.

5. These three key socio-economic indicators were used by the Canadian Labour Force Development Board, in its 1994 Report *Aboriginal Peoples Making Transitions.*

6. Tables 6.1, 6.2, and 6.3 were produced from the following data:

- *The 1991 Aboriginal Peoples Survey,* including subsequent special reports such as *Language, Tradition, Health, Lifestyle and Social Issues* (Catalogue 89-552, Statistics Canada), *Age and Sex* (Catalogue 94-327, Statistics Canada), and *Schooling, Work and Related Activities, Income, Expenses and Mobility* (Catalogue 89-534)
- the 1991 and 1996 *Canadian Census,* including such special reports as the *Profile of Canada's Aboriginal Population* (Catalogue 94-325)
- various Department of Indian Affairs and Northern Development publications, such as *Highlights of Aboriginal Conditions,* 1991, 1986: *Demographic, Social and Economic Characteristics* (Ottawa: Department of Indian Affairs and Northern Development, October 1995); and *Basic Departmental Data, 1995* (January 1996)
- The Royal Commission on Aboriginal Peoples, including separate volumes such as *Gathering Strength* (Vol. 3), *Perspectives and Realities* (Vol. 4), and various background studies, like *Bridging the Cultural Divide: A Report on Aboriginal People and the Justice System* (1995).

7. Wedge and Prosser.

8. *The 1991 Aboriginal Peoples Survey,* p. 108.

9. National Indian Brotherhood, p. 2, p. 9.

10. National Indian Brotherhood, pp. 27–38, p. 31.

11. Cobb and Elder, "The Politics of Agenda-Building," pp. 892–915; and *Participation in American Politics.*

12. Government of Canada, *Federal Policy Guide: Aboriginal Self-Government,* p. 1.

13. Government of Canada, *Federal Policy Guide: Aboriginal Self-Government,* p. 2.

14. Ponting, p. 359.

15. Schaan.

16. Government of Canada, *Federal Policy Guide: Aboriginal Self-Government,* p. 2.

17. Brock, p. 190.

18. Jhappan, p. 175.

19. Government of Canada, *Federal Policy Guide: Aboriginal Self-Government,* p. 19.

20. For example, see Riddell, pp. 127–44.

21. Government of Canada, *Success in the Works* and *Adjusting to Win.*

22. *Success in the Works,* p. 2.

23. *Success in the Works,* p. 5.

24. *Success in the Works,* p. 10.

25. Canadian Labour Force Development Board, p. 1.

26. Clatworthy, p. 25.

27. Satzewich and Wotherspoon, p. 115.

28. Satzewich and Wotherspoon, p. 145.

29. International Labour Office, p. 87.

30. Advisory Group, p. 33.

31. Betcherman and Lowe, p. 26.

32. *Financial Post,* 29 April 1995.

33. Morissette et al.; and Habtu.

34. Shields.

35. Advisory Group, p. 7.

36. Osberg, p. 66.

37. Government of Canada, *Success in the Works,* p. 2.

38. Livingstone, pp. 83–86.

39. Osberg, pp. 57–58.

40. Osberg, p. 61.

41. Eberts, pp. 131–32.

42. Universalia, p. 2.

43. Young and McDermott.

44. Eberts, p. 130.

45. Human Resources Development Canada, *Structural Review: Stage 1,* p. 1.

46. Universalia, p. 3.

47. Universalia, p. 17.

48. Universalia, p. 16.

49. Universalia, pp. 68–69.

50. Human Resources and Development Canada, *Structural Review: Stage 1,* p. 7.

51. Assembly of First Nations, p.1.

52. Interview, HRDC official, 6 January 1997. (All interviews were conducted on terms of confidentiality.)

53. Joint Government of Canada–Mi'kmaw Kina'masuti (Education) news release, p. 1.

54. Mi'kmaw Kina'masuti (Education) "Backgrounder."

55. Joint Government of Canada—Mi'kmaw news release, pp. 1–2.

56. Mi'kmaw Kina'masuti (Education) "Backgrounder," p. 2.

57. Mi'kmaq Agreement-in-Principle, May 1996, p.2.

58. Mi'kmaq Agreement, p. 5.

59. Mi'kmaq Agreement, pp. 4–7.

60. Mi'kmaq Agreement, p. 7.

61. Mi'kmaq Agreement, p. 9.

62. Mi'kmaq Agreement, p. 11; pp. 15–18.

63. Mi'kmaq Agreement, p. 61.

64. Nisga'a Agreement-in-Principle, pp. 71–77.

65. See Gaskell, *Secondary Schools in Canada,* for a discussion of such issues. See also the accompanying 21 case studies of *Secondary Schools in Canada,* CEA, 1996. Several of these profile native studies in the Exemplary Schools Project, such as at Vancouver Technical Secondary School in B.C. and the Peguis School north of Winnipeg, Manitoba.

66. Nicola Valley Institute of Technology, p. 5.

67. Stated by President Chief Saul Terry, in the *Globe and Mail,* 12 August 1995.

68. Paul Chartrand, President of the Institute of Indigenous Government, quoted in *Ubyssey,* 23 January 1996, p. 3; and Chief Saul Terry, quoted in the *Vancouver Sun,* 27 December 1995: p. B1.

69. Interview, Official from the British Columbia Ministry of Skills, Training, and Labour, October 1996.

70. Royal Commission on Aboriginal Peoples, *People to People, Nation to Nation,* Vol. 1.

71. Royal Commission on Aboriginal Peoples, *Highlights,* Vol. 4, pp. 15–16.

References

Advisory Group. *Report of the Advisory Group on Working Time and the Distribution of Work*. Ottawa: Human Resources and Development Canada, 1994.

Assembly of First Nations. *Press Release,* 23 January 1996.

Banting, Keith G., and Charles M. Beach, eds. *Labour Market Polarization and Social Policy Reform*. Kingston, Ont.: Queen's University School of Policy Studies, 1995.

Banting, Keith G., and Ken Battle, eds. *A New Social Vision for Canada?* Kingston, Ont.: Queen's University School of Policy Studies/Caledon Institute of Social Policy, 1994.

Betcherman, Gordon, and Graham Lowe. *The Future of Work in Canada*. Ottawa: Canadian Policy Research Networks, 1997.

Brock, Kathy. "Aboriginal People: First Nations." In *Canadian Public Policy: Globalization and Political Parties,* eds. Andrew F. Johnson and Andrew Stritch. Toronto: Copp Clark, 1996.

Canadian Labour Force Development Board. *Aboriginal Peoples Making Transitions*. Ottawa: CFLDB, 1994.

———. *Labour Force Development Review: Research Report 6*. Ottawa: CLFDB, 1994.

Cardinal, Harold. *The Unjust Society: TheTtragedy of Canada's Indians*. Edmonton: Hurtig, 1969.

Clatworthy, Stewart J. "The Effects of Education on Native Behaviour in the Urban Labour Market." Ottawa: Federal Task Force on Labour Market Development, Department of Employment and Immigration, 1981.

Cobb, Roger, and Charles Elder. "The Politics of Agenda Building: An Alternative Perspective for Modern Democratic Theory," *Journal of Politics*. Vol. 33, No.4, November 1971, pp. 892–915.

———. *Participation in American Politics: The Dynamics of Agenda Building*. Boston: Allyn and Bacon, 1972.

———. *Participation in American Politics*. Baltimore, Md.: Johns Hopkins University Press, 1983.

Dunk, Thomas, Stephen McBride, and Randle Nelsen, eds. *The Training Trap*. Halifax: Fernwood, 1996.

Eberts, Tina. "Pathways to Success: Aboriginal Decision-Making in Employment and Training." In *Aboriginal Self-Government in Canada: Current Trends and Issues,* ed. John H. Hylton. Saskatoon: Purich Publishing, 1994.

Gaskell, Jane. *Secondary Schools in Canada*. Toronto: Canadian Education Association, 1995.

Government of Canada. *Success in the Works: A Profile of Canada's Emerging Workforce*. Ottawa: Supply and Services Canada, 1989.

————. *Adjusting to Win: Report of the Advisory Council on Adjustment*. Ottawa: Employment and Immigration Canada, 1989.

————. *Federal Policy Guide: Aboriginal Self Government*. Ottawa: Public Works and Government Services, 1995.

————. *Highlights of Aboriginal Conditions 1991, 1986*. Ottawa: Department of Indian Affairs and Northern Development, 1995.

————. *Success in the Works: A Labour Force Development Strategy for Canada*. Ottawa: Employment and Immigration Canada, 1989.

Habtu, Roman. "Labour Market Developments in Canada." In the CLFDB's *Labour Force Development Review,* 1994.

Human Resources and Development Canada. *Pathways to Success Structural Review; Stage 1: Report and Recommendations*. Ottawa: mimeograph, 1995.

————. *Pathways to Success Structural Review; Stage II: Strategic Directions: Options for Consideration*. Ottawa: mimeograph, 1995.

Hylton, John H., ed. *Aboriginal Self-Government in Canada: Current Trends and Issues*. Saskatoon: Purich Publishing, 1994.

International Labour Office. *World Labour Report 1995*. Geneva: ILO, 1995.

Jhappan, Radha. "The Federal-Provincial Power-grid and Aboriginal Self-Government." In *New Trends in Canadian Federalism,* eds. Francois Rocher and Miriam Smith. Peterborough: Broadview, 1995.

Joint Government of Canada–Mi'kmaw Kina'masuti (Education) news release, 3 May 1996.

Johnson, Andrew F., Stephen McBride, and Patrick J. Smith, eds. *Continuities and Discontinuities: The Political Economy of Social Welfare and Labour Market Policy in Canada*. Toronto: University of Toronto Press, 1994.

Johnson, Andrew F., and Andrew Stritch, eds. *Canadian Public Policy: Globalization and Political Parties*. Toronto: Copp Clark, 1996.

Leslie, Peter. "The Economic Framework: Fiscal and Monetary Policy." In *Canadian Public Policy: Globalization and Political Parties,* eds. Andrew F. Johnson and Andrew Stritch. Toronto: Copp Clark, 1996.

Livingstone, David. "Wasted Education and Withered Work: Reversing the 'Post-Industrial' Education-Jobs Optic." In *The Training Trap,* eds. Thomas Dunk et al. Halifax: Fernwood, 1996.

Lovick, L. Dale, ed. "Last Words: A Minority Report on Canada's Future." In *Tommy Douglas Speaks*. Vancouver: Douglas and McIntyre, 1979.

Mi'kmaw Kina'masuti (Education), "Backgrounder," 3 May 1996.

Morissette, René, John Myles, and Garnett Picard. "Earnings Polarization in Canada, 1969–1991." In *Labour Market Polarization and Social Policy Reform,* eds. Keith G. Banting and Charles M. Beach. Kingston, Ont.: Queen's University School of Policy Studies, 1995.

National Indian Brotherhood. *Indian Control of Indian Education Policy Paper.* Ottawa: National Indian Brotherhood, 1972.

Nicola Valley Institute of Technology. *Introducing NVIT*. Merritt: NVIT, 1996.

Osberg, Lars. "Jobs and Growth: The Missing Link." In *A New Social Vision for Canada?* eds. Keith Banting and Ken Battle. Kingston, Ont.: Queen's University School of Policy Studies/Caledon Institute of Social Policy, 1994.

Paul, Danny. *We Were Not the Savages: A Micmac Perspective on the Collision of European and Aboriginal Civilization.* Halifax: Nimbus Publishing, 1993.

Ponting, Rick. "The Impact of Self-Government on Indian Communities." In *Arduous Journey: Canadian Indians and Decolonization*. Toronto: McClelland and Stewart, 1986.

Riddell, W. Craig. "Human Capital Formation in Canada: Recent Developments and Policy Responses." In *Labour Market Polarization and Social Policy Reform,* eds. Keith G. Banting and Charles M. Beach. Kingston, Ont.: Queen's University School of Policy Studies, 1995.

Royal Commission on Aboriginal Peoples. *People to People, Nation to Nation: Highlights from the Report of the Royal Commission on Aboriginal Peoples*. Ottawa: Minister of Supply and Services Canada, November 1996.

Satzewich, Vic, and Terry Wotherspoon. *First Nations: Race, Class and Gender Relations*. Toronto: Nelson Canada, 1993.

Schaan, Gary. "Holistic Social and Health Services in Indian Communities." In *Continuities and Discontinuities: The Political Economy of Social Welfare and Labour Market Policy in Canada,* eds. Andrew F. Johnson et al. Toronto: University of Toronto Press, 1994.

Shields, John. "'Flexible' Work, Labour Market Polarization, and the Politics of Skills Training and Enhancement." In *The Training Trap,* eds. Thomas Dunk et al. Halifax: Fernwood, 1996.

Statistics Canada (Schooling, Work and Related Activities: Income, Expenses and Mobility). *1991 Aboriginal Peoples Survey.* Ottawa: Government of Canada, 1992, Catalogue 89–534.

Universalia. *Assessment of the Pathways to Success Strategy: Final Report to the National Aboriginal Management Board*. Montreal: Universalia, 1994.

Wedge, Peter, and Hilary Prosser. *Born to Fail*. London: Arrow, 1977.

Wilson, James. *Canada's Indians*. Report 21 at the Minority Rights Group. London: Minority Rights Group, 1974.

Young, R.A., and P. McDermott. "Employment Training Programs and Acculturation of Native Peoples in Canada's Northwest Territories." *Arctic,* September 1988.

7

Unlocking the Medicine Chest:

The Implications of Transferring Control of Health Services to First Nations

By Lee Morrison and David Fish

This chapter focuses on how transferring control and management of health services to First Nations will affect both the health of both Aboriginal communities and British Columbia's economy. It starts by looking at the current health status of B.C. First Nations.

From there, the discussion moves in two rather different directions. First it examines how the conditions of self-government might improve the health of Aboriginal people. It then addresses the issue of how the federal and provincial governments can best transfer funds to control and manage health care. The chapter identifies the current sources of funding for First Nations health services both on and off reserves, and finally, closes with a discussion of how transferring control of health care will affect the B.C. economy.

The Health Status of B.C. First Nations

This section highlights measures of health that usually guide the development of health care policy and help decision-makers choose appropriate health care programs. All of the data reported here comes from *A Statistical Report on the Health of First Nations in British Columbia,* a report by Health Canada that compiles statistics from a variety of sources for the years 1987 to 1992.[1]

Life expectancy

One overall indicator of how healthy First Nations people are is how long they are expected to live. The 1982 to 1985 average life expectancy for Aboriginal men was 63.2 years, compared to 73.3 years for other B.C. men. For Aboriginal women, life expectancy was 74.2 years, compared to 80.8 for women in the rest of the province.[2] These shorter life expectancies are the result of higher death rates for infants, teenagers, and young adults.

The Health Canada report notes that if we took the higher levels of disability and illness into account, we would see "an even greater discrepancy between First Nations and non-First Nations in terms of disability-free life expectancy at birth (that is, the number of years expected to be lived free of serious disabilities)." The report comments that this wider gap would actually be a more accurate reflection of the overall quality of life for First Nations people.[3]

Birth rates and infant death

The general birth rate for First Nations people is double that of other British Columbians, but the birth rate for teenage Aboriginal mothers is four times the provincial rate. This substantially higher rate also contributes to higher numbers of premature births and stillbirths. The Health Canada report believes these higher infant mortality rates are caused by "poor nutrition, cigarette smoking, and alcohol and substance abuse."[4]

The number of infant deaths is another key indicator of a population's health status. From 1987 to 1992, 13.9 First Nations infants died for every 1,000 live births, a rate about twice that of the province (7.4). Mortality rates for neonatal babies, however, were similar to provincial rates. That means the major causes of the higher infant death rate are those that occur after birth, such as respiratory disease (especially sudden infant death syndrome), accidents, and diarrhea.[5]

The favourable neonatal rate is undoubtedly due to the medical and nursing attention given to birth itself. The high death rates of Status Indian infants probably have their roots in "adverse environmental conditions," which may include not only physical surroundings and nutrition, but also parenting skills, alcohol use, and smoking. This relationship between infant death rates, neonatal mortality, and post-neonatal mortality has been similar to those in other provinces for at least 30 years.

Causes of lower life expectancies

"Age standardized mortality rates" (ASMRs) tell us some of the reasons why First Nations people have lower life expectancies. The Health Canada report showed that the overall death rate for First Nations people is double that for other British Columbians. First Nations have higher ASMRs for digestive system diseases (four times higher than the provincial rate), chronic liver disease and cirrhosis (five times higher), motor vehicle traffic accidents (5.7 times higher), suicide (3.8 times higher), and alcohol-related deaths (5 times higher).

Status Indians have about twice the provincial rates of infectious and parasitic diseases, diabetes, respiratory system failures, and accidental falls. Rates for cancer, circulatory system diseases, and asthma are similar to those for other British Columbians.

Only a small number of Status Indian deaths can be traced to one specific cause (such as lung cancer). This may be blocking our ability to see patterns in the causes of death. Nevertheless, the overall picture suggests that the high death rate is due to environmental and social causes that usually affect First Nations people in the earlier years of their lives.

Using ASMRs allows researchers to make adjustments for the different age structures of the population. The full impact of patterns in causes of death appears in the "raw" data. It tells us that 1,998 Status Indians died between 1987 and 1992 due to circulatory diseases, strokes, coronary heart disease, and cancer. However, 1,319 died from "external" causes, including motor vehicle traffic accidents, poisoning, falls, and suicide. In the same time period, 151,043 other British Columbians died from the chronic diseases, and 18,864 from "external" causes. These actual numbers of deaths, as opposed to the comparative ASMRs, are a stark signal of where priorities should be for future strategies to improve the health of Status Indians.

Disability

Not only are mortality rates higher among Status Indians, but rates of disability among the population are higher, too. "Disability" covers faculties like mobility, agility, hearing, speaking, seeing, and mental disabilities. The Health Canada report shows the following disability rates for B.C. Aboriginal peoples:

- from ages 15 to 24, 22.9% are disabled
- from ages 25 to 34, 25.6% are disabled
- from ages 35 to 54, 38% are disabled
- from age 55 and over, 72.7% are disabled.[6]

The report does not give comparative figures for the rest of the B.C. population, but they are about triple those for the rest of Canada for all age groups up to 55 years. Rates for Aboriginal adults 55 years and older are 50% higher than for the general population.

Clearly the health of Aboriginal adults is considerably poorer than that of other B.C. adults, which likely affects their ability to be economically productive.

Chronic diseases

According to the *1991 Aboriginal Peoples Health Survey*, 30% of "Canadian Indians" 15 years and older reported that they had a chronic health problem. In British Columbia, out of the 6,100 people living on reserves who reported chronic health problems, 57% said they had arthritis and rheumatism, 35% reported high blood pressure, and more than 20% had heart problems, bronchitis, or emphysema.

No comparative figures for the rest of the Canadian population are available. However, we can still see that there are significant numbers of Aboriginal people whose everyday health and activities are compromised in some way.

Interestingly, while diabetes is reported by 14% of those who have chronic diseases, the B.C. rate for diabetes was the lowest of the Canadian provinces in 1990. However, the Health Canada report also quotes a detailed study that shows the diabetes rates have increased by 77% for the total population (and 40% for ages 35 and over) from 1987 to 1995.[7] This suggests diabetes will be a major health problem in B.C. First Nations communities. Aggressive and extensive programs will be necessary to prevent the disabilities and advanced chronic diseases (like end state renal disease) that have troubled the First Nations in eastern Canada.

How Will Treaty Settlements Affect Aboriginal Health?

The disturbing data on the health of Aboriginal people is a dramatic backdrop against which we must assess the process of land settlements. These high rates of illness and death are caused largely by the social and economic status that has been thrust on the First Nations by the dominant culture. Centuries of colonization have brought policies that have swung between isolating the First Nations from the mainstream in remote reserves with no economic support other than from the government, and attempting to integrate them into the dominant culture.

As a result, First Nations communities have found themselves in conditions of economic deprivation. Perhaps more significantly, they have not had access to vehicles of economic development (such as capital), access to natural resources (which had previously been theirs), and education (which might have helped them compete within the larger culture). When treaties are settled that incorporate principles of self-government, and provide access to natural resources, capital, and operating funds, the First Nations will face a new era in which they control their economic future. Communities can control the paths to economic development, and traditional cultural values and ways of life can be restored to full harmony with those of the larger culture.

This process will take time, perhaps several generations. But economic development and the healing process have already begun. Bands across the country are already planning for economic development and seeking ways to ensure that not only children but all those involved in economic activity and public service can get the education they need. They are ensuring that First Nations have access to safe water and housing, and that their nutrition is both consistent with their traditional ways and with current Western ideals of healthy diets.

In the area of health, First Nations communities have re-embraced traditional ways of healing. They have begun to deal with the problems of social disorganization and lack of moral foundations that are reflected in alcohol and drug abuse, domestic and community violence, and the alienation of the young people from their culture.

How current health programs and future treaty settlements affect the health of the First Nations will not be immediate. In fact, we can predict that indicators such as life expectancy, chronic diseases that arise from social and economic deprivation, and conditions rooted in life styles and environmental factors may continue to be unfavourable for some years compared to the larger Canadian population. Current patterns of smoking, alcohol consumption, environmental contamination, high fat and carbohydrate diets, and sexual activity will contribute to increased rates of lung cancer and respiratory problems, alcohol-related diseases, diabetes and cardiovascular diseases, and perhaps HIV and AIDS in the coming years.

Nevertheless, some factors can be drastically changed by self-government, economic development, and the restoration of cultural and social self-worth. For example, communities will be able to address death and disability rates from motor vehicle accidents and occupational pursuits. Eighty-eight Status Indian males in the age group 25 to 44 died in motor vehicle accidents from 1987 to 1992. Data is not readily available on how many of these were alcohol related, but researchers believe that alcohol abuse may be a major cause of such premature death and disability. As First Nations take charge of their destiny, they can apply the preventive strategies that have become part of the highways and workplaces of Canadian society. Some deaths were undoubtedly due to correctable driving practices, faulty vehicles, and hazardous roads. These can also be remedied within the short term. In fact, First Nations cannot afford to continue losing these community members, who are in their years of prime economic productivity.

The tragedy of suicide rates among Aboriginal youths under 25, which are six times higher than those for the general B.C. population, may be less easy to overcome. The problems that lead to these suicides are deeply rooted in the social and cultural circumstances of the adolescent population that will not easily respond to change. Yet, since treaty settlements promise a meaningful future for those inheriting the responsibilities of the elders negotiating those claims, the rate of suicide may be cut in half. Saving the lives of Aboriginal teenagers will also add to the community's economic strength.

Major steps can also be taken to reduce infant death. Medical and nursing attention now focused on prenatal care and childbirth help keep prenatal mortality rates down. However, no one is solving problems of how Aboriginal infants and children are cared for when they return to the community. Under self-government, the community will take responsibility for the well-being and survival of its children, reducing the environmental hazards and making sure that the young are properly fed by following dietary guidelines suitably adapted to traditional foods. The loss of 40 children every year—double the provincial rate—can and will be reduced as the social, economic, and cultural circumstances of the First Nations change.

The major impact of treaty settlements and the social and economic changes that accompany them will, therefore, be on the younger age groups. In fact, as communities make economic and social plans, they should focus on the new generations. These will be the ones to carry forward plans put into place by their elders.

However, though treaty settlements should help change the social and economic conditions that profoundly affect the health of the younger and emerging generations, they will not be a cure-all for the health problems that now confront communities across the country. The emergence of crippling diseases like arthritis, diabetes, and end state renal disease in the First Nations populations will continue to need extensive medical services. Victims of accidents that continue to occur will need access to both medical care and rehabilitation. If HIV/AIDS does become the "epidemic" that is predicted, First Nations people must also be able to get the help of new therapies. While traditional healing does play a central role among the First Nations, they also need the additional support of Western methods of handling alcohol and substance abuse. And positive results of prenatal care show the need to maintain the medical programs that have proven their value in the First Nations context.

All this takes financial and human resources. Resources that federal and provincial governments now commit to providing health care to First Nations are a significant factor in the evolution of the changing economic landscape. Transfers of control over health service resources must be parallel to the settlement process. Each interacts with and complements the other. When we consider the economic impact that treaty settlements will have on health, we must also consider how current resources committed to health care will be transferred.

Policies and Regulations That Govern the Transfer of Health Care Resources

While the federal government has traditionally taken responsibility to provide health services to the First Nations, what may have begun as a "medicine chest" under certain treaties has developed into a complex set of arrangements and policies. These have partly come about as part of the requirements for provincial health care plans to meet federal guidelines. The need to provide sophisticated medical technologies, drugs and medical devices, dental care, transportation to receive care, and alternative methods to deal with problems like alcohol and drug abuse has also resulted in numerous different programs that are governed by various policies and regulations.

While governments appear to agree in principle that they will transfer control over health care to First Nations, both the timing and the strategies for this transfer are being widely debated. This section outlines the policies and regulations governing the transfer that are now under discussion.

Constitutional principles and legislation

The federal government has promised that any First Nation interested in self-government will not lose any real or potential treaty rights or inherent rights. However, several legal opinions show that transferring responsibility from the federal government to the First Nations may significantly weaken or reduce the federal government's financial responsibilities. The First Nations therefore must rely on overriding constitutional and federal legal principles to protect their traditional right to the resources that ensure they will continue to receive the full spectrum of health services.[8]

These legislative principles include

- recognition in the Constitution that First Nations can continue to seek self-government, inherent rights, and treaty rights through the political process
- laws that set out a formal process to negotiate and enact self-government between the Department of Indian Affairs and Northern Development and the First Nations. When provincial jurisdictions are affected, the provincial government must also be included in the negotiations. The scope of negotiations should include matters that are integral to the First Nations culture, internal to the communities, or are necessary for government.[9] These include health and education.

The 1979 Indian Health Policy

The 1979 Indian Health Policy provides the background to the various methods by which the federal government can transfer control of health services. The policy was based on "the special relationship of the Indian peoples to the federal government"[10] in the area of health. It recognized intolerable conditions of poverty and community decline, and how these caused poor health among Aboriginal people. It expressed the view that only the Aboriginal communities themselves could change the causes of these problems.

The policy had three principles.[11] The first was that developing communities was the most important way to remove conditions of poverty and apathy. This included not only social and economic development, but also cultural and spiritual development.

Secondly, the policy recognized the need to strengthen the traditional relationship between the First Nations people and the federal government in the area of health. This could be done by improving communications with the First Nations and encouraging their involvement in planning, budgeting, and delivering health programs.

Finally, the policy recognized the need to take into account the combined responsibilities of the different levels of government in the Canadian health system. It identified that federal responsibilities were primarily to operate public health services on reserves, promote health, and to detect and remove environmental hazards to health. The provinces were to provide services to diagnose and treat acute and chronic disease, and to rehabilitate people suffering from injuries. The First Nations were to have a significant role in health promotion and in adapting health services to meet the specific needs of their communities.

Methods to deliver health services now available to First Nations

To determine how best to transfer control of health services, we must identify the methods of delivery now available to First Nations communities.[12] First Nations are determined to move away from the dominant strategy of the past, which was that personnel from Health Canada's Medical Services Branch designed, delivered, and managed services, without input from the First Nations.

The Medical Services Branch has stated that the long-term goal is to transfer all health resources to First Nations' control, within a time to be determined during community consultations. In the meantime, it has developed various short-term strategies. How much control each method gives to the First Nations varies. These methods of management include, in order of the extent of control exercised by First Nations, contribution agreements, integrated agreements, transfer agreements, single funding agreements, and self-government.

Contribution agreements

Contribution agreements govern how specific programs are managed. These include

- community health representation
- community health
- the "brighter futures" program
- medical transportation
- dental therapy
- North and Native Drug and Alcohol Program (NADAP) treatment programs
- various clerical and support functions for each program.

Alternatively, a community may make a contribution agreement that includes all community health services. To do so, the community must agree to creating a system to manage a community health management structure and enter into a planning process resulting in a comprehensive community health plan. Under this method of management, mental health programs, home nursing services, and solvent abuse programs may be included in addition to the programs mentioned above.

It is important to note that contribution agreements impose certain financial limitations. First Nations cannot carry forward unspent balances and cannot transfer funds from one budget line to another. They must also deliver the programs exactly as Medical Services Branch would under the direct delivery system.

Integrated agreements

A community may seek an agreement that encompasses all community health services. This gives the community the option to include not only the specific programs designated under a contribution agreement, but also mental health programs, home nursing services, and solvent abuse programs. In doing so, the community must agree to establish a community health management structure and enter into a planning process resulting in a comprehensive community health plan. While it provides more flexibility in allocating resources to the various programs under the label of community health, this option also does not allow the First Nations to keep any unspent money from their funding budget.

Transfer agreements

Medical Services Branch developed a broad transfer process to respond to the individual requirements of each First Nations community. Under this process, the community may enter into health transfer discussions involving the full spectrum of health services. In addition to the programs identified under contribution agreements, integrated agreements, and single funding agreements, transfer agreements may include environmental health services, medical and dental service, Medical Services Branch hospitals, and various contracted professional services. Such agreements may also include a proportional share of the administrative resources of Medical Services Branch.

Single funding agreements

Another strategy is to manage services through the single funding mechanisms that Indian and Northern Affairs Canada have established with other federal departments. Health Canada and the First Nation first develop an amendment to their alternate funding agreement, then Indian and Northern Affairs Canada moves it through the system. The same services are available as under the contribution agreements. Currently, only one tribal council in B.C. has amended an alternate funding agreement to include community health resources and entered into a single funding agreement.

Self-government

The option that provides First Nations with the most control over health services is self-government. Under this management option, the First Nation has complete authority to allocate health resources according to priorities set by the community, as long as it also delivers Health Canada's required programs. In addition to the community-based programs listed under contribution agreements, First Nations also would have control over non-insured health benefits (described in detail in a following section). Each First Nation must develop a framework agreement with Indian and Northern Affairs Canada, although final authority to negotiate health resources remains with Medical Services Branch.

Since 1988, the only legislated self-government agreement implemented in B.C. has been with the Sechelt First Nation.

Health transfers from the federal government

The progress of health transfer

Health Canada has stated that health transfer is not the perfect solution for self-government, because although there are positive aspects, there are many limitations.[13] First Nations themselves appear to agree with this assessment. Not surprisingly, health transfer under the existing policies has achieved only limited success.

Since January 1996, ten years after the health transfer policy was introduced, 58 transfer agreements have been signed with 111 communities. Although 210 more communities have accepted initial funding to conduct "health needs assessments" and to begin community health planning, they have not yet made a commitment to implement transfer. In addition, four single funding agreements have been signed with 23 communities, and 22 integrated agreements have been signed with 27 communities. So, out of 605 First Nations communities, transfer of health services has occurred in only 161 of them. The next sections discuss some of the limitations that may account for this lack of enthusiasm.

The "envelope" system of budget control

The federal government's introduction of the "envelope" system of budget control has limited resource allocations to community health services from growing beyond the maximum allowed by the Treasury Board. In the 1996/97 fiscal year, Medical Services Branch's budget growth is limited to 3%, with a further 3% increase allowed for the 1997/98 fiscal year. The rate of growth for 1998/99 has been limited to a 1% increase.

First Nations believe this "envelope" system has reduced the funding available for health resources at the community level because their population growth has been greater than the rate of budget growth. This population growth continues to exceed the Canadian national average, at a steady 3% for each year from 1991 to 1996.[14] This is further compounded by the addition of those people reinstated to First Nations status under Bill C-31.

Health care reform

Health care reform throughout Canada has changed the emphasis from institutional to community care. There is an increasing need for home nursing services and comprehensive home care. These services have been underfunded by the federal government, and are usually not provided on reserves by provincial health care systems.[15] One survey found that 57% of the communities it interviewed said that changes in the provincial health systems had put more pressure on home-care systems in Aboriginal communities.[16]

Limits on additional funding

The community health transfer process does not allow First Nations communities in the transfer process to get additional funding. As a result, although the pre-transfer "health needs assessment" may identify the need for additional funding, no further resources would be provided in the transfer process to fulfill these health requirements.[17]

The Non-Insured Health Benefits Program

The Non-Insured Health Benefits Program (NIHB) has evolved over the years to provide health-related benefits not covered by a provincial or territorial health care program. NIHB has become central to the negotiations to transfer health resources because the programs that it covers are the means for First Nations to receive their rights to a full spectrum of health care. The First Nations will settle for no less.

Medical Services Branch holds the position that in providing NIHB benefits, it must be the "payer of last resort." This means that First Nations must obtain benefits or services from other funding sources first, either provincial or private. This has a significant effect on provincially funded programs like Pharmacare, since through NIHB, Medical Services Branch is only required to pay for the remaining portion of a professional fee or the cost of an item. The First Nations almost universally reject this policy. They believe that health care is a treaty right, and that in the transfer process, the federal government must pay the full cost of NIHB programs.

Current NIHB benefits and services

NIHB now pays for all of the following:

- prescription drugs, including over-the-counter medications prescribed by a medical or dental practitioner
- medical supplies and equipment, such as wheelchairs, crutches, hearing aids, and prosthetic and orthodontic devices
- vision care services, including the cost of eyeglasses and repairs to frames
- dental procedures and services listed under the NIHB Schedule of Dental Benefits

- transportation to medical and dental services, including meals and accommodations when people must be away from their home community
- individual counselling in crisis situations
- the cost of daily fees for extended care for patients between the ages of 19 and 64
- the full cost of daily fees for in-patient attendance at alcohol or drug treatment facilities.

In addition, NIHB pays provincial health care premiums for First Nations residents in British Columbia. It also makes co-payments for physiotherapy, massage, podiatry, and chiropractic and naturopathic treatments approved by the B.C. Medical Plan.

How much does NIHB cost?

Reported NIHB expenses for the fiscal year 1995/96 were $505.3 million nationally, excluding administrative expenses.[18] Total NIHB expenses for the Pacific Region were $72 million for the same period, or 14.24% of the national total (although 16.21% of eligible NIHB clients live in the Pacific Region).[19] Table 7.1 below shows the expenses for the Pacific Region by benefit category.

Table 7.1: NIHB Expenses for the Pacific Region, 1985–96

NIHB Benefit Category	Expenses
Transportation	$ 12,520 million
Prescriptions	$ 23,752 million
Dental	$ 20,855 million
Health Care	$ 3,627 million
Provincial premiums	$ 8,797 million
Vision care	$ 2,463 million
Total	**$ 72,014 million**

Source: Health Canada, *Year End Variance Report: 1995/96* (Vancouver: Pacific Region Director, Medical Services Branch, June 1996).

Transferring NIHB benefits to First Nations

When Medical Services Branch originally got authority to transfer health services to the First Nations, NIHB benefits were specifically excluded from the legislative authority granted them, except under conditions of self-government. Nevertheless, in 1993, Medical Services Branch sought and obtained the authority to create a maximum of 30 pilot transfer projects to complete a time-limited transfer of the NIHB Program.

At the time they got this additional authority, the Joint Assembly of First Nations and Medical Services Branch Task Force was examining the various options for the future management of NIHB. The Assembly of First Nations, supported by the majority of the First Nations members consulted, strongly recommended that these two-year pilot projects be used to test the viability of various NIHB management options. They also strongly recommended that Medical Services Branch stop seeking additional transfer authority until the pilot projects were completed and evaluated.[20] Medical Services Branch, however, states that many First Nations wish to proceed to the transfer of NIHB, and are placing pressure on them to obtain transfer authority as soon as possible.

Current problems with NIHB program transfers

Limitations of pilot projects. Although NIHB categories of "prescription drugs and dental services" make up about 60% of its expenses, they were excluded from transfer in the pilot projects.[21] This exclusion was because of the terms of the contract for automated claims processing that Medical Services Branch had entered into with Liberty Health. Under these circumstances, the pilot projects could test only the administrative responsibility for these benefit categories.

The Assembly of First Nations maintains that NIHB pilot projects were established to test the various delivery and management options open to the First Nations. As such, pilot project participants should be able to include all aspects of NIHB.

Losing portability of benefits. Under the existing NIHB, clients can obtain benefits at no direct cost anywhere in Canada. This portability exists because there are nationally defined benefit levels and because claims for drugs, dental services, medical supplies, and equipment are processed and paid through one contracted agent.

In the case of transfer to individual First Nations communities, this portability could be lost. Suppliers may require direct payment from the beneficiary, who in turn must seek reimbursement from the First Nation. This will cause financial hardship, especially to those living outside their home community or in a different province.

The effects of the "envelope" system. Before the "envelope" system of budget control, the benefit expenses for NIHB were determined directly by the practices of prescribers. If additional funding was required because of unexpected demand, Medical Services Branch got additional funding. Unexpected demand now may result in less funding being available for other health programs and initiatives. NIHB has thus become "capped," as opposed to operating as an open-ended insurance program.

If a First Nation accepts the responsibility for delivering NIHB benefits with a capped budget, this change could be highly restrictive at the community level.

Reduced purchasing power. Transferring NIHB to individual First Nations communities or even to tribal councils may result in reduced purchasing power. Individual bands or councils would have less power to negotiate reduced prices for higher volumes of service, resulting in higher prices.

For example, Medical Services Branch, Pacific Region, negotiated a preferred rate for the B.C. health care premium, based on the total Status Indian population in the province. Such a preferred rate may not be immediately available to an individual First Nations community or council.

Differences in policy interpretations. Medical Services Branch states that NIHB is a national program with nationally established goals and standards. The interpretation of these standards, however, is left to regional discretion. This has resulted in regional differences in the level of NIHB benefits provided. Variations between the provinces are between $623 and $888 per capita, although Alberta is an outlier with a figure of $1,309.

These variations are believed to be caused mainly by how regions are interpreting the policy for medical transportation. Most regions have interpreted the policy to include transportation for dental services. But Ontario Region specifically excludes transportation to dental services from the list of provided benefits. They refuse, for example, to provide orthodontic services unless parents agree to cover the transportation costs. Transfers from Medical Services Branch to individual communities and bands will inevitably result in inequities in the availability and quality of health services across the country.

Financial resources available under devolution

Before assessing how transferring health services to First Nations will affect the B.C. economy, we must identify how much the federal and provincial governments actually spend to provide health care now. This is by no means an easy task in view of multiple sources of funding; the complexity of various transfer arrangements between levels of government and from governments to First Nations; and identifying the many services now provided to First Nations. We begin with federal funding.

Federally funded Aboriginal health programs and services

Annual budget of Medical Services Branch. The 1996/97 budget of Medical Services Branch, Pacific Region, for Status Aboriginal peoples living in B.C. shows a total of over $130 million in a variety of categories covering both services and administrative costs.[22]

The 1996/97 budgeted expenditures for the "headquarters" of Medical Services Branch amounts to some $76 million of this total.[23] It is not clear how much of this money is committed to providing direct health services to First Nations. However, a considerable portion is likely for general "overhead" expenses that First Nations would be eligible to receive after control had been transferred.

Programs and initiatives funded by Health Canada. Under self-government, the First Nations will also seek to obtain a proportionate share of all funding that has an Aboriginal component, on the basis that First Nations people also receive programs directed to the general Canadian population. The full implications of this have not been fully explored. For example, programs such as those embedded within the Health Protection Branch are not easily segmented into Aboriginal and non-aboriginal components. We assume, however, that most of Health Canada's budget would thus be open for negotiation. In 1995/96, this budget, not including the total Medical Services Branch budget, was $8,500 million.[24]

Canada Health and Social Transfer (CHST) payments. A major source of funding for the provincial health care plans was provided by the federal government under the Established Programs Funding, a program that has now been incorporated into the Canada Health and Social Transfer Payment Program (CHST). CHST transfers to the provinces, provided in the form of cash and tax points, fund health services, post-secondary education, and social assistance.

In 1996/97, British Columbia is budgeted to receive $3.3 billion in CHST payments, although the specific amount allocated to health services is not indicated.[25] An analysis of the 1995/96 data reported by Health Canada suggests that health services expenses would make up 60% or over $2 billion.[26]

Total federal funding for Aboriginal health. To arrive at the total funding that may be available to B.C. First Nations for negotiated self-government, we can allocate the federal expenditures outlined above to British Columbia on the following assumptions:

- the percentage of Status Indians living in B.C. (16.21%)[27]
- the percentage of the B.C. population who are Aboriginal (2.7%)[28]
- the percentage of the total Canadian population (including Aboriginal people) who live in B.C. (12.9%).[29]

Based on these assumptions, Table 7.2 estimates the amount of money the federal government spends on health services for Aboriginal people in British Columbia.

Table 7.2: Potential Health-Related Funding Available under Self-Government

Funding Source	Calculation	Potential Budget
Medical Services Branch:		
Pacific Region	100% of total	$ 130,097.10 million
Headquarters	16.21% of total	$ 12,417.54 million
Health Canada:		
Health Programs	2.6% of 12% of national expenditures for health programs, excluding Medical Services Branch	$ 1,738.79 million
Health Transfer Payment	2.6% of B.C. total	$ 50,930.00 million
Total		**$ 195,183.43 million**

Provincial health care expenses for Aboriginal peoples in British Columbia

While we can pinpoint health services funding provided by the federal government fairly specifically, determining provincial government expenditures is more complex. The various British Columbia health plans do not reliably record the Aboriginal status of the recipients.

In theory, we might assume that Status Indians in B.C. use provincial health plans proportionally to the general population. If this assumption were valid, we could calculate an equitable allocation of health services resources under self-government.

However, a paper prepared for the Aboriginal Health Policy Branch states that allocating resources based on the population ratio would not reflect how much the province actually spends on health care. Nor would it show rates of use. In fact, the estimated expenses are greater than those that would be derived from the population ratio. According to the paper, in 1992/93, it was estimated the total actual cost to the province for the provision of health services to Status Indians was $97.14 million. In the same fiscal year, the total funding provided by the federal government was estimated at $60.68 million, including CHST payments and health premiums.[30]

This analysis suggests that British Columbia subsidized health care for Status Indians by \$36.5 million in 1992/93, and that additional funding to provide the full spectrum of health services for First Nations people comes from provincial tax revenues.

How Will Transferring Health Services Affect the B.C. Economy?

How transferring health services to First Nations will affect the B.C. economy depends on the type of transfer, how extensive it is, and how quickly it will come about. The most far-reaching impact would come through the process of self-government.

Part of the self-government process will likely involve First Nations negotiating to assume control of all the health resources they now receive, through either federal or provincial programs. Each First Nation may negotiate for the entire band membership, including people living on and off reserves, or may make arrangements only for those living on reserves.

The federal government has taken the position that they will continue to make CHST payments to the provinces. Therefore, each First Nation and the provincial government will have to settle how all resources except those the federal government spends on Indian health services and NIHB benefits will be transferred. And the First Nations have said that the B.C. government is very reluctant to begin such discussions.

Nevertheless, Status First Nations leaders expect that a proportionate share of the federal money spent on health services in B.C., estimated as \$195.2 million will be available for transfer. In addition, an analysis by J.F. Lamarche suggests that paying the costs of health care for Status Indians in B.C. would require additional money, approximately \$36.5 million, from provincial sources.[31] Clearly, both parties need more detailed information before they can begin meaningful negotiations.

Even if a First Nation were to negotiate receiving a fair and equitable portion of the resources contributed directly and indirectly by the federal government, this money would not be enough to pay for the current total health services expenses for First Nations in the province.

Unless the provincial government is prepared to continue the subsidy from its tax base, it may seek to set a significantly higher health care premium for the First Nations. Another option is for the First Nation to obtain third-party coverage and move towards private health care, possibly through an Aboriginal health maintenance organization.

Even so, as treaties are settled and First Nations assume more control over the various services provided to their communities, the health services sector could contribute significantly to the economic development of those communities. This is already beginning to occur with the transfer of community-based programs. They provide additional local employment as band members become trained to both manage and deliver those programs. In addition, as Medical Services Branch obtains authority to transfer the NIHB, band and tribal councils could have many opportunities to create new economic benefits. Here are some examples drawn from the pilot projects:

- One First Nation has built a pharmacy on reserve, and has recruited a salaried pharmacist. The quality and quantity of professional advice has improved, and dispensing fees formerly paid by NIHB are directed to other health programs. The cost of medical transportation has decreased, since band members no longer have to travel off the reserve to fill a prescription. Another tribal council has negotiated with a large national chain to provide pharmacy services at a preferred rate.
- Several First Nations and tribal councils have contracted directly with dentists to provide dental services for a fixed monthly fee. This move away from payment on a "fee-for-service" basis has saved a notable amount of costs.
- In the case of vision care services, some First Nations have negotiated preferred vendor status, where they get better quality frames at no extra cost. Other negotiated improvements are the inclusion of lens coatings and tints in filling basic prescriptions.
- One First Nation has entered into partnership with an airline that provides medical transportation. Not only does this provide employment for band members, but the First Nation participates in controlling the costs, thus channelling savings to other health programs.

Such projects not only give First Nations more control over service delivery, they also provide a means of economic growth through employment and the introduction of new money into the economy. They also pave the way for new initiatives like health centres, where First Nations people can find employment and health services that are consistent with the cultural values of their society.

Pathways to transferring control of health service resources are clearly complex, as is providing health services at any level. It is crucial that the government change its policies for transferring health programs to meet the needs of First Nations people. The First Nations are asking for the government to maintain and improve all resources now committed to health-related programs, to allow flexibility in using the funding, and to recognize that the First Nations should themselves be the ones to determine which programs are most appropriate to meet the needs of their people.

The process of treaty settlements will undoubtedly place pressures on the federal and provincial governments, and the communities themselves, to fully transfer control in the health sector. The resources at stake are huge. They offer the opportunity to improve both the physical and the economic health of the First Nations. This can only contribute to the economic productivity of the First Nations peoples.

Notes

1. Health Canada, *A Statistical Report.*

2. *A Statistical Report,* pp. 101–102.

3. *A Statistical Report,* p. 102.

4. *A Statistical Report,* p. 107.

5. *A Statistical Report,* p. 109.

6. *A Statistical Report,* p. 55.

7. *A Statistical Report,* p. 56.

8. Health Canada, *Introduction to Health Transfer,* p. 45.

9. Department of Indian Affairs and Northern Development.

10. Health Canada, *Indian Health Policy 1979,* p. 3.

11. *Indian Health Policy 1979,* p. 3.

12. Health Canada, *Pathways to First Nation Control.*

13. *Indian Health Policy 1979,* p. 3.

14. Health Canada, *Non-Insured Health Benefits Program, Annual Report,* p. 3.

15. Lamarche, p. 3.

16. Health Canada, *Long Term Evaluation of Transfer,* p. 60.

17. *Long Term Evaluation of Transfer,* p. 9.

18. *Non-Insured Health Benefits Program, Annual Report,* p. 26.

19. *Non-Insured Health Benefits Program, Annual Report,* p. 33.

20. Health Canada, *Report on the Future Management of the Non-Insured Health Benefits Program,* p. 33.

21. Health Canada, *Non-Insured Health Benefits Pilot Project Handbook,* p. 7.

22. Health Canada, *1996/97 Medical Services Branch, Pacific Region Budget.*

23. *1996/97 Medical Services Branch, Pacific Region Budget.*

24. Health Canada, *1995/96 Operations Budget.*

25. Department of Finance, Federal-Provincial Relations, *1996/97 Canada Health and Social Transfer Budget.*

26. *1995/96 Health Canada Operations Budget.*

27. Health Canada, *Analysis and Reporting Division Annual Report: Non-Insured Health Benefits Program, 1995–96*, p. 5.

28. *A Statistical Report*, p. 9.

29. *A Statistical Report*, p. 9.

30. Lamarche.

31. Lamarche.

References

Department of Finance, Federal-Provincial Relations. *1996/97 Canada Health and Social Transfer Budget*. Ottawa: Minister of Finance, Supply and Services Canada, 1996.

Department of Indian Affairs and Northern Development. *Federal Policy Guide for the Implementation of the Inherent Right*. Ottawa: Minister of Health, Supply and Services Canada, 1979.

Health Canada. *Analysis and Reporting Division Annual Report: Non-Insured Health Benefits Program, 1995–96*. Ottawa: Minister of Health.

———. *Indian Health Policy 1979*. Ottawa: Minister of Health, Supply and Services Canada, 1979.

———. *Introduction to Health Transfer*. Ottawa: Minister of Health, Supply and Services Canada, 1989.

———. *Long Term Evaluation of Transfer—Final Report*. Ottawa: Institute for Human Resources Development, October 1995.

———. *Non-Insured Health Benefits Pilot Project Handbook*. Rev. ed. Ottawa: Joint Assembly of First Nations and Medical Services

Branch Task Force on the Future Management of the Non-Insured Health Benefits Program, November 1995.

————. *Non-Insured Health Benefits Program, Analysis Division Annual Report*. Ottawa: Minister of Health, Supply and Services Canada, 1995.

————. *1995/96 Health Canada Operations Budget*. Ottawa: Minister of Health, Planning Analysis and Reporting Division, Corporate Services Branch, 1995.

————. *1996/97 Medical Services Branch, Pacific Region Budget*. Ottawa: Minister of Health, Department of Financial Systems, 1996.

————. *Pathways to First Nation Control: Report on Project 7— Strategic Planning Exercise*. Ottawa: Minister of Health, Supply and Services Canada, 1995.

————. *Report on the Future Management of the Non-Insured Health Benefits Program*. Vol. 1, Sec. 5. Ottawa: Director General, Non-Insured Health Benefits, 1994.

————. *A Statistical Report on the Health of First Nations in British Columbia*. Ottawa: Minister of Health, Supply and Services Canada, 1995.

————. *Year End Variance Report: 1995/96*. Vancouver: Pacific Region Director, Medical Services Branch, June 1996.

Lamarche, J.F. *Economic Analysis of Health Services Utilized by British Columbia's Status Indian Population*. Victoria: Division of Vital Statistics, Ministry of Health and Ministry Responsible for Seniors, Canadian Cataloguing in Publication Data, 1995.

8

Degrees of Separation:

First Nations Self-Government in British Columbia

By Ken Coates

The movement for aboriginal self-government has come a long way in the past thirty years. If it is to continue to proceed forward and if difficult issues such as achieving a balance between the right of aboriginal peoples as aboriginal peoples and as Canadians are to be resolved, then Canadians are going to have to look deep into their own history and culture. Canadians are going to have to think about their country, its past and future, in vastly different ways than those to which they have become familiar. It might be agreed that this is not very likely. And that may be so, but such an argument should not obscure what is necessary for the full recognition of the aboriginal right of self-government in Canada today.[1]

The quest for Aboriginal self-government sits at the centre of the land claims debate in British Columbia. The movement to give political power back to the province's First Nations has a history and life separate from treaty negotiations. However, it is a central issue in the discussions now under way between more than 70 First Nations in B.C. and the federal and provincial governments.

Chafing under the controls of the *Indian Act,* and angry about the lingering paternal attitude of agencies managing Aboriginal affairs,

First Nations now insist that governments give them greater freedom to manage their affairs. When the federal government announced it recognized First Nations' "inherent right" to self-government in August 1995, it agreed that many elements of First Nations' Aboriginal demands were legitimate. This started a process that could rapidly change the nature of Aboriginal government across the country.[2]

Even though all First Nations and many non-aboriginal people support the idea of self-government, exactly what that would mean is uncertain and often misunderstood. Some of the most important questions are:

- Will First Nations people pay taxes?
- Will First Nations governments operate within the confines of federal and provincial laws?
- How will self-governing communities be accountable for their finances and programs?
- What relationship will local First Nations governments have to municipalities and regional districts?
- If specific bands or tribal councils provide public services, will First Nations peoples have their rights to similar government services restricted?
- Will Aboriginal communities still struggling with the effects of decades of colonial control and racism be able to cope with the pressures and difficulties of increased authority?[3]

The fact that so many questions engulf the discussion about Aboriginal self-government shows how serious the concerns and disputes about First Nations' rights and responsibilities are.[4]

This chapter examines some of these crucial questions to discover how First Nations self-government might work in B.C. Specifically, it will discuss

- government paternalism and the beginning of Aboriginal activism
- how national politics have stalled First Nations self-government
- the creation of the federal "inherent right" policy as a new agenda for self-government
- how self-government is now working in B.C.
- the challenges of self-government, from seeing it as a cure-all to reducing bureaucracy, removing paternalism, managing the costs

and complications of program delivery, and paying for the costly transition

- the outlook for First Nations self-government in B.C.

Government Paternalism and the Beginnings of Aboriginal Activism

For thousands of years before Europeans arrived on the west coast of North America, Aboriginal peoples managed their affairs with success. Systems of government varied dramatically among the various cultures of the region. Coastal tribes were more sedentary, more hierarchical, and more status oriented. The mobile peoples of the North had much more informal structures, built around controlling land and resources for the protection and regulation of all. Neither system was like the government structures that the newcomers imported into the region. This largely explains why the Europeans found it so easy to displace systems of administration, power, wealth distribution, and social control that had served the First Nations for many generations.[5]

For a few years after newcomers encountered First Nations in British Columbia, government officials did treat First Nations as central political organizations.[6] However, once Britain won the struggle to control the Coast, British colonial officials placed very little importance on maintaining relations with Aboriginal peoples, except to make sure that they were not a threat to the incoming population. Even James Douglas, long praised for his more considerate approach to managing Aboriginal affairs, was concerned primarily with reducing tensions and controlling conflicts. His handful of minor treaties were only a small project to gain clear title to land of immediate interest to settlers.

The governing of Aboriginal peoples has long been tied to the level of European interest in First Nations territories. Governments moved in during the gold rush era to supervise, if not to regulate, Aboriginal life, but only for those areas they wished to develop. Bands in the isolated Northern Interior had little direct interference from government officials. Even the establishment of a network of First Nations agencies under the federal Department of Indian Affairs after British Columbia joined Confederation did not immediately bring First Nations under the government control. As federal authorities became more active— ordering First Nations children to attend day and residential schools, trying to stop the potlatch, and encouraging settlement of small reserves—the hand of government became more noticeable and at times more oppressive. But right through to the 1950s, many First Nations along the West Coast and in the Interior, away from the major areas of new settlement, were considerably free from government interference.[7]

After World War II, new government programs increased its influence. Government housing projects and Mother's Allowance subsidies encouraged First Nations to settle permanently on reserves. Educational programs like residential schooling expanded, as did attempts to integrate First Nations people into the Canadian mainstream.

Although First Nations had some say in their affairs by electing band chiefs and councils, government Indian agents had more and more authority. Armed with the controlling mechanisms of the *Indian Act,* better funding, and greater administrative powers, Indian agents operated quite freely on reserves. Some used their powers gently; others ruled more firmly. In general, however, they were the ultimate in government paternalism, the embodiment of the idea that non-aboriginal governments knew what was best for Aboriginal peoples.[8]

The First Nations chafed under this control, just as they routinely expressed their frustration that the government would not settle land claims. In the late 1960s, the federal government considered abandoning the *Indian Act* and managing Aboriginal life through the Department of Indian Affairs. The Liberal White Paper of 1969 proposed that the government eliminate "Indian" status and remove all special privileges for First Nations people. Aboriginal organizations moved into action, using their opposition to the White Paper to criticize the very foundations of government paternalism in Canada.

In the process of insisting that government recognize their special rights as "Indians" and Aboriginal peoples, First Nations across the country also began to assert their right and their ability to manage their own affairs. The roots of the modern land claims and self-government movements lie in this burst of late 1960s radicalism and activism. At first wrapped in the language of anti-colonialism and the rhetoric of the American Indian movement, protests quickly became more measured and culturally specific in tone. First Nations began to make clear that they wanted and deserved the power to govern their own lives.[9]

How National Politics Have Stalled First Nations Self-Government

First Nations people have been pushing for major changes in how the Department of Indian Affairs and Northern Development operates and asserting the right to have greater control over their local affairs since the 1960s. Negotiations to bring about such changes have gone on almost as long. Public attention has focused on the highly volatile debates over Aboriginal rights to self-government in the Canadian constitution. As discussions unfolded on the patriation of the Constitution, Aboriginal organizations fought to include rights to Aboriginal treaties and rights of self-government.

In 1978, the government drew attention to Aboriginal constitutional issues by including in the major government policy document a statement, "A Time for Action," on the importance of entrenching Aboriginal rights. With the issue firmly on the nation's constitutional agenda, First Nations leaders pressed their demands. At one meeting after another, provincial governments resisted their position, calling for a more concrete and precise definition of what self-government meant before they agreed to include the principle in the Constitution. As a result, section 35(1) simply established "existing aboriginal and treaty rights." The governments of and in Canada also agreed to a series of meetings to hammer out other differences on Aboriginal constitutional rights, raising the profile of First Nations government to an unprecedented level.

The federal government wanted to clarify exactly what the vague and unspecified "existing aboriginal and treaty rights" were. They launched a parliamentary task force on Aboriginal self-government. Chaired by Liberal MP Keith Penner, it began work late in 1992. Its report marked a turning point on the issue, arguing that governments had to recognize that the concept of Aboriginal self-government was valid and significant.

The recommendations of the task force, which were built on lengthy consultations with Aboriginal organizations, were sweeping in scope and substance. They called for the government to accept that First Nations needed freedom to determine their future, freedom to govern their own actions, freedom from federal and provincial control, and power to create their own laws. First Nations organizations saw the Penner report as a major leap forward in government recognition of their aspirations. However, the federal government quickly pushed it aside, preferring a much slower process of administrative and structural change.[10]

In the Constitution, the governments of and in Canada agreed to discuss further constitutional reforms with Aboriginal peoples. Through a series of national meetings in 1983, 1984, 1985, and 1987, governments and First Nations organizations attempted to define Aboriginal rights more precisely. They failed. Federal and provincial governments were prepared to provide "delegated" powers, but would not agree that Aboriginal peoples had an "inherent right" to self-government. The First Nations, on the other hand, presented the matter as one of self-determination. They argued that their pre-existing right to govern themselves should be included in the national constitution.

As the debates continued, the gap seemed to widen rather than narrow. First Nations leaders spoke of creating a "third order" of government, and of establishing Aboriginal peoples as permanent decision-makers at the highest level of national administration.[11] Provincial premiers, in particular, would have none of it. They demanded that Aboriginal rights be more specifically defined and narrowly focused.

Canadians continued this constitutional dance for some time, which became both an endemic disease and national hobby. The focus of provincial and federal governments was mainly to bring Quebec back into the political family. In 1987, the governments agreed to the Meech Lake Accord, a compromise arrangement that seemed to satisfy Quebec's demands. Native leaders launched a major campaign against the agreement. They charged that they had not been involved in drafting it, that it failed to include their demands for self-government, and that under its terms, any further amendment (such as one granting the Aboriginal right to self-government) would require the unanimous approval of the provinces and the federal government. The Meech Lake Accord ultimately failed, perhaps appropriately because of Aboriginal MLA Elijah Harper's determined stand against it.

The failure of the Meech Lake Accord did not stop self-government discussions. Nor did it halt deliberations on constitutional change.

Governments came back in 1992 with another more comprehensive package—the Charlottetown Accord. This time it included a very complete statement on Aboriginal self-government. Although some First Nations were divided over the terms of its provision for self-government, the Charlottetown Accord appeared to address most Aboriginal demands. Everything was wrapped in a complex package of Senate reform and provisions recognizing Quebec's unique position within Confederation, then presented to the Canadian electorate in a referendum.

But the referendum failed. In fact, even a majority of First Nations people voted against it. Reasons for this failure varied among concerns over giving First Nations too much power, anger over the special status provisions for Quebec, and a groundswell of public opposition to the fact that political and intellectual elites had great influence in creating the Accord. It seemed that major constitutional change for Aboriginal peoples had failed.

First Nations leaders continued their efforts through an ambitious consultation process, the First Nations Circle on the Constitution, that in turn was linked to the Aboriginal Consultation Process, a national endeavour. Not surprisingly, the First Nations Circle presented strong arguments in favour of Aboriginal self-government. However, the level of its demands, its assertions of autonomy (even sovereignty), and its limited attention to practical and financial matters did little to convince governments to support the sweeping recommendations.

A year before the Charlottetown referendum, Prime Minister Brian Mulroney had established the Royal Commission on Aboriginal Peoples to try to appease First Nations for the political conflicts stirred up by the Meech Lake Accord. It was jointly chaired by René Dussault, from the Quebec Court of Appeal, and George Erasmus, former chief of the Assembly of First Nations. The second item in the Royal Commission's mandate directed it to investigate self-government, and further observed:

> The Commission's investigation of self-government may focus upon the political relationship between aboriginal peoples and the Canadian state. Although self-government is a complex concept, with many variations, the essential task is to break the

pattern of paternalism which has characterized the relationship between aboriginal peoples and the Canadian government.[12]

In a variety of statements, the Royal Commission has shown it strongly supports expanding Aboriginal self-government. Indeed, this concept has been at the centre of its initiatives and recommendations. But because it was millions of dollars over budget and several years overdue, the Royal Commission lost much of its steam. The final report was at last released in the fall of 1996, and argued strongly for both self-government and increased government funding on Aboriginal programs. However, it did not catch the public's imagination, and the government has yet to respond to it in detail.

The federal government did not wait for constitutional change in order to begin taking slow steps to First Nations self-government. In the late 1980s, it introduced the concept of community-based self-government under a program called "Indian Self-Government Community Negotiations." It transferred some administrative authority and funding to First Nations communities.

Many First Nations leaders and groups rejected the approach. They felt that it still involved paternalistic centralizing government control, and that it rejected the idea that Aboriginal peoples had the inherent right to govern themselves. Nevertheless, some Aboriginal communities entered into negotiations to transfer control into their hands. The Sechelt Band in British Columbia was the first to capitalize on the opportunity, negotiating a self-government agreement in 1988. Their model of self-government was rebuffed by most other First Nations as being little more than municipal administration.[13]

Community-based self-government had proven to be an expensive failure. Negotiations dragged on, with little success. As late as 1993, over 175 First Nations were negotiating with the government and, according to one study, 50 were near agreements. But almost all of them stalled. First Nations leaders continued to push for sweeping constitutional change, and the negotiations were tightly limited to community self-government. They were a pale reflection of what First Nations really wanted. Similarly, the federal government program failed because it required the provinces to participate in the negotiations and implementation—a measure of cooperation that has been only rarely achieved in Aboriginal affairs.[14]

The Federal "Inherent Right" Policy: A New Agenda for Self-Government

Even though millions of dollars and thousands of days were spent in exhaustive negotiations, the community-based self-government program did not work. Nor did the hard-won consensus between the Assembly of First Nations, the federal government, and the provincial leaders in the Charlottetown Accord. The failure of the national referendum in October 1992 seemed to be the death knell to the campaign for Aboriginal self-government. Even the arguments presented at the hearings of the Royal Commission on Aboriginal Peoples, which showed strong support for the concept in First Nations communities, seemed unlikely to move the constitutional agenda.

Even so, the federal government, anxious to move on this front, found a way to push the concept forward and, most significantly, to make sure that the rights negotiated with First Nations would be protected under section 35 of the *Constitution Act, 1982*. In August 1995, the Hon. Ron Irwin, Minister of Indian Affairs and Northern Development, announced the "inherent right" policy. Arguing that "the status quo, paternalistic system has just not worked—and the proof is all around us,"[15] Irwin introduced a comprehensive program to transfer powers to First Nations and to ensure that those powers remained in Aboriginal hands. The government agreed to recognize Aboriginal self-government as a right defined in the Constitution, and then made plans to negotiate that right with First Nations across the country. This was a sweeping admission that several decades of government administration of Aboriginal affairs had failed, and the beginning of new movement on the long-standing debate about the meaning and nature of self-government.

The inherent right policy fell short of some First Nations' more comprehensive demands, particularly those pushing for an open-ended acceptance of Aboriginal sovereignty.[16] The government clearly intended to pass substantial and meaningful decision-making power to First Nations, but it would do so only within fairly clear limits:

• The policy did not recognize Aboriginal sovereignty as commonly understood in international terms. First Nations people will be Canadian citizens and will continue to have a strong relationship with federal and provincial governments.

- Despite controversy within First Nations on the issue, self-governing groups will not be exempt from the *Canadian Charter of Rights and Freedoms*. Given that the Charter makes specific reference to the special rights of Aboriginal peoples, this policy is intended to provide flexibility and to protect the national charter.[17]

- Self-government will not be a time-limited, take-it-or-leave-it offer. Agreements will be negotiated when First Nations are ready to assume certain responsibilities. Arrangements for self-government will therefore vary in timing and specifics among First Nations groups.

- Some government powers over First Nations cannot be negotiated. The legal authority of First Nations will "likely [extend] to matters that are internal to the group, integral to its distinct Aboriginal culture, and essential to its operation as a government or institution."[18]

- First Nations will be able to choose to control government structures, membership lists, marriage, adoption, child welfare, Aboriginal culture and language, education, health, social services, the creation and enforcement of local laws and Aboriginal customary law, police powers, property rights, land management regimes, natural resources management, agriculture, taxation (direct and property taxes), public works management, housing, and licensing of businesses.

- First Nations can also have some controls over a second list of areas, subject to negotiation with federal and provincial governments. However, broader laws governing these areas will still apply. These include divorce, labour and training, justice issues and criminal codes, jails, environmental protection, gambling, and emergency procedures.

- There is a third list of government powers "where there are no compelling reasons for Aboriginal governments or institutions to exercise law-making authority."[19] These powers include defense and international relations, immigration, international trade, monetary policy, commercial laws, national criminal law, health and safety issues, postal service, shipping and transportation, broadcasting, census, and several others. In these areas, the federal government is willing to negotiate managerial responsibility, but not law-making authority.

Debate continues about the list of powers and the federal government's unilateral implementation of the policy, but the fact remains that the self-government initiative is a sweeping departure from past practices. And the relatively quick negotiation of several substantial deals, including an agreement with the Union of Manitoba Indian Chiefs, made it clear that the government is serious about implementing the policy. This, in turn, was in keeping with Irwin's determination to abandon the idea of a single national agreement and rely on negotiations with the Assembly of First Nations. The goal was simply to demonstrate that the policy could work by actually negotiating several agreements.

The federal government's implementation strategy provides several options. The self-government agreements can be

- new treaties between the federal government and specific First Nations groups
- additions to existing treaties
- included in comprehensive land claims deals (as with the Nisga'a Agreement-in-Principle and plans for other groups now negotiating in British Columbia).

Other less permanent measures will assist the expansion of self-government, including federal and provincial legislation, contracts with First Nations groups, and legal "memoranda of understanding." The policy

- makes broad commitments to community consultation, particularly with municipalities and economic interest groups
- requires ratification by provincial (or territorial) and federal legislatures
- promises that federal commitments to Aboriginal peoples required by law and the Constitution will not decrease
- guarantees that self-governing groups will be fully accountable
- provides for a gradual process of negotiation and transition.

The federal government has moved quickly to implement the new inherent rights policy, even though many questions about it remain unanswered. As a starting point, and as a policy that can be applied across the country, it promises major changes in the way that governments and First Nations people interact. It also accomplished this task without reopening the contentious constitutional arguments that had plagued the country for a generation.

In British Columbia, negotiations over self-government have been merged with treaty negotiations (again, as with the Nisga'a Agreement-in-Principle). This inclusion of self-government considerations in treaty discussions added another layer to already complex negotiations. However, self-government is so integral to the principle of empowerment that underlies the treaty process that they fit easily together. Provincial officials saw that the inherent-right principle could be accommodated within the existing treaty-making process, and agreed to participate on that basis. Given that many of the powers open to negotiation are either provincial or overlap with federal responsibilities, this is an important concession.[20]

Self-Government in British Columbia

While governments wrangled over constitutional initiatives, and while politicians debated the finer points about self-government, the process of implementing it began.[21] The steps were small for the most part: local control over schools or health units, Aboriginal administration of federal post-secondary education grants, band management of economic development initiatives, and participation in government resource-management programs. Although the emotions and ceremonies for local government of schools in particular revealed the intense feeling First Nations people had about gaining control over their lives, these activities lacked the political grandeur of full self-government. Nevertheless, they provided numerous practical limited examples of what was possible.

Some of the initiatives were unsuccessful. Several of the schools run by band or tribal councils had difficulty attracting and keeping teachers and administrators, especially in their first years of operation. Teachers complained of interference in school affairs, but local residents praised the fact that they had managerial control over the education system. When teachers expressed their dissatisfaction by resigning, school boards soon discovered more effective means of working with education professionals.

Many of the locally managed economic development programs also ran into trouble. Some were poorly planned, others poorly managed.

Many had difficulty making the transition from government support to competing in the open market. The isolated location of most First Nations reserves also limited the financial viability of all but a few projects.

That some attempts at self-government failed is hardly evidence that the concept as a whole is weak, though critics of the process tried to use it as such. The absence of trained managers, the difficulties of getting non-aboriginal professionals to work under First Nations guidance, and the financial and administrative difficulties of operating in isolated settings simply proved difficult to overcome. The federal government didn't help matters by continually haggling over funding levels, demanding program evaluations, and otherwise overseeing First Nations operations. In some instances (Aboriginal management of post-secondary training is perhaps the best example), the federal government changed promised funding arrangements, transferring financial problems into the hands of First Nations managers.

Other self-government programs were more successful. The Nisga'a, for example, established an array of locally managed initiatives. The school system (with a strong emphasis on language and culture), a post-secondary institution (the Nisga'a House of Learning), health and community care services, and economic development operations proved extremely popular with residents and became a model of First Nations management. In communities like Alkali Lake, self-managed operations (especially in the forest industry) were crucial to renewing local culture. Aboriginally run schools in the Lower Mainland and on Vancouver Island became the focus for community pride and Aboriginal assertiveness. And in the Interior, the ability of First Nations groups like Westbank and Kamloops to assume greater responsibility in local administration was greeted with enthusiasm.

What did this period of partial and limited self-government prove? While the results were mixed, the experience revealed that stereotypes about First Nations' inability to manage their affairs were unfounded. Many of the key difficulties that Aboriginal communities faced were those of location, history, and the skill level of the population. All were problems common to small, remote, and externally dominated communities in general. In those areas where major initiatives began, community pride and the development of trained and able managers were marks of the gradual rejection of paternalism.

These first initiatives proved that self-government is not easy, simple, or painless. As decision-making power shifted from the government to local leadership, First Nations people found themselves arguing with their managers, not with bureaucrats from Victoria or Ottawa. Given the frequent shortage of resources, First Nations governments faced inevitable and difficult choices, and quickly discovered that in such situations it was impossible to please everyone.

Aboriginal self-government is not an untested concept. Governments moving to implement self-government in British Columbia are not operating in a vacuum. Because the process is entangled in treaty negotiations, it is integrated into discussions of land rights, resource control, and financial transfers. This has added to public suspicion and Aboriginal insistence. By extending the discussions on this issue across the country, and by giving self-government agreements constitutional protection, the inherent rights program has taken some of the sting out of the arguments, but has not resolved all of the uncertainty. The simple reality is that making the shift from concepts and legalisms to practical issues will certainly be difficult.[22]

The Challenges of Self-Government

Support for First Nations' self-government dominates the Aboriginal political agenda in British Columbia.[23] Chief Saul Terry of the Union of British Columbia Indian Chiefs rejected the federal government's inherent rights policy as a "cookie-cutter approach" that was little more than municipal-style administration. But Chief Joe Mathias of the First Nations Summit observed: "It means we will have our own jurisdictions, an opportunity to run our own lives without veto power from bureaucrats and politicians."[24]

Unlike other "new" initiatives, however, self-government has been around in various forms and at various levels for quite some time. British Columbia and the federal government are not moving into uncharted territory in attempting to understand the potential effects and difficulties of this large and bold initiative. There are many reasons to be optimistic about the future of First Nations government under negotiated self-government. But there are, at the same time, more than a few concerns that are often left unspoken or unresolved, submerged in the rhetoric and enthusiasm for the empowerment of First Nations communities. This section examines some of those major challenges.

Seeing self-government as the latest cure-all

First Nations policy in Canada has tended to lurch from one "cure-all" approach to another, from Christianization to residential schools, and from a conviction that segregating First Nations on reserves would address their needs to an equally strong expectation that integration was the answer. Federal governments have sought to develop strategies and programs that would solve the social, economic, and cultural difficulties facing First Nations communities, but with little success. The past 20 years have seen many of these attempts, from costly and unproductive programs of limited community self-government to highly promoted Aboriginal economic development schemes. None has achieved the desired result. First Nations communities were not empowered, economic difficulties did not disappear, social problems were not solved. And critics began to complain, more loudly and persistently than in the past, that vast amounts of government funds were being spent with little return on the investment.

For the first time, a policy initiative has now emerged that has the strong support (although not unanimous) of the First Nations themselves. Unlike earlier "solutions" to the "Indian problem" proposed by those outside the Aboriginal community, plans for a more complete form of self-government have been created largely by the First Nations. A few Aboriginal groups in B.C. do not support the move toward self-government. They feel that it is too limited and not properly respectful of their sovereign rights to administer their land and their affairs. However, surprisingly enough, this initiative has the solid backing of the federal government, the support of the British Columbia government, and widespread support from non-aboriginal groups.

In fact, the high level of enthusiasm is in itself a cause for concern. Expectations are running very high. The chorus seems to be that self-government will solve the problems of the past and present, give First Nations communities the power they deserve, and build the foundation for a new relationship among Aboriginal and non-aboriginal peoples, and their governments. No matter how broadly supported it is, no one policy initiative can fulfil everything expected of it.

Each party has different expectations. As with the treaty process itself, the idea of First Nations self-government gets support from many non-aboriginal people who simply want to end the protests and demands, and finally resolve a decades-old debate. At the other extreme, many First Nations leaders see the current round of self-government negotiations as only the first step toward greater autonomy, even sovereignty. Self-government will clearly not fulfil everyone's hopes, and as a result will be judged by some observers to be a failure. More realistic forecasts about the timing, cost, difficulties, and effects of First Nations self-government would help control public expectations. However, with earlier "solutions" to the challenges facing Aboriginal peoples, few are reluctant to challenge such a popular campaign.

Reducing the weight of bureaucracy

At present, First Nations communities in British Columbia face a bewildering forest of administrations and government. The Department of Indian Affairs and Northern Development plays a major role in the lives of Aboriginal peoples, but they also have additional relationships with numerous federal and provincial departments, municipal governments, and regional districts. Self-government will reinforce First Nations' own administrative systems, but it should substantially reduce the weight of existing bureaucracies.

Instead of making many and occasionally contradictory presentations to different government agencies, self-governing communities will be able to manage programs and initiatives on their own. And instead of waiting for occasional visits from Ottawa or Victoria officials, and then waiting even longer for them to make decisions, First Nations will have the authority to proceed after minimal consultation with other levels of government. The current round of negotiations, discussions, appeal procedures, and administration absorbs a great deal of First Nations' time and effort. Self-government is designed to free up human and financial resources for community-based concerns.[25]

Removing paternalism

Reducing if not eliminating outside involvement in some First Nations affairs has a cultural and social benefit that goes beyond purely practical considerations of time and money. For generations, First

Nations have been governed by outsiders, principally agents of the Department of Indian Affairs. The paternalistic attitude that usually came with this administration was a major cultural imposition on Aboriginal peoples. It gave people without a family or strong personal connection to the First Nations power to make decisions about their lives.

At best, this arrangement allowed well-meaning outsiders to control community affairs. At worst, it gave power to culturally insensitive and manipulative administrators, some of whom were as interested in shoring up personal power as they were in good management. In all cases, government by outsiders left the First Nations without control over their affairs, forced to ask government to handle the most basic matters of community life.

The symbolism of self-government is highly significant. It signals that Aboriginal communities are again running their own affairs, gives them direct managerial responsibility, and reduces community dependence on outsiders. Because individual self-government agreements allow local autonomy, they can substantially reduce the false belief that outsiders know what is best for First Nations communities, which has governed the First Nations for over a century.

Including cultural principles in government administration

Even with the growing anti-government feeling in B.C., the majority of British Columbians want democratically elected governments, an established civil service, and legal guidelines for how elected officials and staff manage local, district, and provincial affairs. People generally accept that tight accountability controls, appropriate hiring systems for staff, public tendering of contracts, and numerous other government regulations are the best possible means to ensure fair and honest government.

First Nations people, however, have a slightly different agenda. Their goal is the same: effective administration of the community. But the First Nations prefer to achieve it according to their own cultural principles.[26] The overriding purpose of self-government is to make sure that First Nations' culture drives First Nations government. This occurs in a variety of ways: selecting representatives by culturally based methods, including prayers and ceremonies in the decision-making process, giving a larger role to community elders in making government judgments, giving cultural concerns a top priority in fund allocations, and giving primary consideration to local needs in forming policy.[27]

Understanding the politics of smallness

Talk about self-government that speaks of "nation to nation negotiations," "community-based administration," and the like ignores one very fundamental reality: size. Most First Nations in British Columbia are very small. The larger ones typically divide their populations among several reserves.

Smallness is a vital and often overlooked political issue. It is not a concern only for Aboriginal peoples, but applies across the political landscape. Governments of small populations, whether it be Norfolk Island in the South Pacific or Greenland, face special circumstances: political intimacy, personal relationships, the interconnectedness of individuals and administrative decisions, and the "goldfish bowl" experience of public life. (We can also add the challenge of less local expertise, which we will discuss in the following section.)

Smallness creates an enormous set of difficult political and operational problems. Budgetary spending has a direct and immediate effect on people whom the decision-makers know or are related to. The need to consider family ahead of or equal to the community is very strong. (This in turn is a major problem for businesses in small towns.) Nepotism is extremely difficult to avoid, particularly in First Nations communities, where anecdotal evidence shows a very strong relationship between family and educational attainment. Within Aboriginal communities, one can add the extra difficulties of clan or other affiliations, and the often difficult relationship between modern and traditional ways of making decisions. Overriding all of these factors is the relative absence of privacy. Everyone knows what goes on in everyone else's life. An individual having marital difficulties, for example, might discover that the community is unwilling to follow their lead on social or cultural matters, precisely because they know about the domestic situation.

This is not an "Aboriginal problem." It is the politics of size. The larger the political body, the less likely personal considerations are to influence day-to-day administration. As governments become smaller—whether in a small farming settlement, a remote mining town, or a tiny coastal fishing village—pressures intensify on the individuals involved, and domestic and administrative matters overlap. Many of the problems of community-level politics that are assumed to be Aboriginal in nature are in fact the challenges of smallness. Since the self-government process is based at the community or band level rather than the tribal or regional level, the politics of smallness will intrude on Aboriginal decision-making.

Overcoming shortages of local expertise

Of all the questions surrounding First Nations self-government, the one that is perhaps the most important has been the least discussed. Self-government requires people—trained, skilled, able managers, comfortable in local cultural situations and capable of working effectively with several layers of government. Most First Nations have few such people available. Those who have these skills are fully absorbed in land claims negotiations, court cases, and other projects. This is no criticism of First Nations people. Because of a long history of marginalization and neglect, and because their very best people have been preoccupied for the last 30 years in seemingly endless confrontations, the First Nations do not have a strong, well-educated core of leaders ready to step easily and smoothly into the administrative positions that will be created by the self-government process.

Who, then, will govern? One option is to bring non-aboriginal professionals in, perhaps only as a transitional phase. The First Nations are strongly committed to education and professional upgrading, so over time, this shortage will likely be remedied. Governments have attempted to shape First Nations training by preparing strong support programs in certain academic areas (like education, health, and law), but have generally done little for students interested in other fields. Recent land claims deals in the Yukon and with the Nisga'a include plans to expand educational programs. However, these are coming after the fact of administrative change.

The supply of trained professionals varies dramatically from First Nation to First Nation. In most cases, only a small group of talented leaders take on most of the responsibilities for the community as a whole. Over the past few years, these leaders have been under withering pressure from land claims, constitutional talks, major political issues, roadblocks and standoffs, debates over resources, and community education. Not surprisingly, the burnout rate has been considerable.

Self-government simply raises demands on Aboriginal leaders to new levels, providing at the same time a level of freedom and responsibility, autonomy from government, and intense local scrutiny. Will the First Nations be able to cope with the rapid implementation of self-government? In most cases, the answer is no. This is one of the main reasons why the national inherent right policy is designed to be a gradual process.

It is distressing that the shortage of First Nations expertise does not get discussed in public. Non-aboriginal people familiar with the personalities of First Nations communities do wonder aloud about it, but government leaders rarely pick up on their concerns. First Nations talk about the need for accelerated educational programs, but do not wish to publicly express anything that might be perceived as a weakness. Governments, in turn, are wary of being seen as openly critical of First Nations leadership, or as having a paternalistic attitude. As a result, one of the most fundamental issues of the entire self-government process gets discussed in hushed tones and private conversations.

Most First Nations communities (except the very small ones) have the local expertise to tackle self-government if they have enough training and time to prepare. Only a very few First Nations now have enough skilled and experienced leaders to handle a more rapid expansion in local administration. It would be foolish for the First Nations to expand self-government beyond their ability to handle the responsibilities.

If self-government is implemented too quickly, major problems and administrative failures would almost certainly be the result. Perhaps the most crucial element in the entire self-government process is the opportunity to go slow, to bring duties and responsibilities on line as the community develops experience and expertise. Modern politics encourages haste, but logic and reason dictate caution.

Overcoming the costs and complications of program delivery

First Nations face special administrative difficulties related to location. First, most Aboriginal communities are located in remote regions, often a considerable distance from other government services and with poor road and air access. Many communities now have half or more of their band members living off the reserve. As self-government expands, managing programs and people under these conditions will be very expensive.

Providing innovative educational programs in the Lower Mainland is a very different challenge at Fort Ware. Providing appropriate health care is much easier in Kelowna than in Prophet River. And economic development programs are much easier to implement around Victoria than along the west coast of Vancouver Island. Expectations of what is possible and what is reasonable will have to take considerations of distance into account.

The second difficulty is that urbanization has resulted in a sizable shift in population from rural reserves to towns and cities.[28] The Nisga'a, for example, have four main communities in the Nass Valley, but have also planned for their urban populations in Terrace, Prince Rupert, and Vancouver. There are probably more members of the Ahousat First Nation in Victoria than in the village. So it goes across the province, presenting serious difficulties to First Nations governments. Will services be available only on reserves? Will First Nations be required to provide for members who live off the reserve? What happens if more than half the population moves off the reserve? How will government structures and decision-making procedures accommodate dispersed populations?[29]

Program delivery presents some very serious practical problems for First Nations governments. Isolation, remoteness, distance, and dispersed band members all add to the costs and complications of government. The fact that self-government is based on membership in a specific First Nation and not on geography or place of residence adds to the difficulties. These practical problems, which trouble First Nations and governments but that the public only rarely considers, can make the already difficult challenge of bringing government closer to Aboriginal people even tougher.

Deciding who pays: The financial aspects of self-government

Self-government is not free. It will require very careful financial negotiations among three major parties: First Nations, the federal government, and provincial governments. The first order of business will be to figure out the relationship between governments, and how payments are calculated. The options are considerable, ranging from allocating a certain amount of money per First Nations member, to creating a provincial or national funding agency that would make sure each First Nation is funded the same way.[30]

Governments will be looking for clarity and simplicity in their financial arrangements, if this is possible given the tensions in federal finances in Canada. They will have to ensure that the arrangements are fair compared to those of non-aboriginal communities in similar regions. On the other hand, the First Nations will likely press for flexibility, for ongoing attention to specific circumstances and changing needs, and for the right to lobby for future increases in funding. These negotiations will ultimately determine whether Aboriginal self-government is viable. Expect them to be very long and difficult.[31]

Once general financial arrangements are set, more serious challenges will emerge. Accountability for public funds will be a crucial issue. The public has always demanded a high level of accountability from First Nations, often more than for other organizations, which reveals an inherent distrust of their administrative ability.

But the first level of accountability for self-governed communities must and should be to the community itself, and only secondarily to the federal and provincial governments. Self-government is and must be a statement of faith in First Nations' ability to govern themselves successfully and to take full responsibility for errors of judgment. High levels of cynicism, some of it from within First Nations communities, make it likely that the public will insist on this issue.

Looming in the background is the prospect of taxation.[32] Under both the treaties and the self-government provisions, First Nations will be expected to raise a significant but unspecified portion of the costs to run their governments. This issue has many different implications. Will First Nations be expected to use tax revenues from businesses established with funds from a land claims settlement to pay for the cost of administration? Will the gradual removal of tax exemptions for First Nations, as required under recent treaties, pay for the costs of self-government? Have First Nations carefully considered what expectations will follow when they establish property taxes and other fees to cover basic administrative operations?

The taxation issue has long been a major one for all governments. As treaties are settled and as self-government agreements are implemented, it will become a major concern for First Nations as well. Given the current level of poverty in most Aboriginal communities in British Columbia, the prospect of paying significant taxes and fees may not sit well with First Nations people. They will see this as another example of governments making them buy their freedom.

Beyond the inevitable posturing and hard feelings that will surround the financial negotiations is a very basic concern for the long-term sustainability of self-government. Governments expect that First Nations will pay an increasing share of the cost of local administration. In addition, they also expect to continue honouring both legal and moral obligations to First Nations, to ensure that Aboriginal communities are not dealt with more harshly than nearby non-aboriginal communities. First Nations also expect governments to honour their historic and legal commitments. It is not yet clear whether they have fully considered the implications of paying a significant portion of the costs of self-government. This issue will figure very prominently in the next few years, as governments and First Nations wrestle with the financial implications and procedures.

Addressing the concerns of municipal and regional governments

If First Nations self-government is the stuff of high-level politics and treaty-making, it is also the source of tremendous local and regional concern, and in many quarters, hostility. Particularly in the Interior and northern parts of B.C., municipalities are extremely worried about what implications First Nations self-government has for them. They are also concerned about what they see as a lack of attention to local issues. British Columbia municipalities and regional districts have repeatedly expressed their severe misgivings about the current land claims process and self-government negotiations. They have made numerous statements, requests, and demands to federal and provincial authorities, requesting seats at the negotiating table and regular updates on the treaty and self-government discussions.

The potential problems are many: expectations of unequal taxes, questions about who will pay for water and sewage systems, fire protection and policing, local zoning regulations, and access to municipal services (like libraries, swimming pools, and recreational facilities). There are also no formal consultation processes with existing municipalities.[33] Add the inevitable rumours about First Nations using their right to set up gambling casinos, or, as in the case of the Mohawk reserves in Quebec, to completely ignore provincial and municipal regions.[34]

The practical concerns of municipal and regional government are in many ways the "sleeper" in the self-government process. Many have dismissed them as the uninformed doubts of local borough politicians, or as attempts by opponents to derail the process. In reality, the issues of how municipal and First Nations administrations will interact are critical.

After the formal negotiations and public signings are over, the task of making self-government work will rest at this level. If municipal governments continue to be hostile to self-government, and particularly if they feel that independent First Nations communities will create difficult financial and operational burdens for local councils, very serious barriers and conflicts could develop. Failure to consider the concerns of municipal and district governments could therefore harm implementation, and aggravate relations between Aboriginal and non-aboriginal peoples in the province.

Handling the effects of government cutbacks

Government plays a more active role in First Nations communities than in almost any other part of Canadian society (with the exception of the Yukon, Northwest Territories, Newfoundland, and the Greater Ottawa Region). The service requirements under the *Indian Act* and attempts to improve social, cultural, and economic conditions for Aboriginal people has meant that federal and provincial government departments have emerged as major influences in the lives of First Nations people. Some First Nations have become extremely adept at playing the administrative and political funding games, are very successful in applying for grants, and have otherwise found ways to increase government programs in their communities.

Gone is the paternalistic attitude and single-office approach of the old Department of Indian Affairs agency. In its place is a complex and often inefficient network of departmental activities and involvements. As government has expanded across Canada from the 1960s onward, it assumed an even more prominent role in First Nations communities.

Recent fiscal policies have changed the focus of government programming. Federal and provincial governments are downsizing, shifting whatever administrative responsibilities possible to local governments. (In this context, of course, First Nations self-government takes its place among other strategies to improve administrative efficiency.) Non-aboriginal Canadians have either supported, agreed with, or resented the downsizing of government responsibilities. First Nations communities have so many pressing needs and concerns that they expect government to continue to play an active role. In the short term, the problem is not terribly pronounced, but if federal and national governments make sharper cuts in community support and social welfare programs (as appears to be under way in Ontario), a new issue will emerge for First Nations.

Self-government processes, including the inherent right initiative, allow First Nations to take responsibility for certain areas of government. To use a particularly striking (and unlikely) example, if the government were to stop making social welfare payments, funding and authority for First Nations in this area would also decline. In an era of government cutbacks and a very rapid shift to users paying for services, this has serious implications for self-governed Aboriginal communities. The move toward self-government supports the current trend toward handing responsibilities to local administration, but conflicts with the prevailing tide that suggests governments are reducing their level of intervention in the lives of their people. In a dramatic, New Zealand-style scenario, First Nations governments could gain self-government, but then face a reduction in the list of responsibilities and the level of funding they get to carry it out.

Defending collective rights in the era of the individual

Giving Aboriginal communities more power also goes against some of the most powerful political forces on the Canadian (and international) landscape: asserting the rights of the individual, and the freeing of societies from the shackles of government.[35] The Reform Party's position on treaties and self-government is often dismissed as the racist ramblings of rural "red-necks," but their arguments have some logic. They criticize the concept of collective and particularly "special" rights, arguing that individuals should have common rights and common opportunities. Much as it runs counter to the ideal of collective rights that has governed Canada since World War II, this view is becoming more and more widely held. It is often held up as the answer to the demands of Aboriginal people.[36] Mel Smith, a former constitutional advisor to the provincial government, expressed some of these feeling when he wrote:

> The outcome of these treaty negotiations, as presently contemplated, with the self-government arrangements which are likely to follow, could re-shape the economic, social and political face of British Columbia. If this process goes ahead, at the end of the day, B.C. may create dozens of fiefdoms, or so-called "First Nations," each with their own law-making body, territory, justice system and economy. In process and in substance the present B.C. treaty-making process is ill-conceived, unworkable and unjust.[37]

Some authors have predicted the global victory of the liberal, capitalist model over socialist and communist systems—an overly simple reading of political and cultural complexities. But it does appear likely that the needs and rights of the individual will be at the forefront of international politics for some time. The very intellectual and political underpinnings of aboriginal self-government will fly in the face of national and international priorities. First Nations will generally not have difficulty maintaining their "collectivist" position. Although there are blocks of support for "individual" rights among aboriginal peoples, they may well find that the arguments marshaled to defend this position will fall on increasingly uncomprehending ears.

The Outlook for First Nations
Self-Government in British Columbia

Accepting that many questions about implementation are unanswered, and will remain so for many years, the negotiation of self-governing rights is forging ahead. Aboriginal self-government already exists, if in a fairly limited form, and will expand rapidly in the years to come. As the political and administrative relationships change, so too will British Columbia. It is impossible to predict what the precise effect of self-government will be, but we can put forward some strong possibilities of what may happen.

More powerful Aboriginal communities

Self-government gives Aboriginal people power.[38] When agreements are negotiated and implemented, First Nations will very quickly face a sharp change in internal management. Decisions made by external agents will be made at home. Distant civil servants, notorious for their short visits and lengthy decision-making processes, will be replaced by local managers—friends, relatives, and tribal members. Priorities once set hundreds if not thousands of miles away will be debated openly in the town hall. The people leading and listening to them can act on community consensus.

The freedom and control that accompanies self-government, even if limited at first to management of a few programs, brings numerous benefits to the First Nations. Solutions are not instant, and having to make difficult choices about neighbours and relatives can add tension and uncertainty. But the power to make changes now rests within the community: a much desired change from long reliance on the Department of Indian Affairs and the confusing array of federal and provincial agencies.

New relationships with other British Columbians

One of the central purposes of Aboriginal self-government is to redefine relationships between First Nations people and other British Columbians. At one level, self-government is a separatist initiative, expanding and even cementing divisions between these groups. But at the same time, self-government changes the structure of the subordinate and dominant relationship entrenched in the *Indian Act* and in more than 100 years of outside control. It makes more equitable arrangements possible.

Self-governed communities will have clear and defined arrangements with federal and provincial governments, and will have an ongoing obligation to work with nearby municipalities and other government agencies. With resources, responsibilities, and authority of their own (based on the federal government's inherent right policy and, over time, constitutionally entrenched in treaty agreements), First Nations governments will be in a much better position to meet other governments on an equal footing. Negotiations certainly carry the potential for conflict, but they should eventually provide a foundation for new relationships between First Nations peoples and other British Columbians.

Disappointments and criticism

There are no assurances that implementing self-government will go smoothly, and no guarantees that the communities involved will find it an easy task. Non-aboriginal critics of self-government expect the initiative to fail, and will be quick to pounce on any and all signs of weakness. And there will be difficulties. No project of this scale, involving numerous services, millions of dollars, dozens of communities, three levels of government, and hundreds of negotiators and administrators, could be expected to proceed without conflicts, controversies, and perhaps administrative chaos. Those who feel that self-government is a bad idea will be ready to bring these occasions to the public's attention, which could erode general support.

Most First Nations people support the shift to self-government, but implementing local control will nevertheless cause conflict and criticism here, too. Decisions made by outsiders are viewed very differently than local judgments are. People tend to expect that self-government will avoid the arbitrary, hasty, and wrong choices made in the past by civil servants not connected to the community. Like all other governments, Aboriginal governments will make mistakes. From time to time, favouritism will emerge, leaders will make bad choices and poor investments, and local residents will be offended. First Nations people will then vent their frustration at "the government," only to find that it is at their doorstep.

First Nations self-government is a very high-profile initiative. It is engulfed in unrealistic expectations, carrying the aspirations of Aboriginal peoples on the tide of administrative change. Because of this profile, because a significant number of non-aboriginal people expect failure, and because the decisions made under self-government will inevitably cause divisions within communities, the effort is bound to disappoint some people. And they'll make much of the difficulties, likely more than deserved. (This could be described as the "Rafe Mair factor," for the influential talk-show host has staked out a place at the front of the parade of self-government critics.) By the same token, some First Nations people have invested self-government with an aura of invincibility, thus making the administrative restructuring an open target for criticism from those unsure of change.

Mel Smith, one of the most articulate critics of First Nations self-government, offered a biting critique of Canadian Aboriginal policy in his book, *Our Home or Native Land?* After making it clear that he opposes special rights for First Nations people, he argues that self-government should be built on the Sechelt model: powers transferred should be municipal in character, and all local laws should be bound by the *Canadian Charter of Rights and Freedoms*. Under Smith's plan, ownership of reserves would be transferred to the band, local governments would have to be elected, and self-government would only be granted where there was a clear plan for economic viability and governmental sustainability.[39] With outspoken and well-informed opponents like Mel Smith monitoring the process, self-government will have regular and constructive review.[40]

Steps toward broader political goals

For the past ten years, those who support self-government have established new administrative arrangements as a major goal of First Nations politics in British Columbia (as they have done with the treaty process). This has diverted attention from the broader more fundamental goals of First Nations political action. Some of these are to preserve culture and language; re-establish healthy communities; provide for local economic, social, and cultural development; eliminate reliance on external organizations and officials; and give First Nations peoples control over their future. In this context, we must remember that self-government is a means to a much larger, more ambitious, and more crucial end. It is not an end in itself.

The test of self-government should not be whether First Nations people can manage their affairs as well or better than outsiders. They have passed it on numerous occasions across the province. The more substantial task for the First Nations is to capitalize on the opportunities presented by self-government to address the wider set of challenges facing their communities. This is a long, more difficult, and less precise goal, but it is the one that underpins the extensive and continuing effort to replace external with local control.

No magic solutions

The ultimate question, of course, is whether self-government will actually work, and it has no certain answer. It is important to remember that self-government is a process rather than an event. First Nations have been getting control of certain administrative responsibilities, service by service, and have been gradually getting used to the responsibilities and opportunities involved. We can expect more of the same.

Self-government will not come to British Columbia in one quick government action. It will be implemented community by community, at their own pace, after extensive negotiations with federal and provincial officials. Local communities and neighbours will have time to adjust to the differences in structure. For some First Nations, self-government will arrive quickly, as with the Nisga'a. Others who are not as ready to take on the responsibilities will move much more slowly. And inevitably, the results will depend on the people and circumstances involved.

A more troubling issue is whether the First Nations will become truly autonomous, or simply responsible for administering their own dependency. First Nations and other observers alike have identified the existing culture of dependency as one of the central challenges facing Aboriginal peoples. Critics of federal affirmative action programs in the United States have often pointed out that a process designed to bring equality of opportunity and circumstances has had few direct results beyond creating a nucleus of African-Americans to manage welfare and social assistance programs.

A similar concern needs to be addressed in British Columbia, for the potential exists for self-government to become little more than a shift in who controls welfare dependency. First Nations leaders are anxious to use the treaty process in combination with self-government to gain the resources, freedom, and administrative power necessary to carve a new path for their communities. Time will tell whether they achieve their goals.

The push for self-government in British Columbia has been invested with so many expectations that it will clearly disappoint some. Self-government is not a cure-all. It is a complex, difficult political process designed to transfer administrative responsibility and accountability. There is no magic, no instant solution, no immediate cure for social, cultural, and economic problems. Self-government could, in fact, create division amongst the First Nations and aggravate rather than ease tensions between Aboriginal and non-aboriginal communities. One thing is certain: self-government will arrive before we really know it's here, in a seemingly endless series of small agreements, short advances, occasional stumbles, brilliant successes, and tragic failures.

Conclusion

We know enough about First Nations self-government in British Columbia to be confident in its ultimate success, provided rapid changes are kept firmly in check. Self-government can and does work. The First Nations manage their affairs as well as (and often considerably better than) federal or provincial agencies. And gaining control of administrative affairs will bring undoubted benefits to First Nations communities: pride, local control, and freedom in decision-making. It will also bring high expectations. Few government initiatives will be watched with as critical an eye as First Nations self-government. Fewer still are expected to address as many community difficulties.

Self-government will not come quickly, nor without struggle. But the process of giving power back to the First Nations is long overdue. It begins a process of reversing generations of paternalistic control, distant administrators, and rule by outsiders. First Nations seeking to expand their self-government powers will discover that history creates a heavy burden that cannot easily be laid aside. We will do well to remember that burden, and the role of federal and provincial governments in creating the social, cultural, economic, and political difficulties facing these communities, to support First Nations in the effort to regain control over their lives.

Notes

1. Cassidy, p. 191.

2. For an overview of the debate on self-government, see

- Dan Smith, *The Seventh Fire: The Struggle for Aboriginal Self-Government*
- Douglas Brown, *Aboriginal Government and Power Sharing in Canada*
- John Hylton, *Aboriginal Self-Government in Canada: Current Trends and Issues*
- Patrick Macklem, *Aboriginal Self-Government: Legal and Constitutional Issues.*

3. D.C. Hawkes tries to answer these questions in *Aboriginal Self-Government: What Does it Mean?*

4. The best study of Aboriginal self-government in Canada is Menno Boldt's *Surviving as Indians: The Challenge of Self-Government.* For a more ideological critique of the politics behind self-government, see Anne-Marie Mawhiney, *Towards Aboriginal Self-Government: Relations Between Status Indian Peoples and the Government of Canada, 1969–1984.* See also John Hylton's *Aboriginal Self-Government in Canada.*

5. For an overview of Aboriginal cultures in the region, see Alan McMillan, *Native Peoples and Cultures of Canada.* On colonial and government policy, see Robin Fisher, *Contact and Conflict: Indian-European Relations in British Columbia, 1774–1890.*

6. Gough.

7. The better studies on this theme, particularly as government policy relates to British Columbia, are

- Douglas Cole and Ira Chaikin, *An Iron Hand Upon the People: The Law Against the Potlatch on the Northwest Coast*
- J.R. Miller, "Owen Glendower, Hotspur, and Canadian Indian Policy"
- Tina Loo, "Dan Cramer's Potlatch: Law as Coercion, Symbol and Rhetoric in British Columbia, 1884–1951"

- Brian Titley, *A Narrow Vision: Duncan Campbell Scott and the Administration of Indian Affairs in Canada.*

The best overview is Paul Tennant's *Aboriginal Peoples and Politics: The Indian Land Question in British Columbia, 1849–1989.*

8. For a strongly worded critique of this process, see Howard Adams, "Red Powerlessness: Bureaucratic Authoritarianism on Indian Reserves." On how this related to Canadian Aboriginal people in the 1960s, see H.B. Hawthorne, *A Survey of the Contemporary Indians of Canada.*

9. Weaver.

10. Asch.

11. For a politician's analysis of the concept of a third level of government, see K. Penner, "Their Own Place: The Case for a Distinct Order of Indian First Nation Government in Canada."

12. Royal Commission on Aboriginal Peoples, *Summary and Terms of Reference.*

13. Etkin.

14. For a critical analysis of this era, see Menno Boldt and J.A. Long, "Native Indian Self-Government: Instrument of Autonomy or Assimilation."

15. Ron Irwin, as quoted in the Government of Canada's *Federal Policy Guide: Aboriginal Self-Government,* p. 2.

16. One of the best recent studies of the sovereignty issue relates to Australia. See Henry Reynolds, *Aboriginal Sovereignty: Three Nations, One Australia.*

17. Luke McNamara writes on the relationship between the Charter of Rights and Freedoms and self-government in "Aboriginal Self-Government and Justice Reform in Canada: The Impact of the Charter of Rights and Freedoms."

18. Government of Canada, *Federal Policy Guide: Aboriginal Self-Government,* p. 5.

19. Government of Canada, *Federal Policy Guide: Aboriginal Self-Government*, p. 6. Many First Nations would disagree with the federal government's position, but that stance is unlikely to change.

20. The provincial government's approach to self-government negotiations is spelled out in "British Columbia's Approach to Treaty Settlements and Self-Government." The federal government's position appears in *Federal Policy Guide: Aboriginal Self-Government*. For a more general overview, see the Federal Treaty Negotiation Office's *Treaty News: Special Edition on Aboriginal Self-Government*.

21. For an overview of this process, see Menno Boldt, *Surviving as Indians*; and R.H. Bartlett, *Subjugation, Self-Management and Self-Government of Aboriginal Land and Reserves in Canada*.

22. The best study on self-government in B.C. is Frank Cassidy and Robert Bish's *Indian Government: Its Meaning in Practice*.

23. Other countries have made efforts toward Aboriginal self-rule. Interested readers might consult Augue Fleras, *The "Nations Within": Aboriginal State Relations in Canada, the United States and New Zealand*; or Guntram Werther, *Self-Determination in Western Democracies: Aboriginal Politics in a Comparative Perspective*.

24. Both statements are from the Federal Treaty Negotiation Office's *Treaty News*, p. 1.

25. Hudson.

26. Durst.

27. Perhaps the most important exception on this point is the insistence by First Nations women that Aboriginal self-government must not work to their disadvantage. They have played a major role in ensuring that the Charter of Rights and Freedoms remains in effect in self-governing communities. On this issue, see H. Hammersmith, "Aboriginal Women and Self-Government," and H. Morry, "Doubly Disadvantaged and Historically Forgotten? Aboriginal Women and the Inherent Right of Aboriginal Self-Government."

28. The issue of what government structures are most appropriate for First Nations people living away from reserves has attracted little attention up to now. John Weinstein discusses it in *Aboriginal Self-Determination Off a Land Base*.

29. On the unique aspects of Aboriginal self-government in urban centers, see Evelyn Peters, *Aboriginal Self-Government in Urban Areas: Proceedings of a Workshop* and "Self-Government for Aboriginal Peoples in Urban Areas: A Literature Review and Suggestions for Research."

30. This proposal appears in Vicky Barham and Robin Broadway's *Financing Aboriginal Self-Government*.

31. Hawkes and Maslove. See also M. Malone, *Financing Aboriginal Self-Government in Canada*; and Barham and Broadway's *Financing Aboriginal Self-Government*.

32. Bish.

33. Dust.

34. On the special issues surrounding Aboriginal self-government in Quebec, see Kerry Cannon and Bruce Hodkins, *On the Land: Confronting the Challenges of Aboriginal Self-Government in Northern Quebec and Labrador*. See also Secretariat of the Parliamentary Committees, *The Political and Constitutional Future of Quebec: Relations Between the State and Aboriginal Nations*.

35. For a provocative introduction to this theme, see Francis Fykuyama's *The End of History*, and also Lester Thurow, *The Future of Capitalism: How Today's Economic Forces Shape Tomorrow's World*. One important element in this process is the rapid economic growth of Asia, and the emergence of the "Asian way" as the dominant form of national government. The Asian way places very low priority on government intervention in personal lives and emphasizes the role of the family. For further information, see John Naisbitt, *Megatrends Asia*.

36. The 1996 Australian election featured extensive public debate on this issue. In New Zealand, polls suggest that a solid majority of electors favour settling legal obligations under the Treaty of Waitangi, but that an equally large group do not believe that the Maori have, or should have, any special rights under New Zealand law.

37. Smith.

38. For a very powerful statement on how this issue relates to Australia, see Christine Fletcher, *Aboriginal Non-Democracy: A Case for Aboriginal Self-Government And Responsive Administration.*

39. Smith.

40. The provincial press has been full of negative and often hostile opinions on the prospects for Aboriginal self-government. In particular, back issues of *BC Report* have carried regular commentaries on this issue. The more liberal magazines in British Columbia and Western Canada have generally published little material on the subject, except for those published by Native organizations (like *Windspeaker*).

References

Adams, Howard. "Red Powerlessness: Bureaucratic Authoritarianism on Indian Reserves." *Cornell Journal of Social Relations* 18/1 (Fall 1984), pp. 28–40.

Asch, M. "Penner and Self-Government: An Appraisal." *Canadian Dimension* 19/5 (1985), pp. 14–17.

Barham, Vicky, and Robin Broadway. *Financing Aboriginal Self-Government.* Report submitted to the Royal Commission on Aboriginal Peoples. Unpublished research paper, 1994.

Bartlett, R.H. *Subjugation, Self-Management and Self-Government of Aboriginal Land and Reserves in Canada.* Kingston: Institute of Intergovernmental Relations, 1986.

Bish, Robert. *Aboriginal Government Taxation and Service Responsibility: Implementing Self-Government in a Federal System.* Victoria: Institute for Research on Public Policy, 1992.

Boldt, Menno. *Surviving as Indians: The Challenge of Self-Government.* Toronto: University of Toronto Press, 1993.

Boldt, Menno, and J.A. Long. "Native Indian Self-Government: Instrument of Autonomy or Assimilation." In *Governments in Conflict: Provinces and Indian Nations in Canada,* eds. J.A. Long and Menno Boldt. Toronto: University of Toronto Press, 1988.

Brown, Douglas. *Aboriginal Government and Power Sharing in Canada*. Kingston: Institute of Government Relations, 1992.

Cannon, Kerry, and Bruce Hodkins. *On the Land: Confronting the Challenges of Aboriginal Self-Government in Northern Quebec and Labrador*. Toronto: Betelyeuse Books, 1995.

Cassidy, Frank. "Troubled Hearts: Indigenous People and the Crown in Canada." *Pacific Viewpoint* 35 (2), 1994.

Cassidy, Frank, and Robert Bish. *Indian Government: Its Meaning in Practice*. Halifax: Institute for Research on Public Policy, 1989.

Cole, Douglas, and Ira Chaikin. *An Iron Hand Upon the People: The Law Against the Potlatch on the Northwest Coast*. Vancouver: Douglas and McIntyre, 1990.

Durst, Douglas. *Aboriginal Self-Government and Social Services: Finding the Path to Empowerment*. Ottawa: Department of Social Services, 1993.

Dust, Theresa. *The Impact of Aboriginal Land Claims and Self-Government on Canadian Municipalities: The Local Government Perspective*. Toronto: Inter-Governmental Committee on Urban and Rural Research, 1995.

Englestad, Diane, ed. *Nation to Nation: Aboriginal Sovereignty and the Future of Canada*. Concord: Anansi, 1992.

Etkin, C.E. "The Sechelt Indian Band: An Analysis of a New Form of Native Self-Government." *Canadian Journal of Native Studies* 8/1 (1988), pp. 73–105.

Federal Treaty Negotiation Office. *Treaty News,* Vol. 2, No. 3 (October 1995).

————. *Treaty News: Special Edition on Aboriginal Self-Government*, Vol. 2, No. 2 (October 1996).

Fisher, Robin. *Contact and Conflict: Indian-European Relations in British Columbia, 1774–1890*. 2nd ed. Vancouver: UBC Press, 1992.

Fleras, Augue. *The "Nations Within": Aboriginal State Relations in Canada, the United States and New Zealand*. Toronto: Oxford, 1992.

Fletcher, Christine. *Aboriginal Non-Democracy: A Case for Aboriginal Self-Government and Responsive Administration*. Darwin: North Australia Research Unit, Discussion Paper No. 23, 1994.

Fykuyama, Francis. *The End of History*. New York: Avon Books, 1993.

Gough, Barry. *Gunboat Frontier: British Maritime Authority and Northwest Coast Indians, 1846–1890*. Vancouver: UBC Press, 1984.

Government of British Columbia. "British Columbia's Approach to Treaty Settlements and Self-Government." (http://www.aaf.govt.bc.ca/aaf/ministry/policydc/s-gsumm.html) 19 March 1996.

Government of Canada. *Federal Policy Guide: Aboriginal Self-Government*. Ottawa: Department of Indian Affairs and Northern Development, 1995. (Also http://www.inac.gc.ca/pubs/selfgov/policy.html)

Hammersmith, H. "Aboriginal Women and Self-Government." In *Nation to Nation: Aboriginal Sovereignty and the Future of Canada,* ed. Diane Englestad. Concord: Anansi, 1992.

Hawkes, D.C. *Aboriginal Self-Government: What Does it Mean?* Kingston: Institute of Intergovernmental Relations, 1985.

———. *Aboriginal Peoples and Government Responsibility*. Ottawa: Carleton University Press, 1989.

Hawkes, D.C., and A. Maslove. "Fiscal Arrangements for Aboriginal Self-Government." In *Aboriginal Peoples and Government Responsibility,* ed. D.C. Hawkes. Ottawa: Carleton University Press, 1989.

Hawthorne, H.B. *A Survey of the Contemporary Indians of Canada*. 2 vols. Ottawa: Indian Affairs Branch, 1966–67.

Hudson, P. "Aboriginal Self-Government and Social Services: First Nations-Provincial Relations." *Canadian Public Policy*, Vol. 18, No. 1 (1992).

Hylton, John. *Aboriginal Self-Government in Canada: Current Trends and Issues*. Saskatoon: Purich Publishing, 1994.

Long, J.A., and Menno Boldt, eds. *Governments in Conflict: Provinces and Indian Nations in Canada*. Toronto: University of Toronto Press, 1988.

Loo, Tina. "Dan Cramer's Potlatch: Law as Coercion, Symbol and Rhetoric in British Columbia, 1884–1951." *Canadian Historical Review* 73, 2 (June 1992).

Macklem, Patrick. *Aboriginal Self-Government: Legal and Constitutional Issues*. Ottawa: Royal Commission on Aboriginal Peoples, 1995.

Malone, M. *Financing Aboriginal Self-Government in Canada*. Kingston: Institute of Intergovernmental Relations, 1986.

Mawhiney, Anne-Marie. *Towards Aboriginal Self-Government: Relations Between Status Indian Peoples and the Government of Canada, 1969–1984*. New York: Garland, 1994.

McMillan, Alan. *Native Peoples and Cultures of Canada*. Vancouver: Douglas & McIntyre, 1988.

McNamara, Luke. "Aboriginal Self-Government and Justice Reform in Canada: The Impact of the Charter of Rights and Freedoms." *Australian-Canadian Studies*, Vol. 11, No. 1–2 (1993).

Miller, J.R. "Owen Glendower, Hotspur, and Canadian Indian Policy." In *Sweet Promises: A Reader on Indian-White Relations in Canada*, ed. J.R. Miller. Toronto: University of Toronto Press, 1991.

Morry, H. "Doubly Disadvantaged and Historically Forgotten? Aboriginal Women and the Inherent Right of Aboriginal Self-Government." *Manitoba Law Journal*, Vol. 21 (1992).

Naisbitt, John. *Megatrends Asia*. New York: Avon, 1996.

Penner, K. "Their Own Place: The Case for a Distinct Order of Indian First Nation Government in Canada." In *Governments in Conflict: Provinces and Indian Nations in Canada,* eds. J.A. Long and Menno Boldt. Toronto: University of Toronto Press, 1988.

Peters, Evelyn. "Self-Government for Aboriginal Peoples in Urban Areas: A Literature Review and Suggestions for Research." *Canadian Journal of Native Studies*, Vol. 12, No. 1 (1992).

Peters, Evelyn, ed. *Aboriginal Self-Government in Urban Areas: Proceedings of a Workshop*. Kingston: Queen's University Press, 1994.

Reynolds, Henry. *Aboriginal Sovereignty: Three Nations, One Australia*. Sydney: Allen and Unwin, 1996.

Royal Commission on Aboriginal Peoples. *Summary and Terms of Reference*. Ottawa: Royal Commission on Aboriginal Peoples, August 1991.

Secretariat of the Parliamentary Committees. *The Political and Constitutional Future of Quebec: Relations Between the State and Aboriginal Nations*. Quebec: SPC, 1991.

Smith, Dan. *The Seventh Fire: The Struggle for Aboriginal Self-Government*. Toronto: Key Porter, 1993.

Smith, Mel. *Our Home or Native Land? What Government's Aboriginal Policy is Doing to Canada*. Victoria: Crown Western, 1995.

Tennant, Paul. *Aboriginal Peoples and Politics: The Indian Land Question in British Columbia, 1849–1989*. Vancouver: UBC Press, 1990.

Thurow, Lester. *The Future of Capitalism: How Today's Economic Forces Shape Tomorrow's World*. New York: William Morrow and Company, 1996.

Titley, Brian. *A Narrow Vision: Duncan Campbell Scott and the Administration of Indian Affairs in Canada*. Vancouver: UBC Press, 1986.

Weaver, Sally. *Making Canadian Indian Policy: The Hidden Agenda, 1968–1970*. Toronto: University of Toronto Press, 1981.

Weinstein, John. *Aboriginal Self-Determination Off a Land Base*. Kingston: Institute of Intergovernmental Relations, 1986.

Werther, Guntram. *Self-Determination in Western Democracies: Aboriginal Politics in a Comparative Perspective*. Westport: Greenwood, 1992.

9

Financing
First Nations
Treaty Settlements

By Brian Scarfe

The issue of financing First Nations treaty settlements clearly goes beyond finding sources for potential cash payments.[1] Settling treaties will mean transferring property rights over certain lands to First Nations peoples. How extensive these property rights are will help determine both the total costs of the settlements themselves, plus the "spill-over" costs that may accrue to third parties if the treaties affect how they now access and use resources. In addition, self-government status will create "transactions" costs attributable to setting up systems to coordinate the relationships between tribal councils and other orders of government, from municipal to federal.

The focus of this chapter is to discuss a possible financial framework for settling First Nations treaties in British Columbia. This discussion will identify the costs of each element within this framework, examine the financial implications of agreements already made, and forecast possible financial arrangements for future settlements. Specifically, the next sections will discuss

- sharing responsibilities and costs
- current systems of land tenure and resource use
- the effects of settlements on local communities and other third parties
- a possible financial framework for treaty settlements
- tax status and services for First Nations people
- the Nisga'a Agreement-in-Principle
- financing future B.C. settlements.

The issues to be addressed are broad. The nature and extent of the property rights transferred to First Nations will have a major influence on how workable the proposed framework is. Cash payments will also have a major effect, as will possible changes in tax status of First Nations peoples and the nature of the government services to which they are entitled. Indeed, we need to face the whole question of who should pay for First Nations treaty settlements upfront.

Sharing Responsibilities and Costs

The traditional perspective of a whole series of B.C. governments has been that Aboriginal rights were long ago extinguished, and that even if the courts decided otherwise, the federal government would have the sole responsibility to deal with them anyway. Over the past few years, however, this point of view has changed. The provincial government has now entered into negotiations with First Nations peoples and the federal government to settle treaties, based on the recommendations set out in the British Columbia Treaty Commission Agreement of September, 1992.

Under this agreement, the governments must negotiate separately with each First Nations applicant. At least 47 different tribal councils or Aboriginal communities have entered claims so far.[2] The federal and provincial governments have also negotiated a cost-sharing formula where the federal government would pay about 80% of the overall cash settlement costs, and the provincial government about 20%. However, the provincial government will also transfer property rights to certain Crown lands.

Setting the value of these transferred property rights will likely create difficult technical issues, which will arise when applying the cost-sharing formula to any particular situation. Disputes over how to interpret their value are inevitable. Nevertheless, a 1996 KPMG report estimated that the cash settlements will cost about $6 billion, and the land transfers more than $3 billion (1995 dollars), with between 3% and 5% of the total lands in B.C. changing hands. So altogether, the two levels of government will share costs roughly equally. Approximately 103,000 First Nations people are likely to benefit from the settlement process, which is about 3% of B.C.'s population.

The provincial government is not expected to purchase any land now privately owned in "fee-simple" for inclusion in the properties to be transferred to First Nations communities. (Holding land in "fee-sim-ple" means having the most absolute ownership possible. Technically, the land still belongs to the Crown, but titleholders have few restrictions on how they use or transfer the land.) However, land transfers could well affect the property rights that other local residents and resource-based firms now have on B.C. Crown lands. These property rights in-clude the ability to extract mineral resources, to harvest Crown timber, to graze animals on provincial range land, and to use provincial water resources. If the Province must reduce these rights to settle First Na-tions treaties, then the issue of how it will compensate third-party in-terests becomes central to the settlement process. Much will depend on what conditions for access are negotiated, and indeed on exactly what property rights Aboriginal title includes. Aboriginal land title could, and arguably should, stop short of granting proprietary or "freehold" own-ership of major territories that now lie outside of Aboriginal reserves (that is, outright ownership for all time). The Province should, never-theless, extend existing reserve lands, and grant tribal councils or Abo-riginal communities proprietary ownership of them.

First Nations communities may be able to pay some of the costs of title settlements themselves. If treaty settlements abolish or phase out the tax-free status of First Nations peoples living on reserve lands, and also reduce the federal government's responsibilities through Aborigi-nal self-government, then Aboriginal communities will bear part of the settlement costs. Admittedly, these savings will be much smaller than the value of resource and cash transfers.

At present, only representatives of First Nations and of the two main orders of government are allowed a place at the negotiating table. Lo-cal communities and private resource interests are not directly repre-sented. This lack of direct representation is understandable, provided that either (or both) levels of government will effectively represent these interests. There is, therefore, an important element of trust that is nec-essary. If the negotiation process is to lead to conclusions that can withstand political opposition, these third parties must be able to trust government to act in their best interests.

Although the government could improve this level of trust by prom-ising to pay compensation to any sacrificed third-party interests, explicit up-front promises of compensation would dramatically increase the costs of settlement, particularly for the provincial government. As a result, local communities and resource businesses are uneasy. They feel that if the government has to change access rights to arrive at an agreement, they will have to pay. On the other hand, the current lack of clarity about property rights in British Columbia is already adding to the uncertainties, and therefore the costs, of resource development in the province. For these reasons, all First Nations treaty settlements must be approved by the Legislative Assembly, and affected third parties should be allowed to speak their cases to government before such approval occurs.

Current Systems of Land Tenure and Resource Use

Systems of property rights for land and natural resources can be classified by their basic characteristics. These include how exclusive and secure the rights are, how long the holders can possess them, whether they can transfer them, and what benefits they get from them.

The economic issues associated with property rights and land tenure systems include

- how holders acquire rights
- how extensive and secure the rights are
- whether government can change and possibly reduce rights
- what the holder's management responsibilities are
- how the holder can renegotiate and renew rights
- how the profits from resource use are distributed.

We can illustrate how some of these issues are important to the settlement of Aboriginal land title by discussing B.C.'s forest tenure system.

Property rights and resource use in B.C.

In British Columbia, third parties can get access to Crown timber by obtaining a variety of licences. Table 9.1 below shows how much timber was harvested in 1993 to 1994 under the most important of these licences, along with some of the basic characteristics of each licence.

Table 9.1: Timber Harvested in B.C. in 1993–94, by Licence

	Millions of cubic metres harvested	Percentage of B.C. harvest volume	Base: land area or harvest volume	Normal initial duration*	Obligations	Methods of pricing
Forest licences	39.2M m³	50.2%	Volume	15 years	Major	Stumpage appraisals
Tree farm licences** (Schedule B lands only)	12.9M m³	16.6%	Area	25 years	Major	Stumpage appraisals
Timber sale licences (SBFEP)***	10.2M m³	13.1%	Area	2 years	Minor	Stumpage plus bonus bids
Timber licences (royalty-bearing)	4.5M m³	5.8%	Area	Until timber removed	Major	Appraised royalties ****
All other licences	3.0M m³	3.8%	Various	Various	Various	Stumpage appraisals
Total for Crown land	69.8M m³	89.5%				
Private and other land	8.2M m³	10.5%				
Overall Total	78.0M m³	100%				

Notes to Table

*Most licences are renewable. The times given here refer to the normal initial duration of a licence.

**The total volume actually harvested from tree farm licences (TFLs) is greater than the number recorded in this table for Schedule B lands. TFLs also include other lands that are either under timber licences or held privately.

***SBFEP stands for the Small Business Forest Enterprise Program.

****In 1995–96, royalties were set at 60% of the appraised stumpage. They will rise over the next six years to reach 100% of appraised stumpage on April 1, 2001.

Source: Adapted from B.C. Ministry of Forests, *Annual Report, 1993–94*, Victoria, B.C., 1995.

The B.C. forest tenure system has evolved over the last 100 years. Timber licences are the modern form of the old temporary tenures established before December 24, 1907. These early licences gave the holder rights to the original timber within the licence area, in return for yearly rent payments and for royalty to the Crown when the timber was actually harvested. The licences could be transferred, and renewed for either 16 or 21 years, depending on when they were first issued. However, the Crown retained the right to change both rental payments and scheduled royalty payments, depending on what it decided was in the public interest and on the market value of the timber.

Historically, timber licences gave holders a right to harvest mature, old-growth timber that was exclusive, durable, and transferable. They gave no right to the land itself, nor to any other resources such as water, wildlife, fish, or minerals. Moreover, the land itself reverted to the Crown once the timber it contained had been harvested. Under the modern system, a "timber licence" within a "tree farm licence" becomes "Schedule B lands" once the original timber has been harvested. This means holders eventually pay "stumpage" charges for second-growth timber at appraised rates. In addition, holders must get approval from the Minister of Forests to transfer a timber licence.

The property rights question for timber licences comes down to what benefits the "exclusive right" to harvest is meant to give the holder. Does it give some right to the resource rents that the timber may provide over time as it is harvested, or simply the exclusive right to harvest itself?

This question has been partly resolved by the Independent Review of Timber Royalty Rates in British Columbia. Its main recommendations became law in June 1995. Royalty payments to the Crown must reflect appraised stumpage charges on equivalent timber within six years. These legislated changes are an example of the Crown's right to regulate and alter the terms on which licence-holders exercise their property rights to the timber over time. Timber licences give the holder a conditional right to take a profit from soil owned by another. They are essentially "sharecropping" arrangements that give the holder a conditional legal right to make profit from something the land produces.

It is especially important to note that, in British Columbia, many of the current tenures (and not just timber licences) have come about as a result of investments in timber-processing mills. Sustaining these investments, and the stability of employment they provide to forest-based communities, requires secure long-term supplies of wood fibre. The need for such long-term supplies has led to forest tenures with long durations. Additional requirements for tenureholders to invest in silvi-culture and reforestation have only increased the need for such security. Replacing this system with one that would give harvesting rights on shorter-term contracts, with no guarantee of continuing timber access, could seriously disrupt rural communities.

The timber-pricing or stumpage appraisal system recognizes the fact that the B.C. Crown is the owner, as well as the regulator, of the vast majority of B.C.'s forest land and the timber supplies it contains. When harvested, Crown timber is priced according to a complicated stumpage appraisal system, known as the "comparative value pricing system." There are separate systems for the Coast and for the Interior. Under this system, the relative value of each stand of timber being sold depends on estimates of both the selling price of products that could be made from the timber and the cost of making these products. Stumpage prices are then set so that the average rate charged will approximate a prede-termined target rate per cubic metre harvested. The target rates are adjusted every three months in response to movements in softwood lumber prices.

The comparative value pricing system allows for different species of timber, for differences in timber quality, and for differences in har-vesting costs in the establishment of stand-specific stumpage prices. It provides a financial system for the B.C. forest industry that is both reasonably stable and sensitive to overall market developments. It also collects for the Crown a significant proportion of the profits from higher prices (particularly for softwood lumber) in the marketplace. But whether the comparative value pricing system actually collects forestry resource rents as fully and effectively as it could is not easy to deter-mine.

The B.C. forest tenure system gives the forest industry medium-term rights to use land and profit from it. Several forms of licence, particularly tree farm licences, grant area-based tenures. But the most common form of licence, the forest licence, gives the holder volume-

based rights in specified timber supply areas. Private forest lands fall-
ing both within and outside of existing tree farm licences yield about
10% of the annual harvest in the province. However, private ownership
of forest lands is clearly not the main means of holding property rights
in timber resources in B.C. As a result, the forest industry has little
reason to recognize the value of B.C.'s forest lands for uses other than
timber production in its profit-and-loss calculations.

A similar situation exists for mineral, water, fisheries, and other
resource-based property rights in British Columbia. In general, the
private sector has rights to use resources (and in the case of some fisheries, only rights to capture certain stocks) but does not own them.
Collisions between competing rights to use land and resources are thus
inevitable, especially when many types of use are involved. The government has a natural role of mediating among different interests, and
of regulating access to land and resources. Clearly, mediation among
all potential users is also central to settling First Nations treaties.

The implications of current tenure systems for treaty settlements

Because of the increasingly pressing likelihood of conflict among
resource users, large-scale transfers of provincial Crown lands to proprietary or fee-simple ownership by tribal councils and Aboriginal
communities are unlikely. But even if the Crown continues to be the
ultimate landowner, it can still transfer important rights to use and profit
from the land. These can include rights to

- harvest timber
- influence the pace of exploration for mineral resources and the rate
  at which established mineral deposits are developed
- catch a certain amount of renewable fish stocks
- hunt or trap particular wildlife species
- harness or consume water resources
- control access to recreational resources
- use pasture and grazing lands.

All of these are important property rights, with considerable economic
value. None of them necessarily imply fee-simple ownership, although
granting all of these rights on a parcel of Crown land could look very
much like proprietary ownership.

So far, the courts have not stated that Aboriginal land title would mean proprietary ownership over large tracts of land within the province. In the case of *Delgamuukw v. British Columbia*, the B.C. Court of Appeal decided that Aboriginal rights were limited to traditional uses of resources.[3] Clearly, some of these traditional rights have been the "rule-of-capture" right to "common-pool" resources such as wildlife stocks, fish stocks, and limited timber harvests, in order to meet personal consumption needs, if not plans for commercial harvests. These traditional rights have also involved cultural and spiritual attachment to certain territories, and to at least some of the renewable resources they contain. Traditional rights have often implied tribal dominance over a specific territory, but they may not have generally involved the proprietary rights of fee-simple ownership.

Traditionally, Aboriginal property rights have quite naturally been similar to the right to consume abundant public goods in a way that does not compete with and exclude others from their use. They have not been like the right to consume private goods from which others must be excluded because there is competition for them. Nor have they been like the right to consume goods owned by a "club," as one of its members. Indeed, in today's world, transferring fee-simple title to major areas of land and resources to Aboriginal communities would be like granting special and discriminatory access to limited common-pool resources. Doing so might help to protect resources by giving stewardship over them to certain groups. But in the same breath it would deny most of B.C.'s residents the right both to access these lands and resources, and to develop or conserve them for various present and future purposes.

Let's look at this another way. We can classify resources into two types:

- "private" goods that individuals have proprietary ownership rights to, and can exclude others from using
- "public" goods that individuals have rights to use, but cannot exclude others from using.

We can also classify resources by how much demand there is for them. As time has passed, resources that were previously abundant and used by few people have become more in demand as congestion has increased the pressure on land and resources. Increasing demand turns "public" goods into congested common-pool resources, whereas it turns resources that were previously accessible to members of a "club" into private goods. The point is that the property rights involved in Aboriginal title are more like "public" rights to use a pool of common resources in high demand, than they are like "private" or proprietary rights to exclude others from benefiting from them.

Although the courts have not yet precisely defined which property rights are included in Aboriginal title, they have found that these rights are not absolute, and must therefore take into account other legitimate social interests. The courts have also held that Aboriginal title is a unique interest in land which is not equivalent to fee-simple ownership. Therefore, First Nations cannot claim such ownership as part of their traditional Aboriginal title.[4] If Aboriginal title is to be meaningful at all, it must include certain (possibly quite comprehensive) property rights to use land and resources, but generally not exclusive ownership of large tracts of land, which is a concept that does not apply to the uncongested world of B.C.'s early history. This does not of course mean that First Nations communities cannot hold *any* land as proprietary owners. For example, existing reserve lands and some important additions to those lands could be transferred to Aboriginal communities as fee-simple property.

Effects on Local Communities and Other Third Parties

In the previous section, we used the forest industry to illustrate the property rights issues involved in systems of land tenure and resource use. We also explained why Aboriginal title is unlikely, in general, to imply private fee-simple ownership. Identifying Aboriginal title as proprietary ownership would not only be historically inaccurate, it could also be unfair to British Columbia's taxpayers. They could lose access to significant public revenues from natural resources, and lose their third-party interests in resource development without compensation for these rights to use property transferred in treaty settlements. If the value of the property rights to be transferred in treaty settlements becomes too large, Canadian taxpayers could be worried enough to suggest that the federal government withdraw from its agreement to share costs with the province. In addition, the frustration of important economic opportunities might prevent the B.C. government from having the resources to meet its share of the costs. A provincial economy where the resource industries have shrunk enough to create large pools of unemployment, particularly in rural communities, is a provincial economy where major transfers of resource ownership rights would meet with overwhelming public resistance. Resource industries still directly or indirectly create the most jobs in the B.C. economy. Arranging treaty settlements that are beyond our ability to pay will ultimately serve nobody well. Unfortunately, this also includes the First Nations people.

Some take the view that, once transferred to First Nations communities, federal funds would create a local economic boom due to the substantial "multiplier" effects that would occur as these monies were spent. (See, for example, KPMG's report, 1996.) Unfortunately, federal cash is not "manna from heaven." It must ultimately be covered by higher federal tax revenues or reductions in other federal spending, which would have its own offseting "multiplier" effects. The contribution of federal taxpayers from other provinces to B.C. treaty settlements will likely be roughly offset by the contribution of federal taxpayers in B.C. to treaty settlements in other Canadian provinces and territories. There is ultimately only one taxpayer and "no free lunch."

Wherever the losses to local communities and third-party resource interests are both clear and substantial, compensation is justified. Given past cases, it also seems likely, either through court challenges or through negotiation processes. (See Schwindt, 1992.) However, where actual losses are less easy to demonstrate, they may remain uncompensated, which could lead to friction between First Nations and their surrounding communities. These frictions could in turn undermine co-operative business ventures. If the treaty settlement process is to avoid collapsing under the political weight of these "spill-over" issues, it must create a financial framework that considers and accommodates third-party interests.

In the forest sector, three major spill-over issues need to be resolved. The first of these is how treaty settlements will affect forest industry tenures and allowable annual cuts in various timber supply areas. The second is how settlements will affect the industry's ability to operate efficiently, and without major delays, in harvesting timber on Crown lands. The third involves what access the industry will have to timber on lands to be transferred to Aboriginal communities, particularly what stumpage fees and other costs they might have to pay for this access. At present, answers to all three issues are unclear. (For further discussion, see Bowden, 1996.)

In the case of other third parties, First Nations may simply re-create rights to use resources now held on any lands to be transferred to their proprietary ownership. Resource rents paid to the provincial Crown would then shrink (with implications for provincial taxpayers), since they will be paid to the particular First Nations community. In this case, compensation for loss of resource interests no longer applies. Much will depend on how interested First Nations communities are in developing transferred lands and resources, and thus how willing they are to grant access and receive rents. This may also apply in cases where treaty settlements grant First Nations rights to use the land instead of proprietary ownership of it.

A Possible Financial Framework

What are the financial implications for each party?

The basic financial framework for treaty settlements is best illustrated in graphic terms. The flow chart below (Figure 9.1) represents the five main parties involved: the federal government, the provincial government, First Nations groups, third-party resource interests, and taxpayers.

Taxpayers provide the funds for both levels of government. Since Canadian taxpayers will bear most of the costs of First Nations treaty settlements, they will have to pay additional taxes. The federal government will need more tax revenues to finance a stream of cash transfers to First Nations groups. However, if First Nations groups lose their non-taxable status as part of the settlement, or lose access to special federal government services, they will, in effect, transfer some of that cash back. (For simplicity, the illustration does not show the parallel transfer of cash to and from the provincial government, or the province's cash contribution to the settlement.)

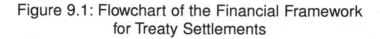

Figure 9.1: Flowchart of the Financial Framework for Treaty Settlements

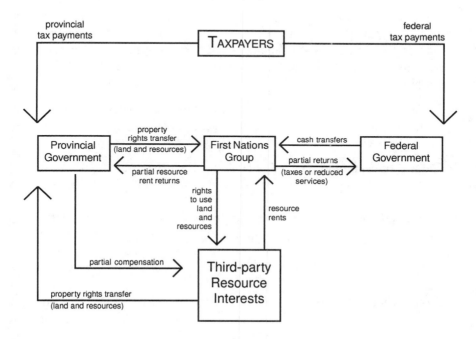

The provincial government will arrange to transfer property rights in land and resources to First Nations groups. Although these property rights transfers are essentially transfers-in-kind, they will diminish the provincially owned stock of resources. The provincial government will then need to replenish its loss of natural resource revenues by imposing additional taxes on provincial residents.[5] These will probably not be taxes on resources, because the land and resource transfer itself will undoubtedly lower the province's ability to increase such taxation. However, the process will also involve the taking of resource interests from the private sector. The provincial government will need to pay partial compensation for these takings.

First Nations groups may then give third parties access to land and resources. Resource rents flowing in the opposite direction to First

Nations communities will compensate for this renewed access. However, if the new arrangements between First Nations communities and third-party resource interests benefit both and they enter into them freely, then the value of the renewed access to resources will be equal to the resource rents. This assumption does not, of course, imply that these new partnerships will be unproductive. Nor does it imply that reducing uncertainty about land ownership and rights to use resources will fail to reduce costs for the private-sector economy in British Columbia.

Here are the financial implications for each of the five players. Each expression nets outlays or losses from receipts or gains.

Federal government: Tax revenues + partial returns from First Nations — cash transfers to First Nations

Provincial government: Tax revenues + third-party property rights takings — property rights given to First Nations — partial compensation to third parties

First Nations: Cash transfers + property rights transfers - partial returns (resource rents, taxes, or reduced services)

Third-party interests: — Property rights to use resources + partial compensation

Taxpayers: — Tax payments to federal and provincial governments

These expressions assume that the value of First Nations granting renewed resource access to third-party interests will equal the value of the rents third parties pay for those resources. They also assume that any rents First Nations pay on property rights transferred from the provincial government will be very small compared to the value of those property rights.

If both major levels of government can arrange their finances so they break even, then

- the gain to First Nations will equal
  - the additional federal tax revenues, plus
  - the net value of the transferred property rights in land and re-sources;
- the loss to taxpayers will be
  - tax payments to both levels of government; and
- the loss to third-party interests will be
  - the net value of the property rights transfers to First Nations, minus
  - the additional provincial tax payments used to compensate them.

There may also be "dead-weight losses" created by the additional tax burdens and transactions costs arising from the transfer process. The overall costs borne by third-party resource interests compared to tax-payers-at-large will depend on the provincial government's actions and policies. Those of the federal government will likely have only a small effect on this division.

Thus, the provincial government will be able to cover its share of the overall costs of settling treaties by making some trade-offs between increasing the burden on general provincial taxpayers and reducing third-parties' property rights. Public choice theory suggests that if third-party interests are represented by strong and powerful lobbies, and supported by the major trade unions of the resource industries, increasing the burden on general provincial taxpayers will be easier to achieve than uncompensated reductions in resource-use rights.

Other questions arising from financial implications

The flowchart gives us a logical structure to answer the financing question, but does nothing to resolve this question. To do so, we would need to construct a cost-benefit analysis of various financing methods, which might include an overall limit on the total scope of First Nations treaty settlements. The B.C. government has done this in part, by plac-ing a ceiling on its land transfer commitment for all treaty settlements in the province. This cap is 5% of the province's total land base. (See the KPMG's report.)

Transferring 5% of B.C.'s total land base to proprietary ownership by First Nations would be an expensive settlement, especially if the representative land selection model applies. However, what is more important than how much of the land base will be transferred is what sort of property rights will be transferred with it. Although the provincial government appears to be thinking in proprietary terms, this approach will likely be very expensive, unless the size of the territories involved is kept to manageable proportions.

In many ways, in comparison to the provincial government, the federal government is in an enviable position. The cash settlements it will negotiate are likely to be spread out over some years, unlike land title transfers, which will occur at one time. In principle, rights to use land can be transferred gradually over time, phasing in additional rights for First Nations communities in stages, as they are taken away from third-party resource interests. But such a strategy of gradual transfer is likely to reduce third parties' incentives to maintain their stewardship of resources at high levels. Transfers of rights to use resources can occur for set durations, and need not always mean one party has exclusive use of the resource in question. Nevertheless, resource transfer at the provincial level is the issue most likely to create political unrest.

The increasing congestion and depletion of the global pool of resources, including provincial lands and resource stocks, has tended to increase the value of rights of access to these resources over time. We can identify this rate of change in the resource rental value as the "capital gain" from rights of access to provincial resources. The treaty settlement process will provide a clear answer to the question of who is entitled to share in this capital gain. First Nations people will argue that land and resources were originally taken from them without due process or compensation, and that they are therefore entitled to the capital gain on lands and resources implicitly held for them in trust by the provincial Crown. Other British Columbians will argue that the capital gain has occurred only because physical and human capital, plus modern exploratory and developmental technologies, have been invested in land and resources that would be much less productive without them. Are capital gains simply due to the scarcity of resources in an increasingly congested world, or are they a product of human and technological ingenuity?

The theory of inter-temporal choice does not provide a clear answer. It supports arguments on both sides. As a result, who should share this capital gain is ultimately a question of both politics and distributional justice rather than one of economics. Nevertheless, it is useful to consider the question of how to settle treaties as how to share the capital gain made available by the appreciation of natural resource values.

Tax Status and Services for First Nations

The process of settling First Nations land title is likely to be balanced by the process of creating self-government. First Nations governments should have at least the powers and authorities of municipal governments. These would include the power to collect appropriate taxes from community residents, and to provide local public services to these residents.

From the perspective of community development, it may be sensible for the two senior orders of government to withhold demands for First Nations people to pay full taxes for an appropriate period of time. As Aboriginal communities become wealthier, the lion's share of additional tax revenues could then go to First Nations governments. Such a strategy would allow provincial and federal governments to transfer responsibility for special services to local First Nations governments. Once Aboriginal communities have sufficient finances from collecting their own taxes, such a transfer of responsibilities is desirable for several reasons.

Although many Canadians will likely argue that the ultimate goal should be for First Nations people to pay the same taxes as all other Canadians, there are important reasons for making only a gradual transition to such a state. During this transition, residents of First Nations communities would still have to pay local taxes to finance public services provided by local governments. The goals of having First Nations pay taxes at the local level, and relying less on goods and services provided by senior orders of government, are important ones to achieve. From a purely financial perspective, they will help offset the costs of the treaty settlement process. But there are clearly other social and economic benefits: self-reliance, cultural independence, and community health.

Even if local First Nations governments have the authority to collect certain taxes, the costs to set up and operate these governments may generate a need for "equalization" payments from the senior orders of government to cover them. The total cost of these equalization payments could easily equal the amount the federal government transfers each year to a small province like Prince Edward Island. Pinpointing exactly how much Aboriginal self-government will cost will be difficult. It will also be important to avoid creating a new dependency on the federal government for support, especially when one of the principal objectives of First Nations treaty settlements should be to create productive resource endowments that gradually release the hold of the current paternalistic system.

The Nisga'a Agreement-in-Principle

The Nisga'a Agreement-in-Principle is clearly a ground-breaking achievement for all its negotiating teams. The fact that an Agreement-in-Principle has finally been achieved after many years of sustained activity by the Nisga'a Nation is very much to the credit of the Nisga'a people. They have demonstrated great patience and faith that a settlement would ultimately be achieved.

Because the Nisga'a Nation has approximately 5,000 members, the Agreement-in-Principle provides significant benefits for each individual. However, it can't easily stand as a precedent for future B.C. settlements. To do so could involve transfer costs too expensive for the provincial, if not the federal, government to sustain, economically or politically.

The Nisga'a Agreement-in-Principle does recognize the difference between proprietary (or freehold) ownership and rights to use property. If the Agreement is upheld in a treaty settlement, the Nisga'a Nation will have communal freehold ownership rights to 1,930 sq. km of land, mostly in the Nass River region, including ownership of all the surface and subsurface resources it contains.

These freehold rights will therefore include ownership of timber lands capable of supporting an allowable annual cut (AAC) of 220,000 cubic metres (about 7% of the total AAC of the Kalum and North Coast forest districts). At today's rates, it could produce at least $2.7 million in stumpage revenues per year (which the province would lose). In addition, the Nisga'a Nation will receive a variety of rights to control the resources of another 10,000 sq. km of land in the same general area. These include rights to commercial back-country recreation holdings, rights to wildlife resources, substantial water rights, and the right to receive revenues from public utilities and rights of way (excluding highways). The Nisga'a Nation will have the right to an AAC of 150,000 cubic metres of Crown timber on the additional 10,000 sq. km.[6] It will be able to develop a large part of the Nass River fishery, including its important salmon runs, for commercial use, essentially as a treaty right. The federal government will give $11.5 million to the Nisga'a Nation for fishing vessels and licences, and a further $10 million to a jointly managed fisheries conservation trust for the Nass River region. Important management rights for all of these resources will also be granted. Altogether, the Nisga'a will receive rights to use property within much of the 10,000 sq. km land base that virtually amount to proprietary ownership, in addition to their communal freehold ownership of the 1,930 sq. km "Nisga'a homeland."

The federal government will transfer $190 million (in 1995 dollars) to the Nisga'a Nation over a time period yet to be decided. This cash transfer is called "Nisga'a capital." All members of the Nisga'a Nation who live on the 1,930 sq. km of Nisga'a homeland will not have to pay transaction or sales taxes for the next eight years, and will not pay income and capital taxes for the next 12 years. Nisga'a lands will always remain exempt from provincial property and resource taxes.

The Nisga'a Nation will get new legislative powers as it gains self-government. These will include the power to make laws concerning their judicial system, local taxation, resource development and access, education, and social services. The federal government will make some form of equalization payments to help provide public services, but the Nisga'a will also be able to benefit from federal programs specifically for Aboriginal people who are Status Indians.

Unfortunately, many people will believe that the Nisga'a Agreement-in-Principle (which has yet to be ratified by the B.C. legislature) "gives away the store." The problem is not really with granting communal freehold ownership to 1,930 sq. km of Nisga'a homeland, or with the substantial cash transfer. It is with the other provisions for resource use. If the Agreement were the only one to be settled, then British Columbians would most likely accept it. But there are at least another 45 to 50 settlements still to come. Several claim overlapping territories, especially in the North Coastal region, which will have to be resolved among the claimants as the title settlement process unfolds.

How much these claims overlap clearly shows that nothing like fee-simple ownership existed in the uncrowded world of the past. Instead, First Nations competed for access to a common pool of resources. Settling these claims by granting freehold rights to these common pool resources needs to be approached cautiously. Negotiators must make careful distinctions between the proprietary rights of "homelands" versus rights to use what have traditionally been shared resources. Finding contiguous territories of land to transfer to freehold status will also be much more difficult, if not impossible, to achieve in other treaty settlements than it has been in the Nisga'a case.

Financing Future B.C. Settlements

Future B.C. settlements will undoubtedly be financed in a similar way to the Nisga'a Agreement-in-Principle. They will involve substantial contributions of cash by both federal and provincial taxpayers, and contributions of existing property rights by third parties forced to part with them. Since much of their livelihood comes from these resource interests, various communities could experience significant adjustment costs. Other third parties could also feel the effects, as access to resources on Crown lands not involved in the settlement process becomes even more crowded. However, this really depends on the pace of development First Nations communities plan for the lands and resources transferred to them. The social value of rights to use natural resources owned by the provincial Crown is likely to keep increasing over time.

If the B.C. government ratifies the Agreement and allows it to set a precedent, then the ultimate cost to British Columbian and other Canadian taxpayers will be considerable. For this reason alone, the Agreement may not be allowed to set the standard for future settlements. If the expectations of other First Nations are based on the Agreement, they may well be disappointed. Moreover, public opinion may yet affect whether the Agreement actually materializes as a firm treaty settlement.

It is important to be realistic about what goals treaty settlements can truly achieve. Unrealistic expectations may ultimately hinder the settlement process. The environmental movement's implicit support for treaty settlements, for example, often has a hidden agenda: to support taking resource rights away from major developers. Although there may be grounds to believe that First Nations communities will provide better stewardship over natural resources, this is less likely to be the result of different value systems than different types of management.

As Elinor Ostrom points out, "when common property resource appropriators design their own operational rules to be enforced by individuals who are local appropriators or are accountable to them, using graduated sanctions that define who has rights to withdraw units from the common property resource and that effectively restrict appropriation activities, given local conditions, the commitment and monitoring problems are solved in an interrelated manner" and effective stewardship over the common property resource is likely to occur.[7] In other words, "small is beautiful." Institutional arrangements that limit the total number of appropriators can prevent "the tragedy of the commons," and the dissipation of resource rents that often results from congested common-pool resources. These arrangements may also involve smaller social discount rates, perhaps because of long-term community attachment to a particular place.

Financing First Nations treaty settlements will undoubtedly be expensive. Yet we must proceed with them, not only because First Nations Aboriginal rights have not been extinguished within B.C., but also because we must treat First Nations peoples equitably. Resolving settlements is also the only way to clarify the legal status of third-party rights to use Crown lands and resources. We must clearly define what Aboriginal land rights are and how they will apply in specific situations.

Giving First Nations peoples freehold ownership of existing reserve lands, plus some additional parcels of Crown lands next to these reserves, would certainly clarify the question of who has title to these lands. Granting further rights to use and profit from other Crown lands that are consistent with how First Nations have traditionally used them would also help to clarify exactly what rights Aboriginal title conveys. The more specific definitions are, the less is the potential for conflict over resource use in the future, as access to the province's resources becomes increasingly congested. Trade-offs will clearly be necessary to balance the amount of land transferred to proprietary ownership, the amount of Crown land on which rights to use resources are conveyed, and the exact definition of these rights.

Establishing how extensive and durable these rights to use resources are is especially important. The increasing intensity of competition for access to congested resources may make it difficult to avoid granting exclusive rights. However, doing so could open treaty settlements to court challenges under the *Canadian Charter of Rights and Freedoms*. One obvious example is the creation of "Aboriginal fisheries." To minimize major conflicts among third-party interests over the resources in territories under Crown ownership, it will sometimes be better to settle Aboriginal title by giving First Nations communal proprietary rights of ownership over smaller tracts of land.

Trade-offs like this will inevitably occur as the treaty settlement process gathers momentum. First Nations communities may have to give up Aboriginal title over larger tracts of land in order to secure communal freehold title over smaller areas. Another compromise would be for First Nations to enter into development partnerships with non-aboriginal business ventures whose operations require access to certain natural resources.

If new resource frontiers were waiting to be explored in B.C. much as they have been in the Yukon and Alaska, such development partnerships would be easier to achieve. However, even in more congested British Columbia, there remain many fruitful opportunities. Pursuing them means obtaining both physical and human capital. First Nations communities could use some of the cash and resource transfers received in treaty settlements to create resource development corporations that could readily enter into partnership arrangements with non-aboriginal businesses. The voting shares in these development corporations could be held by members of the particular First Nations community.

Conclusions

Unless the treaty settlement process creates productive new opportunities for economic development that Aboriginal and non-aboriginal people can share, it will be more difficult to finance. Encouraging co-operative development opportunities, such as joint ventures in the forest industries, is therefore crucial. This cannot be achieved if the parties to the process take an adversarial approach.

Given the unfortunate history of discrimination against First Nations peoples in B.C., most non-aboriginal people understand that redistributing resources is only just, and essential to redressing past wrongs. However, most people also believe that there are limits to the amount of resources that are available for redistribution, even in cases where social conscience is a major motivation. We must set realistic expectations, and then get on with the job of negotiating settlements that allocate ownership of resources in a reasonable way. If the public believes that transfers of property rights make access to resources too privileged, and thus discriminate against third-party interests and the larger public interest, they will find settlements politically unacceptable.

One solution proposed by the Royal Commission on Aboriginal Peoples is to create a reasonably independent Aboriginal lands and treaties tribunal, very much like the existing B.C. Treaty Commission. Such a tribunal would oversee the process of negotiating treaties to settle Aboriginal title and create local self-government, but would not become directly involved in the negotiations. The Commission has also said that Canada needs to invest $30 billion more over the next 15 to 20 years in the economic development and renewal of First Nations communities. The Commission believes that such an investment would succeed if First Nations people had the lands and resources to enable them to regain self-reliance and to reduce their dependency on transfers from other orders of government. As the Commission puts it, "Failure to redistribute land and resources will doom Aboriginal people to a state of dependency on other Canadians—a sure recipe for grievance on both sides."[8] It recommends three categories of land allocation:

1. Lands selected from traditional territories that would belong exclusively to Aboriginal nations and be under their sole control.
2. Other lands in their traditional territories that would belong jointly to Aboriginal and non-aboriginal governments, and be the object of shared management arrangements.

3. Land that would belong to and remain under the control of the Crown but to which Aboriginal people would have special rights, such as a right of access to sacred and historical sites.[9]

Sorting out which property rights are to be proprietary, which are to grant use of certain resources, and which are to be by special privilege lies at the heart of the issue of how to finance treaty settlements in British Columbia. Since the ownership and control of land and natural resources is the central issue rather than the investment or transfer of financial resources, the onus will be on the Province, not the federal government, to make sure settlements are viable—from the perspective of all British Columbians.

Notes

1. The author is indebted to Ken Avio, Lloyd Barber, Rod Dobell, Gordon Gibson, Peter Meekison, Tony Scott, and Zane Spindler for their valuable comments and advice on earlier drafts of this chapter. None of these persons is to be held responsible for the contents of the chapter.

2. The Royal Commission on Aboriginal Peoples identifies just seven tribal and linguistic groups within B.C.: Athapaskan, Haida, Kutenai, Salishan, Tlingit, Tsimshian, and Wakashan. (See *People to People, Nation to Nation,* p. 7.) Although there seem to be more distinct First Nations than these seven groups, many of the 47 applicants are far too small to be considered as separate First Nations. Some amalgamations will likely be necessary as the settlement process continues.

3. As stated on pp. 16–17 of the 1995–96 annual report of the B.C. Treaty Commission:

> The majority of the Court in *Delgamuukw* held that the aboriginal plaintiffs had asked the Court to determine only two issues: "ownership" in the conventional sense, which had not been proved; and non-exclusive aboriginal rights to engage in particular activities and practices, which had been proved. It was not appropriate, they said, to rule on anything that fell between.
>
> They made no determination as to whether the plaintiffs might have been entitled to a finding of aboriginal title of the type described in *Calder* and the Supreme Court of Canada decisions: that is a title less than full ownership but greater than the non-exclusive aboriginal rights that they did accept.
>
> The result is that no court has yet made a finding of aboriginal title in British Columbia beyond rights to engage in particular activities and practices. But *Delgamuukw* repudiated the notion of blanket extinguishment. So the door is open to other First Nations to attempt to establish aboriginal title if they decide to litigate, and if there is supporting evidence.
>
> Thus, when treaty negotiations began in 1993, the following situation existed. The courts had confirmed that aboriginal rights still exist in B.C., that these rights are unique and unlike conventional

property rights, and that the rights are constitutionally entrenched so that neither the federal nor the provincial government can interfere with them, let alone extinguish them, without meeting strict constitutional standards.

Although aboriginal rights are unique and do not fit into the rigid classification of conventional property rights, this does not make them a significantly lesser right. In common with property rights, aboriginal rights directly connected to land can invoke the courts' protection against unlawful infringement by others claiming an interest in that land. That is why these rights have been described by the courts as a "burden" on the title of the Crown. It is also why there can be no certainty about the nature and extent of the Crown's title to land and resources, except through a process of negotiation designed to reconcile the respective rights of the Crown and First Nations. That is one reason First Nations expect lands and resources to be on the negotiating table and why their claims cannot be satisfied by compensation only. And that is why the British Columbia Court of Appeal has urged Canada, British Columbia and First Nations to negotiate their differences, observing that "treaty making is the best way to respect Indian rights."

4. In *Gladstone v. The Queen,* [1996] 2 S.C.R. 723, the Supreme Court of Canada upheld the position that Aboriginal rights include specific rights to use and profit from resources that can be proven to have existed at the time of settlement, and that these rights must be balanced with other societal interests. In his assessment of the earlier Supreme Court judgment in *R. v. Sparrow,* [1990], 1 S.C.R. 1075, K.L. Avio has defined Aboriginal property rights as rights that "accrue only to organised aboriginal communities, require historical grounding, are inalienable except to the Crown, are subject to extinguishment by abandonment, and are accompanied by a fiduciary duty on the part of the Crown" (p. 425).

5. Even if First Nations groups pay some resource rentals to the provincial Crown for the rights to use a subset of these resources, the Province will not get rentals from those lands and resources transferred to proprietary (freehold) ownership. Thus, our framework takes into account the possibility of First Nations paying rents on trans-

ferred property by assuming that such return rents are at most a partial offset to the transfer of property rights.

6. Tree farm licence (TFL) #1, currently operated by Skeena Cellulose Inc., overlaps with Nisga'a lands. The Province will re-acquire the portion of the TFL within Nisga'a lands for the Nisga'a Nation. This land will then be reclassified as Schedule A lands, from which the provincial Crown will not receive stumpage payments (or, in this case, any other charges). If the Crown obtains the remaining portion of the TFL lying outside Nisga'a lands, harvesting operations by the Nisga'a Nation would have to pay normal stumpage charges, as for Schedule B lands.

7. Ostrom, p. 99.

8. Royal Commission on Aboriginal Peoples, *People to People, Nation to Nation,* p. 38. This statement, like many in the Royal Commission report, is open to challenge. Independence may also be achieved through major investments in human capital, as well as by relying on nature's bounty or on the rents from natural resources. However, in common with some hunter-gatherer societies of the past, a rentier society is likely to enjoy more leisure time than one relying on the rewards of investing in the education of its people.

9. *People to People, Nation to Nation,* p. 37.

References

ARA Consulting Group Inc. *Social and Economic Impacts of Aboriginal Land Claim Settlements: A Case Study Analysis.* For the Ministry of Aboriginal Affairs, Province of British Columbia, and the Federal Treaty Negotiation Office. Vancouver: ARA Consulting Group Inc., December 1995.

Avio, Kenneth L. "Aboriginal Property Rights in Canada: A Contractarian Interpretation of *R. v. Sparrow.*" *Canadian Public Policy,* Vol. XX, No. 4, December 1994, pp. 415–29.

Bowden, Gary K. "Land Claims and the Future of the B.C. Forest Industry." Paper presented to the Fraser Institute conference, What is the Future of the B.C. Forest Industry? Vancouver: 13 December 1996.

BriMar Consultants Ltd. *An Independent Review of Timber Royalty Rates in British Columbia.* B.C. Ministry of Forests, Victoria: January 1995.

―――. "Timber Pricing Policies and Sustainable Forestry." In *The Wealth of Forests: Markets, Regulation and Sustainable Forestry,* ed. C. Tollefson. Vancouver: UBC Press, 1997 (forthcoming).

British Columbia Claims Task Force. *The Report of the British Columbia Claims Task Force.* Vancouver: British Columbia Claims Task Force, June 1991.

British Columbia Ministry of Forests. *Annual Report, 1993–94.* Victoria: 1995.

British Columbia Treaty Commission, *Annual Report, 1995–96.* Victoria: 1996.

Cassidy, Frank, ed. *Reaching Just Settlements.* Halifax: Institute for Research on Public Policy, and Lantzville: Oolichan Books, 1991.

Council of Forest Industries of British Columbia. *Native Indian Land Claims in British Columbia: A Background Paper.* Vancouver: COFI, 1989.

Feschuk, Scott, and Rudy Platiel. "Vast Changes Sought to Aid Natives." *The Globe and Mail,* 22 November 1996, p. 1.

―――. "Natives Warn Ottawa Not to Ignore Report." *The Globe and Mail,* 22 November 1996, p. 8.

―――. "Cost of Reforms $30 Billion Report on Aboriginals Says." *The Globe and Mail,* 22 November 1996, p. 9.

Gibson, Gordon. "Back to Reality on Aboriginal Rights." *The Globe and Mail,* 27 August 1996, p. A17.

―――. "Where the Aboriginal Report Takes a Wrong Turn." *The Globe and Mail,* 26 November 1996, p. A23.

―――. "Toward a Better Aboriginal Policy." *The Globe and Mail,* 3 December 1996, p. A23.

Gladstone v. The Queen, [1996] 2 S.C.R. 723, [1996] 9 W.W.R. 149.

Government of British Columbia. *Regional Socio-Economic Assessment of the Nisga'a Agreement in Principle.* Victoria: December 1996.

Government of Canada, Province of British Columbia, and Nisga'a Tribal Council. *Nisga'a Treaty Negotiations, Agreement-in-Principle.* Victoria: Queen's Printer, 15 February 1996.

Hawley, Donna Lea. *The Annotated 1990 Indian Act.* Toronto: Carswell, 1990.

Howard, Ross. "B.C.'s Cuts not Timely for Indian Claims." *The Globe and Mail,* 14 October 1996.

————. "Committee Finds Support for B.C. Treaty." *The Globe and Mail,* 5 December 1996.

Indian and Northern Affairs Canada. *Basic Departmental Data, 1993.* Ottawa: Department of Indian and Northern Affairs, December 1993.

Jones, Sheila. "How Many Citizens in the Métis Nation?" *The Globe and Mail,* 3 August 1996, p. D2.

KPMG. *Benefits and Costs of Treaty Settlements in British Columbia—A Financial and Economic Perspective.* Victoria: January 1996.

Lippert, Owen. "Questioning the Nisga'a Agreement." *Fraser Forum.* Vancouver: The Fraser Institute, March 1996, pp. 13–15.

Ostrom, Elinor. *Governing the Commons: The Evolution of Institutions for Collective Action.* Cambridge: Cambridge University Press, 1990.

Pearse, Peter H. *Introduction to Forestry Economics.* Vancouver: UBC Press, 1990.

Plant, Geoffrey. *Aboriginal Rights in British Columbia: An Overview.* Vancouver: Russell and Dumoulin, Vancouver Board of Trade, 1993.

Porter, David. "Trees and Treaties—Aboriginal Interests in the Forest Industry in British Columbia." Paper presented to the Fraser Institute conference, What is the Future of the B.C. Forest Industry? Vancouver, 13 December 1996.

Royal Commission on Aboriginal Peoples. *Exploring the Options, Overview of the Third Round*. Ottawa: Minister of Supply and Services Canada, November 1993.

――――. *Toward Reconciliation, Overview of the Fourth Round*. Ottawa: Minister of Supply and Services Canada, April 1994.

――――. *People to People, Nation to Nation: Highlights from the Report of the Royal Commission on Aboriginal Peoples*. Ottawa: Minister of Supply and Services Canada, November 1996.

R. v. Sparrow, [1990] 1 S.C.R. 1075, (1990) 70 D.L.R. (4th) 385.

Schwindt, Richard. *Report of the Commission of Inquiry into Compensation for the Taking of Resource Interests*. Vancouver: Resources Compensation Commission, August 1992.

Schwindt, Richard, and Steven Globerman. "Takings of Private Rights to Public Natural Resources: A Policy Analysis." *Canadian Public Policy*, Vol XXII, No. 3, September 1996, pp. 205–24.

Scott, Anthony D., and James Johnson. "Property Rights: Developing the Characteristics of Interests in Natural Resources." In *Progress in Natural Resource Economics*, ed. A.D. Scott, pp. 376–403. Oxford: Oxford University Press, 1985.

Sheppard, Robert. "How You React to the First Page." *The Globe and Mail*, 26 November 1996, p. A23.

――――. "The Rights and the Power." *The Globe and Mail*, 27 November 1996, p. A27.

――――. "The Importance of Land." *The Globe and Mail*, 28 November 1996, p. A21.

Smith, Mel. "What Government Aboriginal Policy is Doing to Canada." *Fraser Forum*. Vancouver: The Fraser Institute, March 1996, pp. 5–12.

Tennant, Paul. "Aboriginal Peoples and Aboriginal Title in British Columbia Politics." In *Politics, Policy, and Government in British Columbia*, ed. Ken Carty, pp. 45–64. Vancouver: UBC Press, 1996.

Biographies

Authors and Researchers

Ken Coates

Ken Coates is Dean of Arts, University of New Brunswick at Saint John. He formerly held the Chair of History at the University of Waikato (Hamilton, New Zealand), the University of Northern British Columbia (Prince George), and the University of Victoria. He works primarily in the fields of the history of indigenous land rights and Northern Canadian history. Among his published works (as editor) are: *Aboriginal Land Claims in Canada*; *Best Left As Indians: Native-White Relations in the Yukon Territory,* and *Canada's Colonies: A History of the Yukon and Northwest Territories*. He has worked as a consultant on land claims issues for the Government of British Columbia, the Government of Canada, the Government of New Zealand, and the United Nations. He is currently working on a study of Aboriginal self-government in Canada and a comparative history of indigenous land claims and rights.

David Fish

David Fish is currently Dean of the Faculty of Health and Human Sciences at the University of Northern British Columbia (UNBC). He joined UNBC in 1992 as a "founding Dean" from the University of Manitoba where he was Head of the Department of Community Health Sciences in the Faculty of Medicine. He has maintained his interest in the health of First Nations and in the transfer of health services to the First Nations since his arrival in British Columbia. Dr. Fish has had extensive experience in developing countries where he has worked with communities to develop community-based health programs within the context of social and economic development.

Steven Globerman

Steven Globerman is a professor of economics at Simon Fraser University. In 1998/99, he will be on leave to assume the position of Ross Distinguished Professor of Canada-U.S. Business and Economic Relations at Western Washington University. He has also served on the Faculty of Administrative Studies at York University and has been a visiting professor at the University of British Columbia, the University of California, and the Stockholm School of Economics. Dr. Globerman holds a Ph.D. in economics. His research and consulting work focus on a variety of industrial economic public policy issues including competition policy, regulation and investment policies. He has published numerous journal articles, monographs, and books, and has consulted widely for both private and public sector organizations. He has also served on the research staffs of two federal government Royal Commissions. Dr. Globerman is listed in *Who's Who in Economics*.

Stephen McBride

Stephen McBride is Professor and Chair of Political Science at Simon Fraser University. Before coming to Simon Fraser University, he taught at McMaster University, Ryerson Polytechnical Institute, and Lakehead University.

Paul Jonathon Mitchell-Banks

Paul Jonathon Mitchell-Banks is a B.C.-based business, forestry, and environmental management consultant. He holds a Master of Science in Planning from the University of Toronto and a Master of Business Administration from the University of British Columbia (UBC). He is a Ph.D. candidate in the UBC Faculty of Forestry and is completing a thesis on tenure reform to facilitate community forestry in B.C. He has presented forestry-related papers internationally and across Canada, and has worked with Forest Renewal B.C., the Science Council of British Columbia, and 15 Indian bands from four First Nations. He consults with numerous small communities, government agencies, and industry on forest policy and economic development, with a particular interest in small-scale forestry, capacity, and relationship-building.

Lee Morrison

Lee Morrison, Ph.D., a First Nation Ojibwa, has over 18 years experience as a consultant and administrator in the health care industry before completing his Ph.D. at Century University New Mexico in Health Care Administration with a specialty in Geriatric Care Management. He holds an M.A. in Education Administration from Northern Michigan University and a B.P.H.E. (Honours) in Health Education from Laurentian University. As a consultant and health care manager, his experience includes hospital administration, health care planning, and First Nation health and social service management. Dr. Morrison has written numerous articles and authored briefs, proposals, and reports for university, government, and First Nations organizations. He is frequently invited to speak at professional conferences, workshops, and public meetings. Representing Canada, Dr. Morrison was invited by the United States Congress to present an overview of the Canadian health care system to the House Committee on Government Operation for Health Care Reform in the United States.

Paul J. Pearlman

Paul J. Pearlman is a partner in the Victoria law firm of Fuller, Pearlman. His practice includes labour and employment law, and administrative and constitutional law. Over the past 18 years, Mr. Pearlman has represented both the Attorney General of British Columbia, and private clients in Aboriginal rights litigation in the Supreme Court of British Columbia, the Court of Appeal, and the Supreme Court of Canada. He has also participated in negotiations for the settlement of various Aboriginal claims. Mr. Pearlman has a B.A. in History from the University of Victoria, a B.A. in Law from Cambridge University, and an LL.B. from Dalhousie University.

Greg Poelzer

Greg Poelzer is Assistant Professor of Political Science at the University of Northern British Columbia. His field research in northern Canada and Siberia on Aboriginal self-government has been published in a number of articles and chapters. He is co-editor of *Polar Geography,* an interdisciplinary journal with a special focus on the Russian North. Greg Poelzer is the co-recipient with Gail Fondahl of a Social Science and Humanities research Grant to research Aboriginal land tenure and self-government in the Sakha Republic, Russia.

Dr. Brian L. Scarfe

Dr. Brian L. Scarfe is President of BriMar Consultants Ltd. in Victoria, B.C., Adjunct Professor of Public Administration at the University of Victoria, and Professor of Economics (formerly Vice-president, Academic) at the University of Regina. He has taught at universities in all four western provinces, and has published widely in the areas of macroeconomics and natural resource economics. BriMar Consultants Ltd. has recently completed several major reports for the B.C. Ministry of Forests, the B.C. Ministry of Environment, Lands and Parks, and the B.C. Environmental Assessment Office.

Harry Slade

Harry Slade has focused his work in the areas concerning Aboriginal peoples and lands for over 17 years. He has extensive experience in the litigation of issues relating to Aboriginal interests and negotiating involving First Nations, federal and provincial government ministries, and resources companies. He acts as counselor for numerous First Nations and was involved in interventions in the landmark cases of *Sparrow* (SCC), *Delgamuukw* (BCCA), and *R. v. Gladstone* (SCC). He has also acted for intervenors in fishing cases at the Appellant Level in British Columbia involving the issue of First Nation Consultations.

Patrick J. Smith

Patrick J. Smith is an associate professor and Past Chair of Political Science at Simon Fraser University (SFU). He is currently Director of the Institute of Governance Studies at SFU. He holds a B.A. (Hons.) and M.A. (Political Science) from McMaster University and a Ph.D. (Government) from the London School of Economics and Political Science.

Reviewers

James R. Aldridge

James R. Aldridge, Ll.M., is a partner in the Vancouver law firm, Rosenbloom & Aldridge. He is a member of the British Columbia Bar and an adjunct professor at the University of British Columbia. Mr. Aldridge has represented the Nisga'a's Tribal Council in their treaty negotiations since 1980.

John Borrows

John Borrows, B.A. (Hons.), M.A., LL.B., LL.M. (Toronto), D. Jur. (Osgoode), is an Associate Professor of Law at the University of British Columbia and the Director of First Nations Legal Studies. He was formerly an associate professor at Osgoode Hall Law School of York University and the Director of the Intensive Program in Lands, Resources and First Nations Governments. His teaching areas cover the fields of First Nations law, land use planning, environment law and natural resources. He has published widely in *Canadian Law Reviews* on the subjects of Aboriginal law, treaties, and self-government, and has acted as an advisor to various First Nations throughout Canada. Professor Burrows is on the Executive of the Canadian Association of Law Teachers. He is Anishinabe and a member of the Chippewa of the Nawash Nation in southern Ontario.

Jane Gaskell

Jane Gaskell is a professor in the Department of Education Studies at the University of British Columbia. She presently serves as Associate Dean. Her background is in the sociology of education and her publications include *Gender Matters from School to Work* (1992) and *Secondary Schools in Canada* (1996). She has served as President of the Canadian Society for the Study of Education and is on the Social Sciences and Humanities Research Council of Canada.

John Helliwell

John Helliwell is Professor of Economics at the University of British Columbia. He was Mackenzie King Visiting Professor of Canadian Studies (1991–1994) and Fullbright Fellow (1995–1996) at Harvard University.

Thomas A. Hutton

Thomas A. Hutton has pursued a career in public policy and scholarly research both in the domestic and international arenas. His principal research and applied policy interests include economic restructuring in the metropolitan context; the changing role of the service sector, with special reference to the producer services; the development of urban systems and networks; impacts of tertiarisation on metropolitan structure; regional and community development in British Columbia; and comparative urbanization processes in the Asia Pacific and Pacific Basin.

Margaret Neylan

Margaret Neylan graduated in nursing from McGill University and did graduate studies from the University of British Columbia. Her extensive varied experience in hospitals, universities, and institutes as nurse, educator, administrator, and consultant in Canada, the United States, and internationally have given her a broad perspective on health issues.

Arthur Ray

Arthur Ray is a professor in the Department of History at the University of British Columbia. He specializes in the research and teaching of the economic history of Native people of Canada and the Pacific Islands. He is also an historical consultant and has served as an expert witness in comprehensive land claims (*Delgamuukw v. Attorney General for Canada*) and treaty rights cases (Robinson Treaties 8 and 9). These cases all involved issues of Aboriginal rights to use fish and game resources.

Anthony Scott

Anthony Scott is a former professor of economics at the University of British Columbia. He specializes in the economics of institutions and organizations. He also specializes in the economics of the environment and natural resources.

Zane Splindler

Zane Splindler is a professor of economics at Simon Fraser University. He has published scholarly articles on public policy issues such as privatization, tax reform, economic sanctions, insurance-induced unemployment, pension-induced single parenthood, proprietary squatting, economic freedom and growth, and constitutional design. He has travelled and lectured worldwide, and has held visiting positions at the universities of Adelaide, Cape Town, Essex, Helsinki, Paris, Singapore, and Stlellbosch.

Editor

Roslyn Kunin

Roslyn Kunin has served the community in many positions, including Governor of the University of British Columbia and the Vancouver Stock Exchange. She is a member of the National Statistics Council. In her career, Dr. Kunin has worked in the private sector, taught at several Canadian universities, including Simon Fraser University and the University of British Columbia, and served 20 years as Regional Economist for the federal government in B.C. and the Yukon. She is now Executive Director of the Laurier Institution, writes a weekly newspaper column on the job market, and is in private practice as a consulting economist.

Publications
The Laurier Institution

Diminishing Returns: The Economics of Canada's Recent Immigration Policy
Published: January 1995   Cost: $21.95 + $5.00 postage and handling

This volume contains information about immigration, an essential building block of the Canadian nation, and about the strength and vitality of people and cultures which have helped create a society that is the envy of the world.

Celebrate
Published: 1994   Cost: $15.00 + $5.00 postage and handling

This booklet introduces the reader to a variety of religious celebrations that take place in BC. It includes Census Canada data showing the statistics of religious groups in BC and Canada.

Youth Gang Study
Published: February 1994   Cost: $15 + $5.00 postage and handling

This study describes and delineates the problem of youth gangs engaged in criminal activity in Greater Vancouver. Various theories are examined, including those that blame crime on the individual and those that look at the social origins of criminal behaviour. Theories about gangs are described and related research is summarized.

Looking to 2005: The BC Job Market in the Future
Published: July 1993   Cost: $45.00 + $5.00 postage and handling

This study gives an overview of the labour market to the year 2005. Population and the labour force growth are the most important highlights in the report.

People, Jobs and Immigration
Published: April 1991   Cost: $20.00 + $5.00 postage and handling

This report identifies the major demographic and labour market trends which will influence the structure of Canadian society in the coming decades. It analyzes these trends in the context of the future labour force supply and assesses the role immigration can play in strengthening Canada's economy.

When Did You Move To Vancouver?
Published: January 1990   Cost: $15.00 + $5.00 postage and handling

This research explores the effects of migration on metropolitan Vancouver's housing market. The analysis examines the impacts of four migrant groups: international migrants, interprovincial migrants, intraprovincial migrants, and interurban movers.

Order Form

Prospering Together:
The Economic Impact of the Aboriginal Title Settlements in B.C.

_____ copies @ $29.95 (Cdn) each _____

Add $5.00 for first book for Shipping & Handling _____

Add $2.00 for each additional book for Shipping & Handling _____

Total enclosed _____

Make cheque or money order payable to:

The Laurier Institution

Ship to:

Name —————————————————————————

Address —————————————————————————

City, Province/State —————————————————————

Postal/Zip Code —————————————————————

Phone (work) ————————— (home) —————————

The Laurier Institution

Suite 608, 1030 West Georgia Street
Vancouver, B.C. Canada V6E 2Y3
Tel: (604) 669-3638
Fax: (604) 669-3626

Thank you for your order!

THE LAURIER
INSTITUTION